Multi-dimensional Review of Peru

VOLUME 2. IN-DEPTH ANALYSIS AND RECOMMENDATIONS

OECD

dev
DEVELOPMENT CENTRE

This work is published under the responsibility of the Secretary-General of the OECD. The opinions expressed and arguments employed herein do not necessarily reflect those of the OECD, its Development Centre or of their member countries.

This document and any map included herein are without prejudice to the status of or sovereignty over any territory, to the delimitation of international frontiers and boundaries and to the name of any territory, city or area.

Please cite this publication as:
OECD (2016), *Multi-dimensional Review of Peru: Volume 2. In-depth Analysis and Recommendations*, OECD Development Pathways, OECD Publishing, Paris.
http://dx.doi.org/10.1787/9789264264670-en

ISBN 978-92-64-26466-3 (print)
ISBN 978-92-64-26467-0 (PDF)
ISBN 978-92-64-26536-3 (epub)

Series: OECD Development Pathways

ISSN 2308-734X (print)
ISSN 2308-7358 (online)

The statistical data for Israel are supplied by and under the responsibility of the relevant Israeli authorities. The use of such data by the OECD is without prejudice to the status of the Golan Heights, East Jerusalem and Israeli settlements in the West Bank under the terms of international law.

Photo credits: Cover © design by the OECD Development Centre.

Corrigenda to OECD publications may be found on line at: *www.oecd.org/about/publishing/corrigenda.htm*.

Foreword

Economic growth matters, but it is just one facet of development. Policy makers should focus their attention on ensuring that their country's development path is sustainable and that the lives of their citizens improve. This requires reconciling economic, social and environmental objectives.

OECD Development Pathways is a new series that looks at multiple development objectives beyond an exclusive focus on growth. It recognises well-being as part and parcel of development and helps governments identify the main constraints to more equitable and sustainable growth by undertaking a multi-dimensional country review (MDCR). Governments trying to achieve economic, social and environmental objectives need to understand the constraints they face and develop comprehensive and well sequenced strategies for reform that take into account the complementarities and trade-offs across policies. The MDCR methodology is based on quantitative economic analysis, as well as qualitative approaches including foresight and participatory workshops that involve actors from the private and public sectors, civil society, and academia.

The MDCRs are composed of three distinct phases: initial assessment, in-depth analysis and recommendations, and implementation of reforms in the identified key areas. This approach allows for a progressive learning process about the country's specific challenges and opportunities that culminates in a final synthesis report to inform reforms in the country.

The MDCR of Peru is the second review, following that of Uruguay, to be undertaken by the OECD in Latin America. The MDCR of Peru – Volume 1, Initial Assessment was launched by the OECD Secretary-General in October 2015 and was the first report to be published as part of the OECD Country Programme with Peru. This second volume, In-depth Analysis and Recommendations, focuses on three key constraints for inclusive development in Peru, namely economic diversification and productivity, transport connectivity and informality.

This MDCR is designed to help Peru formulate development strategies and identify and support the policy reforms needed to achieve further sustainable and inclusive development. This review comes at a time when the newly elected government of Peru faces the challenge to build on and accelerate the progress the country has achieved in recent years. While the recommendations are intended primarily to support public policy action by Peru's national authorities, the findings are also useful for academics, the private sector and civil society.

Acknowledgements

Multi-dimensional Country Reviews are the result of a collaborative effort of the OECD and the country under review. Work on this second phase of the Multi-dimensional Review of Peru was carried out by the OECD Development Centre in collaboration with the International Transport Forum at the OECD, with support from the Ministry of Economy and Finance of Peru.

Mario Pezzini, Director of the OECD Development Centre, guided and oversaw the review. The Multi-dimensional Country Review process is led by Jan Rielaender, Head of the MDCR Unit and Angel Melguizo, Head of the Latin America and Caribbean Unit, both at the OECD Development Centre. Stephen Perkins, Head of Research and Policy Analysis Division at the OECD International Transport Forum, provided supervision to the transport connectivity chapter of this report.

The review was co-ordinated by Sebastián Nieto Parra, Deputy-Head of the Latin America and Caribbean Unit at the OECD Development Centre, and drafted by Juan Carlos Benítez, Juan de Laiglesia, Alejandro Núñez, Juan Vázquez Zamora, Sebastián Nieto Parra (OECD Development Centre) and Aimée Aguilar Jaber (International Transport Forum at the OECD). Deirdre Culley (OECD Development Centre) managed the participatory Foresight process for the formulation and testing of scenarios and provided inputs to the report. Additional inputs were provided by Bénédicte Busquet, Olaf Merk (both at the International Transport Forum at the OECD), Rebecca Lavinson, Lucia Perez-Villar, René Orozco, Annalisa Primi and Caroline Tassot (OECD Development Centre).

The team is grateful for the insightful discussions, data provided and comments made by Catherine Anderson, Rolando Avendano, Federico Bonaglia, Ian Brand-Weiner, Alexandre Kolev, Lahra Liberti, Catriona Marshall, Bakary Traoré and Agustina Vierheller (OECD Development Centre), Bert Brys (OECD Centre for Tax Policy), José-Luis Álvarez-Galán and Raffaele Trapasso (OECD Directorate for Education and Skills), Veerle Miranda (OECD Directorate for Employment, Labour and Social Affairs), Iza Lejarraga (OECD Directorate for Financial and Enterprise Affairs), Balázs Egert and Alain de Serres (OECD Economics Department), José Antonio Ardavín and Jorge Carbonell (OECD Global Relations Secretariat), Anne-Lise Prigent (OECD Public Affairs and Communications Directorate), Andrés Bitar, Guillaume Lecaros de Cossio, Chris McDonald and Adam Ostry (OECD Public Governance and Territorial Development Directorate), and Dalila Cervantes-Godoy and Silvia Surescu (OECD Trade and Agriculture Directorate).

Various ministries and public agencies provided useful support during the authors' visit to Lima in December 2015 as well as throughout the production of the report. The role of the Ministry of Economy and Finance, the main counterpart for this report, was particularly valuable, both technically and analytically. Special thanks go to Javier Roca, José Alfredo La Rosa Basurco and Karen Trujillo for all their support. The Peruvian Embassy in Paris, principally Gonzalo Guillén and Catherine Vennard, members of the OECD Development Centre's

Governing Board provided crucial support to the process. The Ministry of Foreign Affairs, the Ministry of Development and Social Inclusion, the Ministry of Education, the Ministry of Energy and Mining, the Ministry of Foreign Trade and Tourism, the Ministry of Housing, Construction and Sanitation, the Ministry of Labour, the Ministry of Production, the Ministry of Transport and Communications, the National Centre for Strategic Planning (CEPLAN), the National Council of Competitiveness and Formalisation (CNCF), the National Institute of Statistics (INEI) as well as the Supervisory Authority of Investments on Public Transport Infrastructure (OSITRAN) also contributed significantly. Finally, the team is grateful to all the participants of two workshops hosted by the Ministry of the Economy and Finance and the Ministry of Foreign Affairs in Lima in February and December 2015 that brought together stakeholders from a broad set of backgrounds to identify global trends that could affect Peru's future development.

Other institutions, agencies, international organisations and members from the civil society and the academia also gave useful support throughout the production process of the report: the private sector associations and institutions the Bolsa de Valores de Lima, the Cámara de Comercio de Lima, the Confederación Nacional de Instituciones Empresariales Privadas, the Sociedad Agrícola Drokasa (Agrokasa), the Sociedad Nacional de Industrias and the Sociedad Nacional de Minería, Petróleo y Energía; the NGO Fundación Transitemos; the research centres Centro de Investigación de la Universidad del Pacífico, the Centro de Investigación y de Asesoría del Transporte Terrestre (CIDATT) and the Grupo de Análisis para el Desarrollo – GRADE; and the Peru Country Offices of the CAF (Development Bank of Latin America), the Deutsche Gesellschaft für Internationale Zusammenarbeit (GIZ), the Inter-American Development Bank, the International Labour Organization, and the World Bank. In addition, ECLAC (Economic Commission for Latin America and the Caribbean) and UNIDO (United Nations Industrial Development Organization) have been very supportive for this MDCR through discussions and comments during the production of the report.

The team is grateful to Jessica Hutchings for editing the manuscript and to the OECD Development Centre's Communications and Publications Unit, especially Delphine Grandrieux, Aida Buendia, Elizabeth Nash and Vanda Legrandgérard for their excellent support in editing, laying out and producing the report. Linda Smiroldo Herda, from the Director's Office of the Development Centre, made a notable contribution to improve the style and distil the main messages of this report.

Table of contents

Tables

Figures

Boxes

Acronyms and abbreviations

AFP	Administradoras de Fondo de Pensiones del Perú (Pension Fund Administrators of Peru)
APEC	Asia-Pacific Economic Cooperation
ASEAN	Association of Southeast Asian Nations
BCRP	Banco Central de la Reserva del Perú (Central Bank of Peru)
BRT	Bus Rapid Transit
CAF	Development Bank of Latin America
CBA	Cost-benefit analysis
CEPLAN	Centro Nacional de Planeamiento Estratégico (National Centre for Strategic Planning)
CITE	Centro de Innovación Tecnológica (Technological Innovation Centre)
CNCF	Consejo Nacional de Competitividad y Formalización (National Competitiveness and Formalisation Council)
CoG	Centre of Government
CONCYTEC	Consejo Nacional de Ciencia, Tecnología e Innovación Tecnológica (National Science and Technology Council)
ECLAC	Economic Commission for Latin America and the Caribbean
ENAHO	Encuesta Nacional de Hogares (National Households Survey)
EPL	Employment Protection Legislation
EsSalud	Seguro Social de Salud (Social Health Insurance)
FOMITEC	Fondo Marco para la Innovación, Ciencia y Tecnología (Fund for Innovation, Science and Technology)
GDP	Gross Domestic Product
GVA	Gross Value-Added
IDB	Inter-American Development Bank
ILO	International Labour Organization
IMF	International Monetary Fund
INEI	Instituto Nacional de Estadística e Informática (National Institute of Statistics)
ITF	International Transport Forum
ITP	Instituto Tecnológico de la Producción (Technological Insitute of Production)
KILM	Key Indicators of the Labour Market

LAC	Latin America and the Caribbean
LPI	Logistics Performance Index
MDCR	Multi-dimensional Country Review
MEF	Ministerio de Economía y Finanzas (Ministry of Economy and Finance)
MILA	Mercado Integrado Latinoamericano (Integrated Latin American Market)
MINAGRI	Ministerio de Agricultura y Riego (Ministry of Agriculture and Irrigation)
MINCETUR	Ministerio de Comercio Exterior y Turismo (Ministry of Trade and Tourism)
MIT	Middle-Income Trap
MTC	Ministry of Transport and Communications
MTN	Multilateral Trade Negotiations
MVCS	Ministerio de Vivienda, Construcción y Saneamiento (Ministry of Housing, Construction and Sanitation)
NAEC	OECD New Approaches to Economic Challenges
NRUS	Nuevo Régimen Único Simplificado (New Single Simplified Regime)
OECD	Organisation for Economic Co-operation and Development
OSITRAN	Organismo Superior de la Inversión en Infraestructura de Transporte de Uso Público (Supervisory Authority of Investments on Public Transport Infrastructure)
PA	Pacific Alliance
PCM	Presidencia del Consejo de Ministros (Presidency of the Council of Ministers)
PEN	Peruvian sol (national currency)
PENTUR	Plan Estratégico Nacional de Turismo (National Strategic Tourism Plan)
PENX	Plan Estratégico Nacional Exportador (National Strategic Export Plan)
PMR	Product Market Regulation
PPP	Purchasing Power Parity
PRODUCE	Ministerio de la Producción (Ministry of Production)
PROMPERU	Comisión de Promoción del Perú para la Exportación y el Turismo (Commission for the Promotion of Peru for Exports and Tourism)
RCA	Revealed Comparative Advantage
RDA	Regional Development Agencies
REMYPE	Registro Nacional de la Micro y Pequeña Empresa (National Register of Micro and Small Enterprises)
RUS	Régimen Único Simplificado (Single Simplified Regime)
SIS	Seguro Integral de Salud (Comprehensive Health Insurance)
SME	Small and Medium-sized Enterprise
SNIP	Sistema Nacional de Inversión Pública (National Public Investment System)
SNP	Sistema Nacional de Pensiones (National Pension System)

SPP	Sistema Privado de Pensiones (Private Pension System)
SPS	Sistema de Pensiones Sociales (Social Pensions System)
STEM	Science, Technology, Engineering and Mathematics
SUNAFIL	Superintendencia Nacional de Fiscalización Laboral (National Superintendency of Labor Inspection)
SUNAT	Superintendencia Nacional de Aduanas y de Administración Tributaria (National Customs and Tax Administration)
SUNEDU	Superintendencia Nacional de Educación Superior Universitaria (National Supervisory Authority for Higher Education)
TEU	Twenty-Foot Equivalent Units
TfL	Transport for London
TFP	Total Factor Productivity
RER	Regimen Especial de impuesto a la Renta (Special Regime Income Tax)
TiVA	Trade in Value-Added
USD	United States Dollar
VAT	Value Added Tax
VET	Vocational Education and Training
WITS	World Integrated Trade Solution
WTO	World Trade Organization

Executive summary

This is the second volume of the Multi-dimensional Country Review (MDCR) of Peru. It builds on the results of the first volume, which identified the main constraints to achieving well-being and sustainable and inclusive development, and provides recommendations in three key areas to address those constraints: promoting economic diversification and productivity, improving transport connectivity, and tackling informal employment. A forthcoming volume will propose a way of prioritising policy interventions and a framework for measuring policy implementation.

In the last two decades, Peru experienced considerable socioeconomic progress that improved well-being, lifted scores of its people out of poverty and led to a burgeoning middle class. Progress resulted from a combination of sound domestic policies and favourable external conditions. Today, Peru must undergo structural reforms to embark on the next chapter of its development, broadening social inclusion, consolidating its middle class and becoming a high-income economy. Transitioning from a middle-income to a high-income country and overcoming the so-called "middle-income trap" will require economic diversification away from natural resource dependency and higher levels of productivity across sectors. Closely related to higher productivity is the challenge of social cohesion. Peru's middle class has grown considerably in size and in its expectations. Estimated at 38% of the population, twice its share in 2004, the middle class expects more sound policies to expand formal jobs and better public services, such as connectivity, education and skills training.

Economic diversification, better transport connectivity and tackling informality are thus crucial in Peru's inclusive growth agenda.

Promoting economic diversification and productivity

Peru's labour productivity is only about one-third that of OECD countries. Significant gains are then required for Peru to further boost growth and reach high-income status. Even if Peru were able to sustain the strong macroeconomic performance of recent years – 4.6% average per capita GDP growth rate in the past ten years – it would take Peru until 2029 to become a high-income country. In this scenario, the country would have been a middle-income country for more than 80 years. By comparison, OECD countries cruised the middle-income range in around three decades on average.

To design and implement a development agenda for diversification and productivity for all Peruvians, policy actions in several domains should be implemented. These include: market regulation and openness; development of new competitive industries; innovation strategies; taxation and the use of commodity-based resources; enhancement of the strategic institutional framework. First, more efforts are needed to further regional integration with other countries in the region and also to tackle regulatory barriers, such as constraints to entrepreneurship. Second, some pre-conditions, such as specific skills, efficient logistics services, and effective co-operation between private and public sectors, academia and international actors, must be in place to facilitate the development of new competitive sectors. Experiences in agro-industry, tourism, metal-mechanics and forestry are useful for that purpose. Third, increased public and private investment in research and development and more effective interactions with the private sector are needed to promote innovation. Fourth, the allocation of commodity-based fiscal transfers should target all regions in Peru according to their socioeconomic challenges. Fourth, to finance broad-based policies affecting productivity, Peru should move towards comprehensive tax reform by increasing the share of direct taxes (specifically the personal income tax), assessing the impact of some tax benefits and tackling tax evasion and erosion. Finally, Peru needs to adopt more strategic and implementation-oriented public planning for development at both national and sub-national levels. This requires a detailed action plan and highly co-ordinated public administration to improve Peru's institutional framework and fiscal legitimacy.

Improving transport connectivity

Improved connectivity is particularly relevant for Peru, where the ratio of transport costs to tariffs is 20 times higher than in OECD economies. The improved connectivity of goods and people implies going beyond providing transport infrastructure to implementing policies and strategies to increase efficiency and reduce time and financial transport costs for businesses and Peruvians. Increasing connectivity in Peru also means developing other modes of transport beyond roads.

Policy actions are needed to improve the institutional framework to design and implement transport policies at national and urban levels. First, Peru should design a national transport plan that has clear transport policy priorities. Second, the creation of a "logistics observatory" to better assess logistics would help monitor and reduce transport costs. Third, a national urban transport policy should be developed and a lead agency should be identified for its effective implementation. Finally, Peru needs to improve multi-modality transport policies at local levels, particularly in Lima-Callao, to unlock the benefits of walking, cycling and public transport. The limitations created by the lack of coherent policies and investment decisions across administrative boundaries in Lima-Callao highlight the value of creating a single mobility authority for the metropolitan area.

Tackling informal employment

Informal employment remains too high, involving more than 70% of total workers, despite a decline in recent years. Informality and socioeconomic vulnerability go hand-in-hand in Peru: close to 80% of informal workers belong to the so-called vulnerable class and work in low-productivity sectors. Access to formal jobs is particularly difficult for younger workers, women, those with low education and workers from rural areas.

To promote formal jobs and deal with current high levels of informality, Peru should implement an integrated package of labour, tax and social protection interventions, coupled with productive development policies. First, the pervasive impact of informality on working conditions should be mitigated, without reinforcing the incentives to remain informal or, even worse, creating the incentives to move towards informality. This entails such initiatives as integrating existing health regimes into a single one and progressively expanding it to all citizens, as well as extending non-contributing pensions to gradually move towards universal coverage. Second, strengthening inspection and supervision systems, reducing costs of formal hiring, and communicating more effectively about the benefits of formalisation should contribute to job formalisation. Third, to promote the formalisation of firms, Peru should reduce incentives to remain small by simplifying taxation regimes and reducing some administrative and fixed costs of being formal. Finally, to promote more formal job opportunities, Peru should link its formalisation efforts to the broader productivity diversification strategy, aimed at creating more opportunities for formal, better-quality jobs. Increasing skills levels and closing skills gaps are crucial in that context for Peru.

Chapter 1

Overview: Charting Peru's way to a high-income economy with better well-being for all citizens

Many factors play into Peru becoming a high-income country with an expanded and a consolidated middle-class. The changing external landscape – particularly the economic evolution of one of Peru's largest export markets, China – has significant consequences for Peru's traditional economy and for more inclusive development going forward. This chapter also summarises the value of the multi-dimensional review (MDCR) approach and methodology, leading to an overview of the three topics reviewed in this report, their results and the policy implications for more inclusive development in the country: productivity and economic diversification, transport connectivity, and informality. The chapter concludes with three future-state scenarios developed to consider the recommendations in light of major global trends that may affect development prospects for Peru.

After years of impressive economic growth that lifted scores of its people out of poverty and led to a burgeoning middle class, Peru must undergo structural reform to embark on the next chapter of its development. Transitioning from a middle-income to a high-income country will require economic diversification and higher productivity to avoid getting caught in the so-called middle-income trap (MIT).[1] It will also require public policies that improve citizen well-being by providing quality formal jobs and public services.

The model that fuelled Peru's impressive economic growth rates has depended on a global economic landscape that is now shifting. Global demand for natural resources has decreased, driven by a slowdown in China, and is already having an adverse effect on the Peruvian economy, with reduced commodity exports and foreign direct investment. Transitioning to high-income status with a consolidated middle class will entail crafting new development strategies that foster new engines of growth for the Peruvian economy and ensure growth is inclusive and sustainable in the long term.

Peru aspires to be a high-income country with an expanded and a consolidated middle class, where citizens enjoy high living standards. This vision sees an economy that provides quality formal jobs for citizens with the purchasing power to enjoy consumer goods and generates fiscal revenues to provide high-quality public services. In this vision, Peru is a highly connected, inclusive and sustainable society, where educated and healthy citizens trust institutions and actively engage in political and civil life. Peru would be well integrated in the region, with a vibrant business environment that fosters innovation and entrepreneurship. It would have a modern agro-industrial sector and well-managed natural resources. Efforts to improve sustainability will have reaped rewards such that citizens enjoy their country's well-preserved and rich natural heritage and diverse vibrant culture.[2]

To realise this vision for its citizens and to meet their expectations, Peru requires ambitious reforms for the long term. Such reforms should diversify the Peruvian economy away from natural resource dependency and encourage formal job creation. This would enable Peru to consolidate its middle class, while reducing poverty and economic vulnerability. Reforms that improve Peru's institutional framework and fiscal legitimacy should also deliver better public services in the areas of innovation, transport infrastructure and logistics, education and skills, and healthcare. Such an ambitious strategy to realise Peru's high-income aspirations will also require significant financing and state capacity, with a detailed action plan and highly co-ordinated public administration for effective implementation.

This chapter presents an overview of how Peru can pursue development policies that support its vision of becoming an inclusive, high-income country. First, the chapter provides an overview of the major external challenges that Peru faces today in realising inclusive development, including major global trends that may affect future development prospects. Second, the chapter highlights some opportunities the multi-dimensional approach identified for Peru's development, namely the importance of driving productivity and economic diversification, improving transport connectivity and incentivising the creation of formal employment. The three sections following summarise policy implications revealed by the multi-dimensional analysis of these topics. The final section presents three scenarios illustrating global trends that may affect future development prospects. These scenarios are used to test the resilience of recommendations to these structural shifts and changing environment.

Charting inclusive development in a changing global landscape

Favourable external conditions in the past decade were instrumental in the expansion of the Peruvian economy. As one of the largest producers of metals in the world, Peru benefited immensely from the upswing in commodity prices that started a decade ago. Record low international interest rates and sound macroeconomic policy attracted significant foreign capital and boosted economic growth to rates that surpassed those of Peru's regional neighbours.

Today, Peru faces an uncertain global economic environment, with a sharp decline in global commodity prices and increasing volatility in global financial markets.[3] The adverse consequences of some of these shifts are already visible: mining companies, for instance, have reduced their investment plans, leading to a decrease in foreign direct investment and commodity exports.

One important risk to Peru's growth prospects is the shift in the economic model taking place in the People's Republic of China (China), which has become an increasingly important destination for Peruvian exports (in 2015, 19% of Peruvian exports were destined for China, making this market Peru's main export destination). The scale of the impact is significant. Estimates suggest that a decrease in China's investment growth by 1 standard deviation is likely to reduce Peru's terms of trade growth by about 2 percentage points and its gross domestic product (GDP) growth by about 0.2 percentage points (Han, 2014). Furthermore, China's demand for commodities should continue contracting as the country rearranges its imports composition. China's new normal imposes new challenges for Peru. Projections from the 2016 Latin American Economic Outlook foresee Peru's exports slowing down from an impressive 16% annual growth in the period 2001-10 to less than 3% up to 2030 in the baseline scenario (OECD/Development Bank of Latin America [CAF]/Economic Commission for Latin America and the Caribbean [ECLAC], 2015; Chapter 2).[4]

Peru also will have to contend with other emerging global trends, which could have a significant impact on the success of its development strategies. These pertain to the structure and drivers of the global economy, but also to technological trends that could radically affect global production patterns, as well as domestic shifts that could shape the scope and form of Peru's programme of reform. Three scenarios were developed to test the recommendations of this multi-dimensional review against identified global trends to ensure that strategies pursued both mitigate risks and seize opportunities in a shifting world.

Charting the way forward: The value of a multi-dimensional approach

To support Peru's vision of becoming an inclusive, high-income economy, the OECD's MDCR is part of the OECD's Country Programme to support Peruvian authorities in identifying future reforms (Box 1.1).

The first volume of the *MDCR of Peru* described economic development in the country since the 1970s and provides an in-depth assessment of the Peruvian economy and state of well-being today. Since the beginning of the 21st century, Peru has experienced successful socio-economic progress. Coupled with strong economic growth compared to the region, considerable segments of Peru's population were lifted out of poverty, swelling the ranks of the middle class. Peru's success is attributed mainly to sound macroeconomic management, monetary and fiscal policies that reduced inflation and volatility, and a favourable external environment, attracting investment and driving a commodity boom. A stronger emphasis on social policies and redistributive programmes has been crucial for reducing poverty and income inequality to some extent (OECD, 2015a).

Box 1.1. **MDCR in the context of the OECD Country Programme with Peru**

In 2014, the OECD and Peru agreed to set out a joint Country Programme to support Peru in its reform agenda and improve its public policies in priority areas. The programme will facilitate Peru's adherence to OECD legal instruments, participation in OECD bodies and programmes, and effective implementation of OECD standards and best practices. Over two years (2015-16), the programme is and will be conducting a series of policy reviews and activities in five priority areas: removing barriers to growth, public governance, anti-corruption, human capital and the environment. The programme also includes workshops and capacity-building activities in areas such as tax policy, regulatory policy and statistics. In addition to the MDCR, other OECD reviews of the OECD Country Programme include a Skills Strategy Review, a Vocational Education and Training Review, an Environmental Performance Review, a Public Governance Review and a Territorial Review.

MDCR of Peru: Volume 1. Initial Assessment, launched in October 2015 by the OECD's Secretary-General, was the first policy review of this Country Programme to be published. The current Volume 2 analyses and provides recommendations in three areas identified as key to boosting sustainable and inclusive development: economic diversification and productivity, transport connectivity and tackling informality.

The MDCR is composed of three distinct phases:

- Volume 1 identified the main constraints to achieving sustainable and equitable objectives in well-being and economic growth.
- This volume 2 analyses the identified areas to formulate policy recommendations that can be integrated into Peru's development strategy.
- Volume 3 will support implementing these recommendations. As in other Latin American economies, this final phase is particularly relevant in Peru, given the complexity of both the political economy and the policy-making process to make reform happen (Dayton-Johnson, Londoño and Nieto-Parra, 2011).

For each phase, a report is published and workshops are organised. The MDCR methodology is based on quantitative economic analysis, as well as qualitative approaches, including foresight and participatory workshops.

Quantitative methods include standard approaches and a comparative analysis with a selection of countries, referred to as the benchmark countries.

Benchmark countries identified in Volume 1 were selected according to criteria that included their high GDP per capita growth to tackle the MIT, the contribution of natural resources (particularly minerals) to GDP, and the degree to which their successful economic policies could be relevant to Peru. Eight are OECD member countries: Australia, Canada, Chile, Korea, Mexico, Norway, Portugal and Turkey. Australia, Canada and Norway are included because of their important natural resource sectors; Portugal and Turkey are included because of their development path; and Korea serves as an example of a highly successful, export-based economy. In addition to Chile and Mexico, five other Latin American and Caribbean countries are included: Brazil, Colombia, Costa Rica, Ecuador and Panama. Brazil and South Africa, both among the BRICS (Brazil, Russia, India, People's Republic of China and South Africa), are included because of their growing economic power and their mineral resources.

Volume 1 highlighted Peru's good performance in improved ability of households to consume, social connection and life evaluation, along with its underperformance in areas of work, education, skills and health. Analysis of these outcomes drew attention to the issues of informality, inequality and productivity in Peru. These challenges reveal the dynamics underlying Peru's development model, highlighting bottlenecks to inclusive development and identifying cross-cutting issues for further analysis.

A major challenge for Peru is to continue socio-economic progress in reducing poverty and inequality and to identify the new engines for economic growth that are needed to become a high-income country. The current drivers of growth in Peru, which is strongly reliant on labour, capital accumulation and the commodity export sector, seem insufficient to sustain such progress. Peru has a high level of labour utilisation, but low productivity. Structural factors are holding back performance of human capital and total factor productivity. Employment is highly concentrated in the least productive sectors of the Peruvian economy. The most productive sectors – mining, finance, energy, water and telecommunications – represent less than 4% of total employment, while more than half of Peruvian workers have jobs in Peru's two most unproductive sectors: retail and restaurants, and agriculture.

Expanding the middle class has been among Peru's great achievements, but it also created new vulnerabilities and an increasing demand for quality public services and better jobs. Between 2004 and 2014, the middle class jumped from 19% to 37.8% of the population (Figure 1.1). This places greater demands on policies as the middle class demands more and better public services, such as transport connectivity, education and skills. Another challenge is the growing number of vulnerable people in the population, which increased from 36.7% to 40.6% in the same period (World Bank, 2016a). Despite the socio-economic progress achieved in recent years, many people in Peru are in an unstable situation where they could easily slip back into poverty following any turbulence or slowdown in the economy. Most of the vulnerable population hold precarious jobs in the informal sector. Reforms aiming to boost economic diversification and productivity are fundamental to tackling informality.

Figure 1.1. **Peru and Latin American population distribution by per capita income level (% of population), 2004-14**

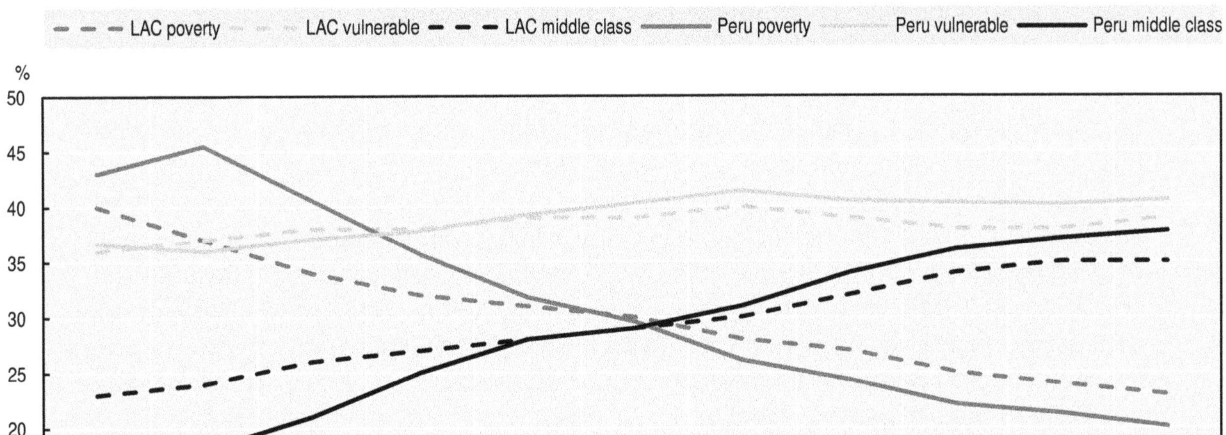

Note: Poverty is defined as the percentage of the population living with less than USD (United States Dollar) 4 (2005) purchasing power parity (PPP) per day. The vulnerable class is defined as the percentage of the population living with USD 4 to 10 (2005) PPP per day. The middle class is defined as the percentage of the population living with USD 10 to 50 (2005) PPP per day. Latin America and the Caribbean (LAC) includes the following countries: Argentina, Bolivia, Brazil, Chile, Colombia, Costa Rica, Dominican Republic, Ecuador, El Salvador, Guatemala, Haiti, Honduras, Mexico, Nicaragua, Panama, Paraguay, Peru and Uruguay.

Source: OECD calculations based on World Bank (2016a), *LAC Equity Lab* (database), World Bank, Washington, D.C., *www.worldbank.org/en/topic/poverty/lac-equity-lab1/overview* (accessed on 1 July 2016).

StatLink http://dx.doi.org/10.1787/888933411179

Thus, economic diversification and productivity, transport connectivity and formal jobs interact with and reinforce each other to achieve a brighter future for its citizens. As such, policies to address these bottlenecks for inclusive development must consider the possible synergies and trade-offs among them. For instance, policies to increase connectivity through infrastructure investment should increase economic diversification and productivity and could result in lower informality rates. However, high levels of informality give low levels of tax revenues, which in turn affect the necessary transport infrastructure investments to boost connectivity.

This Volume 2 of the MDCR presents in-depth analysis of and outlines recommendations for the three topics identified in Volume 1 as key constraints to inclusive development in Peru:

- Promoting economic diversification and productivity (Chapter 2).
- Improving transport connectivity to foster competitiveness and inclusiveness (Chapter 3).
- Tackling informality in the labour market (Chapter 4).

Below is an overview of the main findings and recommendations for these three topics.

Promoting economic diversification and productivity

The shifting global economy and China's new normal require a diversification strategy for the Peruvian economy. As described above, Peru's growth model over the past decade has been heavily reliant on a commodity boom driven by Chinese demand. The shifting environment means Peru needs to diversify to drive new sources of growth.

Peru also needs to diversify its economy to avoid the MIT. MIT is defined as a period of prolonged slowdown once a country reaches a certain level of income (OECD/CAF/ECLAC, 2014; OECD, 2014). This phenomenon occurs when a country can no longer rely on its traditional drivers of growth (e.g. low labour costs or the accumulation of labour as a major source of growth) to make further progress. Peru's recent period of high GDP growth helped it to achieve upper middle-income status in 2008, but this success is not without its challenges.

Overcoming the MIT will require higher productivity and greater diversification (OECD, 2015a). Peru's labour productivity only represents close to 30% of the OECD's labour productivity (Figure 1.2, Panel A), and the productivity gains required for Peru to reach high-income status are significant. Even were Peru to sustain the strong macroeconomic performance of recent years (4.6% of average per capita GDP growth rate in the past ten years), it would take Peru until 2029 to become a high-income country, supposing more than 80 years as a middle-income country.[5] Compared to neighbouring Latin American economies, Peru is not an isolated case in the region (OECD/CAF/ECLAC, 2016). However, the performance of other countries indicates that a more rapid transition from a middle-income to a high-income economy is possible. For instance, it took Korea 27 years, Portugal 46 years and Chile 55 years (Figure 1.2, Panel B).

To design and implement a development agenda for productivity for all Peruvians, certain policy actions should be taken into account:

- Further regional integration and policies to tackle barriers to entrepreneurship should attract foreign capital in productive sectors, expand access to international trade and improve the business environment.
- Micro-analysis of potential sectors (as identified in this report) and pre-conditions in the development of these sectors are fundamental in the strategy to make Peru more productive and diversified. Experiences in agro-industry, tourism, metal-mechanics and forestry are useful for that purpose.

- Higher investment in research and development and more effective interactions with the private sector, for instance through the Centros de innovación y Tecnología (CITEs), are needed to promote innovation.
- To boost productivity and reduce regional inequalities, the allocation of commodity-based transfers should target all regions in Peru according to their socio-economic challenges. Sub-national authorities need to be supported with further technical capacity to manage these resources and interact with civil society, academics and the private sector to improve the allocation of these resources.
- To finance broad-based policies affecting productivity and to make a more fair and efficient taxation system, Peru should move towards a comprehensive tax reform, increasing the share of direct taxes (thanks to personal income taxes).
- Peru needs to move towards more strategic and implementation-oriented public planning for development at national and sub-national levels. Currently, many planning frameworks overlap and are not necessarily co-ordinated. Greater integration between planning agendas and the budgeting process must be a key element of such reform.

Figure 1.2. **Moving from middle-income to high-income in Peru and selected benchmark economies**

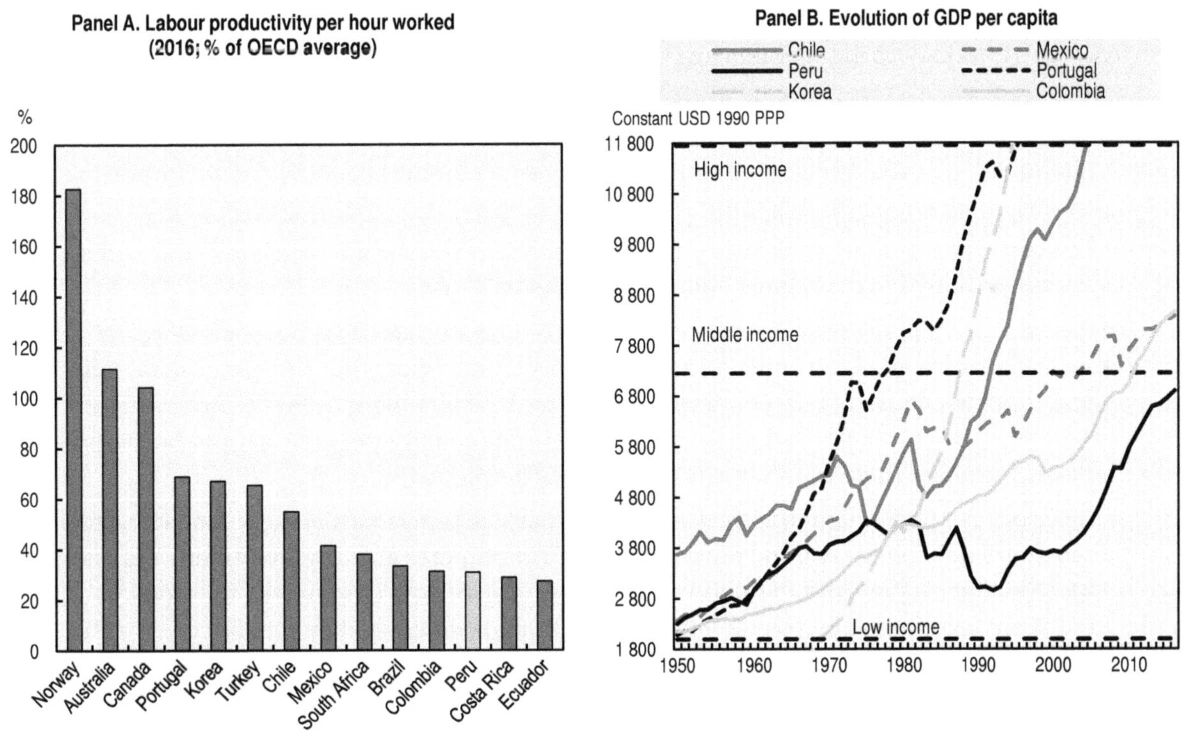

Note: Panel A: Labour productivity per hour worked in USD 2015 (converted to 2015 price level with updated 2011 PPPs).

Source: Panel A: Conference Board (2016), *Total Economy Database* (database), The Conference Board, New York, *www.conference-board.org/data/economydatabase/* (accessed on 1 August 2016). Panel B: OECD calculations based on methodology proposed by Felipe, Abdon and Kumar (2012), Data from International Monetary Fund (IMF) (2016), *World Economic Outlook* (database), International Monetary Fund, Washington, D.C., *www.imf.org/external/pubs/ft/weo/2016/01/weodata/index.aspx* (accessed on 1 July 2016); and Maddison Project (2016), *Maddison Project Database* (database), University of Groningen, Groningen, available at *www.ggdc.net/maddison/maddison-project/home.htm*, 2013 version (accessed on 1 July 2016).

StatLink http://dx.doi.org/10.1787/888933411187

Improving transport connectivity to foster competitiveness and inclusiveness

Good transport connectivity can make Peru more efficient and ensure sustainable and more inclusive development (OECD, 2015a). Improving connectivity requires going beyond transport infrastructure provisions, recognising the need for policies and strategies that focus on increasing efficiency and reducing time and financial transport costs for businesses and the population. This is particularly relevant in Peru, where the ratio of transport costs to tariffs is 20 times higher than in OECD economies (Chapter 3). To take advantage of recent trade agreements, a better use of logistics for the transport sector and the adoption of a multi-modal approach beyond the current focus on roads (e.g. developing railways, ports and waterways) are fundamental.

Despite some recent improvements, logistics and transport infrastructure performance remains below those of benchmark countries. Peru's gap with respect to Germany, the best-performing OECD member country, is 35% larger than that of the region's leading country, Chile, and more than 2.5 times the average gap for OECD member countries.[6] Since Peru has traditionally concentrated on road transportation, the use of other transport modes is low. Furthermore, the quality of ports, rails and roads remains below that in most of the benchmark countries.

A key objective is to define transport strategies to pursue outcomes for the economy and the population rather than exclusively for infrastructure development. Increasing connectivity in Peru means developing a policy framework focused on the reduction of time and financial transport costs and on the promotion of multi-modality. Going beyond transport infrastructure alone involves four key actions:

- Design a national transport plan, which is fundamental to defining transport policy priorities. This should be aligned to wider priorities set for the economy and for improving quality of life for the population.
- Create a logistics observatory to improve assessments on logistics, which is key to including more efficiently "soft" solutions, reducing transport costs.
- Define a national urban transport policy and a lead agency for that purpose. Developing specific objectives, targets and guidelines for urban transport that translate sustainable and inclusive mobility into operational goals, and developing national programmes for enlarging the capacity of urban authorities to fund mobility projects, should be central strategies of the national urban transport policy developed.
- Focus policies implemented at the local level, in particular in Lima-Callao, on unlocking the benefits of walking, cycling and public transport. This requires aligning investment and road space allocation priorities to these modes and setting pricing frameworks that reflect the social costs generated by private vehicles. The limitations created by the lack of coherent policies and investment decisions across administrative boundaries in Lima-Callao highlight the value of creating a single mobility authority for the metropolitan area. The unique authority will have to define key priority areas, while ensuring delivery of public value.

Tackling informal employment and informal economic activities

Informality is both a cause and a consequence of low levels of development in Peru. Despite a decrease in the past years, informal employment remains high at more than 70% of total workers, representing one of the highest ratios in the region. Reducing informality should be a key policy objective and its many manifestations suggest that it should be approached from different policy angles linked not only to productivity but social inclusion. In that sense, a large share of informality is a by-product of certain structural characteristics and will not disappear until those are removed, while other parts of informality can be dealt with from a shorter-term perspective. In addition, policies to promote formalisation of both firms and workers should be accompanied by measures to mitigate the negative impact of informality on working conditions and the functioning of the economy.

The informal sector in Peru is characterised by a vulnerable population. Close to 80% of informal workers belong to a vulnerable class (incomes between USD 4 and 10 per day) and work in low productivity sectors, such as retail and agriculture. Close to 50% of the middle class (incomes between USD 10 and 50 per day) also belong to the informal sector. Access to formal jobs is particularly difficult for younger workers, women, those with low education and workers from rural areas.

To promote formal jobs and deal with current high levels of informality while mitigating its pervasive impact on workers and the economy, four policy interventions stand out as most relevant:

- Mitigate the pervasive impact of informality on working conditions without reinforcing the incentives to remain informal. This entails initiatives such as integrating existing health regimes into a single one and progressively expanding it to all citizens, as well as extending non-contributive pensions to gradually move towards universal coverage.
- Promote the formalisation of jobs through three principle means. One, strengthen inspection and supervision systems, particularly for informal workers in the formal sector. Two, reduce the costs of formal hiring: 1) subsidise the social contributions for low- and low-middle-income workers; 2) provide alternatives to incorporate independent workers in the pension system; and 3) establish a clearly defined mechanism to determine minimum wages and make them less discretionary, allowing for the possibility of a differentiated evolution of minimum wages across regions. Three, improve communication and financial knowledge about the benefits of formalisation.
- Promote the formalisation of firms by reducing incentives to remain small. For instance, simplify existing taxation regimes and decrease incentives to remain in the simplest one, and reduce some recurrent, administrative and fixed costs of being formal.
- Create conditions and opportunities for formal job creation. To close the skills gap, increase skills levels in the country, strengthen and promote technical education and provide training opportunities for informal workers. To better match the skills supply with formal job requirements, certify skills acquired in the informal sector and progress towards the creation of a national qualifications framework. A broader productivity diversification strategy aimed at creating more opportunities for formal and better-quality jobs is also required.

Anticipating global trends: Three scenarios to test recommendations

To ensure that the recommendations in this report not only address current challenges but can withstand shifts in the global economy and global trends, future-state scenarios were developed to test the recommendations.

These scenarios are used to anticipate how these global trends might shape recommendations and, more specifically, how different contexts could affect the incentives and/or prioritisation of policy reform or even create new policy trade-offs.[7] They are also used to ensure that policy recommendations are applicable in each scenario. The end of each chapter discusses the recommendations in light of each scenario and prioritises certain policy actions, depending on the risks and opportunities the scenario presents.

The scenarios for the future of Peru presented in this report were developed using inclusive participatory approaches. Two workshops hosted by the Ministry of the Economy and Finance (MEF) and the Ministry of Foreign Affairs in Lima in February and December 2015 brought together stakeholders from a broad set of backgrounds to identify global trends that could affect Peru's future development. On the basis of these trends, stakeholders developed and elaborated three short scenarios with a time horizon of 2030. Their purpose is to help analysts and policy makers think through the potential consequences of decisions and identify both the risks and opportunities of public policy actions.

The scenarios bring together economic, political and technological trends in changing constellations.

- Scenario 1 describes a revived commodity super cycle, driven by growing demand from India. While providing for a positive growth outlook, this scenario highlights the difficulty of dealing with prolonged resource dependency.
- Scenario 2 assumes a rapid increase in the pace of change and use of technology and the impact on global production patterns. This scenario highlights the importance of education and skills, as well the link between skills, education and inequality.
- Scenario 3 describes an increase in protests throughout Latin America in the 2020s and the successful mobilisation of the middle class to garner better public service provision. This scenario highlights the trade-off between higher social spending to meet increasing expectations and balancing budgets and remaining competitive.

Scenario 1: A new commodity super cycle

After an initial global slowdown, the pace of growth in India accelerates, prompting a new global commodity super cycle with important consequences to global demand on natural resources. In parallel, China's economy continues to grow, albeit at a slower rate, generating an expanding middle class with new habits, diets and appetites for new commodities and consumer goods. The mining sector attracts significant foreign investment, and financial and human resources flow to the natural resource sector.

This scenario presents opportunities for Peru to take advantage of a favourable external environment and improve management and export of natural resource-based commodities. As in the past, growth would drive government revenue, and Peru could seize the opportunity to invest in public services and infrastructure, expand its middle class and reduce poverty rates. Investment in public services, especially health and education, could help to further reduce inequalities and deliver improvements in citizen well-being. This scenario also presents an opportunity to pursue a diversification strategy aimed at supplying the emerging Chinese middle class with new consumer goods and services.

This scenario also presents a number of risks. Renewed global demand for natural resources could create symptoms of Dutch Disease for the larger economy if strong revenues from natural resources removed incentives to pursue a diversification strategy. Investment could flow to the profitable extractive industries and away from the sectors that produce other tradable goods and services, such as agro-business or manufacturing. These sectors could suffer from reduced competitiveness regionally and in other export markets as the exchange rate appreciates with increased investment export inflows. While living standards would increase, in this scenario, Peru remains vulnerable to shocks in global commodity prices.

Scenario 2: Increasing technology and mechanisation

Investment in research and development and agreements for technology sharing between high-income and emerging economies deliver important innovations. The most significant of these are advances in mechanisation and robotics that surpass human capacity and enable the quicker production of higher-quality, cheaper goods. Ability to disseminate this technology radically affects global production patterns, as production costs and labour needs are greatly diminished. A number of service-based industries develop around these technologies. Countries increasingly need to invest in mechanisation and new technologies to ensure their production continues to be competitive. Countries also need to attract high-skilled labour.

This scenario presents an opportunity for Peru to thrive in a future technological revolution. By anticipating this global trend and investing in both research and development and necessary skills, Peru could take advantage of this global shift to position itself as a leading regional player and destination for investment. With a flexible regulatory framework, good business environment and skilled labour force, Peru could both attract firms to set up production in Peru and incubate Peruvian start-ups to supply services around these technologies. Improving intellectual and technical co-operation with other states and actors, such as the private sector, could have a positive effect on other sectors of the economy.

This scenario presents the risk of exacerbating inequality, as demand for highly skilled labour appreciates salaries while low-skill manufacturing, no longer competitive, subsides. Low-skill labour is drawn into the informal sector in low-productivity jobs, and income further depreciates. In this scenario, inequality risks becoming further entrenched between those with high- or low-skilled incomes, with or without skills relevant to new technology, and in formal or informal jobs.

Scenario 3: Rising expectations of the middle class

Popular protest and middle class dissatisfaction intensifies throughout Latin America in the 2020s. By 2030, the region is well integrated economically and politically. Mass demonstrations, marches and strikes have developed into an organised and mobilised social movement across the region. Driven by economic vulnerability and distrust in government and public institutions, the middle class is highly organised and able to represent their interests and extract concessions from governments. Governments respond to these demands by heavily investing in public services, notably improving the quality of education and healthcare, as well as public infrastructure and leisure facilities, to meet citizen expectations.

This scenario presents an opportunity for Peru to improve public governance, increase participation and improve citizen well-being through higher-quality service delivery. Increasing trust in government and public institutions improves the state's fiscal legitimacy, which drives a slow and gradual formalisation of the economy as norms around fiscal participation and civic duty shift. Improved governance also drives high participation rates in political life, with higher turnout at elections and burgeoning connected, local-level institutions.

The scenario also presents risks. The private consumption/public expenditure model presents trade-offs between higher social spending to meet increasing expectations and the difficulty of balancing budgets and remaining competitive. Government financing of expensive public services risks reducing investment in the domestic economy, and strong social policies could drive lower competitive wages. As a result, job creation would dwindle and the Peruvian economy would struggle to integrate into regional value chains. This scenario also presents the risk of increasing regional disparities. As the government strives to respond to constituency expectations, investment in infrastructure is concentrated in unconnected urban centres at the expense of sparsely populated suburban and rural areas.

The following chapters use these three scenarios to consider recommendations against the risks and opportunities each scenario present. This scenario-based reflection is a simple tool to instigate reflection on policy options for different possible futures.[8]

Notes

1. MIT is defined as a period of prolonged slowdown once a country reaches a certain level of income (OECD/Development Bank of Latin America [CAF]/Economic Commission for Latin America and the Caribbean [ECLAC], 2014; OECD, 2014). This phenomenon occurs when a country can no longer rely on its traditional drivers of growth to make further progress.
2. Two workshops hosted by the Ministry of the Economy and Finance (MEF) and the Ministry of Foreign Affairs brought together stakeholders from a broad set of backgrounds in Lima in February and December 2015 to discuss and develop narratives from the citizens' perspective of Peru's vision for the future.
3. High volatility in international capital markets, particularly in the exchange rate market, is a source of external vulnerability to the stability of Peru's financial markets in a highly dollarised economy. Despite macro-prudential tools to contain financial vulnerabilities and a reduction in the exposure to foreign currency, close to 40% of Peru's bank credit to the private sector remains denominated in foreign currency.
4. Two scenarios for China's economy up to 2030 were modelled based on the projections analysis for China 2030 in investment and GDP growth (World Bank-DRC, 2013): a normal-pace transition (baseline scenario) and a high-pace transition (low-investment scenario). The high-pace transition scenario shows a lower GDP growth, especially evident in the period 2021-30. None of these scenarios assume specific external or internal shocks to China's economy, only different trajectories for China's transition from a middle-income and an investment-driven economy towards a high-income and a consumption-based one (OECD/CAF/ECLAC, 2015).
5. To define the lower and upper bounds of the middle-income group, the thresholds are defined as USD 2 000 and USD 11 750, measured in 1990 constant levels and adjusted for PPP (Felipe, Abdon and Kumar, 2012).
6. Based on World Bank (2016b), *Logistics Performance Index* (dataset), *http://lpi.worldbank.org/* (accessed on 1 July 2016) (see Chapter 3 for more details).
7. This approach is consistent with the OECD's focus on and approach to thinking about the future, including the implications of long-term trends. See, for example, the OECD New Approaches to Economic Challenges (NAEC) initiative (*www.oecd.org/naec/*); the use of scenario-based policy discussion at the 2015 Ministerial Council Meeting (*www.oecd.org/mcm/documents/ministerial-meeting-2015-scenario-based-policy-discussion.htm*), and selected publications, such as OECD (2015b), Scarpetta (2016) and the International Transport Forum (ITF) (2015).
8. Many policy recommendations suffer from a static view of time. Even forecasts and projections based on statistical models that portray a dynamic view of the future suffer from the basic flaw that they only can be produced on the basis of past knowledge. Most analysis necessarily assumes the future to be largely similar to the present, as we cannot know what type of changes will occur in the future.

References

Conference Board (2016), *Total Economy Database* (database), The Conference Board, New York, *www.conference-board.org/data/economydatabase (accessed on 1 August 2016).*

Dayton-Johnson J., J. Londoño and S. Nieto-Parra (2011), "The Process of Reform in Latin America: A Review Essay", *OECD Development Centre Working Papers*, No. 304, OECD Publishing, Paris, available at *http://dx.doi.org/10.1787/5kg3mkvfcjxv-en.*

Felipe, J., A. Abdon and U. Kumar (2012), "Tracking the middle-income trap: What is it, who is in It, and why?", *Working Paper*, No. 175, Levy Economics Institute of Bard College, Annandale-On-Hudson, *www.levyinstitute.org/pubs/wp_715.pdf.*

Han, F. (2014), "Measuring external risks for Peru: Insights from a macroeconomic model for a small open and partially dollarized economy", *IMF Working Paper*, No. WP/14/161, International Monetary Fund, Washington, D.C., *www.imf.org/external/pubs/ft/wp/2014/wp14161.pdf*.

IMF (2016), *World Economic Outlook* (database), International Monetary Fund, Washington, D.C., *www.imf.org/external/pubs/ft/weo/2016/01/weodata/index.aspx* (accessed on 1 July 2016).

ITF (2015), *ITF Transport Outlook 2015*, OECD Publishing, Paris, available at *http://dx.doi.org/10.1787/9789282107782-en*.

Maddison Project (2016), *Maddison Project Database* (database), University of Groningen, Groningen, available at *www.ggdc.net/maddison/maddison-project/home.htm*, 2013 version (accessed on 1 July 2016).

OECD (2015a), *Multi-dimensional Review of Peru: Volume 1. Initial Assessment*, OECD Publishing, Paris, *http://dx.doi.org/10.1787/9789264243279-en*.

OECD (2015b), *The Future of Productivity*, OECD Publishing, Paris, available at *www.oecd.org/eco/growth/OECD-2015-The-future-of-productivity-book.pdf* (preliminary version).

OECD (2014), *Perspectives on Global Development 2014: Boosting Productivity to Meet the Middle-Income Challenge*, OECD Publishing, Paris, *http://dx.doi.org/10.1787/persp_glob_dev-2014-en*.

OECD/CAF/ECLAC (2016), *Latin American Economic Outlook 2017: Youth, Skills and Entrepreneurship*, OECD Publishing, Paris (forthcoming).

OECD/CAF/ECLAC (2015), *Latin American Economic Outlook 2016: Towards a New Partnership with China*, OECD Publishing, Paris, *http://dx.doi.org/10.1787/9789264246218-en*.

OECD/CAF/ECLAC (2014), *Latin American Economic Outlook 2015: Education, Skills and Innovation for Development*, OECD Publishing, Paris, *http://dx.doi.org/10.1787/leo-2015-en*.

Scarpetta S. (2016), "What future for work?", *OECD Observer*, No. 305, OECD Publishing, Paris, available at *www.oecdobserver.org/news/fullstory.php/aid/5433/What_future_for_work_.html*.

World Bank (2016a), *LAC Equity Lab* (database), World Bank, Washington, D.C., *www.worldbank.org/en/topic/poverty/lac-equity-lab1/overview* (accessed on 1 July 2016).

World Bank (2016b), *Logistics Performance Index* (dataset), World Bank, Washington, D.C., available at *http://lpi.worldbank.org/* (accessed on 1 July 2016).

World Bank-DRC (2013), *China 2030: Building a Modern, Harmonious, and Creative Society*, World Bank/Development Research Centre of the State Council, People's Republic of China, Washington, D.C., *www.worldbank.org/content/dam/Worldbank/document/China-2030-complete.pdf*.

Multi-dimensional Review of Peru
Volume 2. In-depth Analysis and Recommendations

Chapter 2

Towards higher economic diversification and productivity in Peru

This chapter analyses and provides recommendations to boost economic diversification and productivity in Peru. An analysis of Peru's recent performance in productivity and economic diversification indicates a marked need to boost both in order to achieve a more inclusive development. Several opportunities emerge based on potential new products to export and recent experiences in both successful economic diversification and the promotion of start-ups and entrepreneurship. The chapter identifies policy focuses needed to seize these opportunities, including further innovation; small and medium-sized enterprise (SME) sustainability and reduced barriers to entrepreneurship; and increased regional integration. Better management of commodity-based revenues at the sub-national level and improvements in the taxation system are also relevant to Peru's development goals. The chapter concludes with recommendations for the institutional framework to improve the design and implementation of Peru's strategic development agenda.

Further economic diversification and productivity is needed in Peru to overcome the so-called middle-income trap (MIT) and increase well-being for all Peruvians. Gains in productivity have been slow in the past decade, and further economic diversification would increase formal job creation and reduce dependence on external demand for commodities.

Based on recent experiences and potential new sectors, recommendations and policy actions to increase economic diversification and productivity in Peru are indicated. Key among them is the need to enhance the institutional framework to promote better prioritisation and implementation of policies for greater competitiveness.

This chapter analyses economic diversification and productivity in five sections. First, the chapter analyses the recent performance in labour productivity and total factor productivity, and the external sector composition in Peru. Second, it identifies new activities contributing to further economic diversification based on international experiences. Given the recent growth in non-traditional exports in sectors such as agro-industry, tourism, metal-mechanics and forestry, the chapter also presents the pre-conditions and successful paths for further diversification in Peru. It also analyses recent programmes and initiatives implemented to enhance start-ups and entrepreneurship. Third, the chapter presents policy actions to increase productivity and economic diversification through several channels, including 1) boosting entrepreneurship, SMEs and innovation; 2) increasing regional integration; 3) improving management of commodity-related revenues; and 4) increasing fiscal revenues and implementing a better taxation structure to promote equity and entrepreneurship in Peru. Fourth, the chapter focuses on and provides recommendations for the institutional framework to improve the design and implementation of a strategic plan in Peru at both the national and sub-national level. The chapter concludes with the resulting main policy recommendations.

Peru needs to boost productivity growth and increase economic diversification

Peru's recent period of high and sustainable growth in gross domestic product (GDP) per capita helped it to achieve upper middle-income status in 2008, but this success is not without the challenges of a MIT economy. Sound macroeconomic performance in the past decade has been favourable to high and sustainable economic growth and has been underpinned by better macroeconomic management and an exceptionally favourable external environment.

However, despite this impressive surge in GDP per capita performance, Peru has not been able to close the gap with other emerging markets, and formal job creation remains sparse. Boosting productivity and economic diversification are fundamental to overcoming the MIT and providing better jobs in Peru.

Productivity growth has been slow and heterogeneous across sectors and regions

Escaping the MIT will require increases in productivity and greater diversification of the economy. Like Brazil, the People's Republic of China (China) and Korea, Peru features relatively high labour utilisation, which means that the key barrier affecting GDP per capita is labour productivity (OECD, 2015). Peru's labour productivity represents close to 30% of the average for OECD member countries. Furthermore, although some progress has been observed in the past decade, the labour productivity gap has increased, compared to the 1980s (Figure 2.1).

Figure 2.1. **Labour productivity gap in Peru and selected benchmark countries (% of OECD average), 1980-2016**

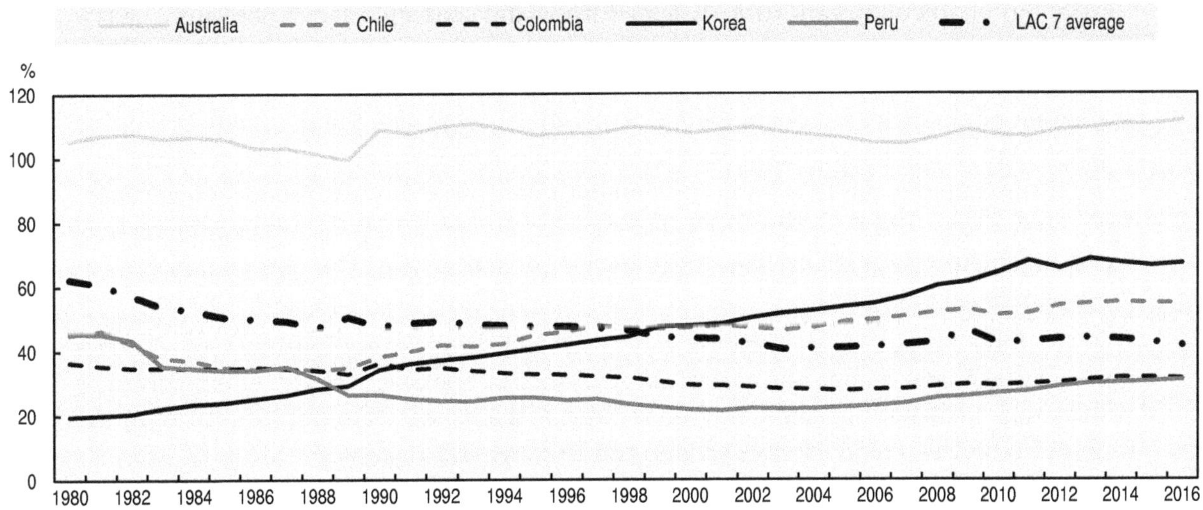

Note: Labour productivity per person employed in 2014 in USD (converted to 2014 price level with updated 2011 purchasing power parities [PPPs]).

Source: Based on The Conference Board (2016), *Total Economy Database* (database), The Conference Board, New York, *www.conference-board.org/data/economydatabase/* (accessed on 1 July 2016).

StatLink *http://dx.doi.org/10.1787/888933411198*

Improving total factor productivity and human capital will be key for promoting labour productivity. Labour productivity, calculated as the output per worker, can be broken down into human capital, physical capital and total factor productivity (TFP). Compared to the United States, Peru's TFP alone accounts for 49% of the labour productivity gap; years of schooling accounts for 27% and quality of education accounts for 22%. Peru's TFP has grown at an annual rate of less than 2% over the last two decades – not enough to close the gap with OECD economies and most of the benchmark countries (OECD, 2015).

Recent policies adopted in education are welcome and these efforts should continue in the years ahead to boost labour productivity and inclusive development. Some recent policies such as incentive mechanisms to improve the quality of teachers, the implementation of "jornada única" (full-time school model) to avoid the prevalence of two or even three-shift schools, the creation of SUNEDU (Superintendencia Nacional de Educación Superior Universitaria) as an independent body for supervision of the quality of higher education, further investment in school infrastructure, in particular in remote areas, and the development of platforms to increase information on labour demand such as "Ponte en Carrera" are determinant to improve the quality of education for all Peruvians. Further fiscal resources and improvements in the effectiveness of public expenditures are fundamental to close the educational gap in Peru (Chapter 4; OECD, 2016a). The importance of these issues is reflected in the OECD's Country Programme for Peru, which includes various reports on these themes: first, a vocational education and training review, focusing on the functioning of the VET system and on ways to improve it. Second, an "Investing in Youth" review, which will deal with issues related to the school-to-work transitions of youth and provide policy options to improve this. Finally, the Country Programme also includes an OECD Skills Strategy for Peru, which provides a comprehensive assessment of the main skills challenges and needs in the country.

Labour productivity varies widely across firms and economic sectors in Peru. The few sectors with high labour productivity, such as mining and finance, create few jobs. By contrast, retail and restaurants, and agriculture create close to half the employment and remain the lowest productivity sectors in Peru (Chapter 4). Furthermore, the productivity of firms exhibits high heterogeneity, compared to other Latin American economies and especially to the United States. While in Peru, the ninetieth percentile of most productive firms are 500% more productive than the tenth percentile, in the United States, it is approximately 200%, highlighting significant disparities in the allocation of production factors in Peru (Vostroknutova et al., 2015).

The total change in productivity can be broken down into a "within-sector" effect (driven by technical change and capital accumulation), a "between-sector" effect (driven by reallocation of labour resources between sectors) and a "cross-sector effect" (driven by the interaction between productivity changes and employment shares).

Within-sector accounted for the largest proportion of total labour productivity growth in the last decade in Peru. Positive within-sector and between-sector largely offset the negative cross-sector (Kaldewei and Weller, 2013). This is the result of the closing productivity gap between growth in slow-growing sectors gaining employment share and fast-growing sectors, such as mining, losing employment share. In the period 2002-12, while cross-sector contracted by more than 2%, within-sector expanded by more than 34%, and between-sector expanded by more than 12%. Most of the within-sector gains come from services and agriculture (Figure 2.2). Regarding the mining sector, most of the labour productivity gains come from the reallocation of labour, while within-sector and cross-sector were negative.

Similarly, at the sub-national level, most of the productivity growth is owing to within-sector and, to some extent, between-sector. However, high heterogeneity in terms of productivity growth was exhibited across departments in Peru (Figure 2.3). Most of the departments abundant in commodities as a percentage of the gross value added (GVA) exhibit high labour productivity, accounting for most of the high levels of GDP per capita (OECD, 2015). However, most of these departments reported negative or low productivity growth in the past decade. In particular, within-sector were negative or close to zero for some of these departments, such as Ancash, Madre de Dios and Pasco. Aspects intrinsic to the natural resources market, such as the reduction of metal prices, are affecting labour productivity in this market.[1]

Figure 2.2. **Labour productivity growth (%) by economic sector in Peru, 2002-12**

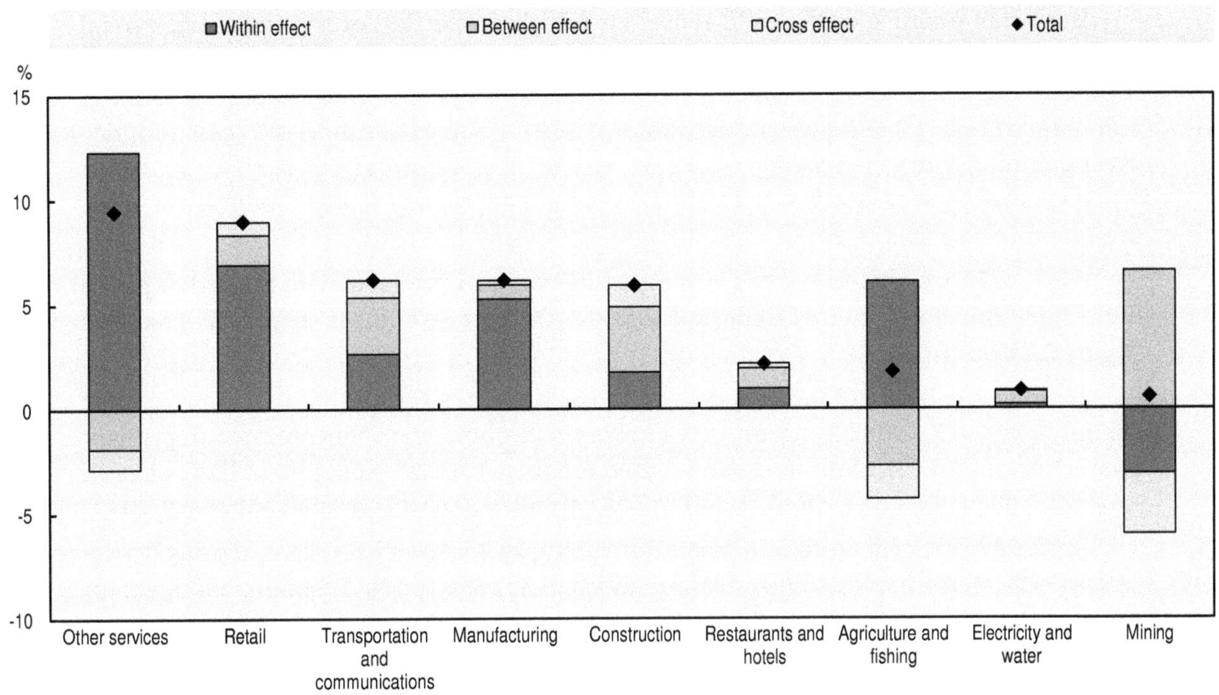

Note: The total economy is the sum of the economic sectors and is represented as PERU in Figure 2.3.

Source: OECD calculations based on data provided by the National Institute of Statistics (Instituto Nacional de Estadística e Información [INEI]).

StatLink http://dx.doi.org/10.1787/888933411205

Figure 2.3. **Labour productivity growth (%) by region in Peru, 2002-12**

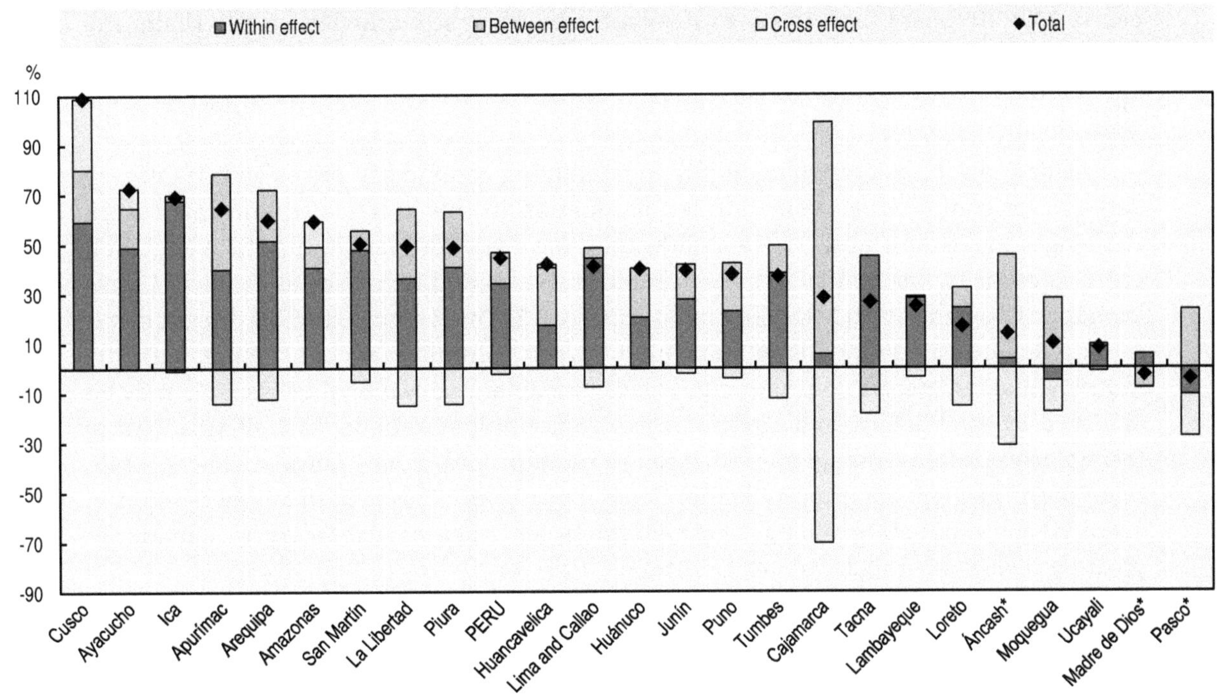

Note: * denotes the three most important departments producing mining in Peru as a percentage of the GVA: Pasco (44%), Madre de Dios (28%) and Ancash (26%).

Source: OECD calculations based on data provided by the INEI.

StatLink http://dx.doi.org/10.1787/888933411219

Towards higher economic diversification

Hard commodities continue to represent a high proportion of the trade and capital accounts in Peru. Despite commodities only accounting for nearly 10% of Peru's GDP in 2015, regarding the external sector, mining attracted about a third of foreign direct investment and represented 61% of Peru's annual exports in 2015.[2] These natural resources comprise several mining components and, to a lesser extent, oil and natural gas. With its abundant and diverse natural resource supply, Peru stands among the top global producers of some of these minerals (OECD, 2015).

Some of Peru's agro-processed and metal-mechanical products have started to play a more significant role in world trade, but together they represent less than 10% of exports (Figure 2.7 below).[3]

Throughout 2015, 19% of exports were destined for China, Peru's largest export destination (ADEX, 2015). By sector, 30% of exports to China were concentrated in primary production and 70% in natural resource-based products (OECD/Development Bank of Latin America [CAF]/Economic Commission for Latin America and the Caribbean [ECLAC], 2015).

Favourable exogenous conditions in the mining sector have been deteriorating. In the period 2004-14, the export value of commodities increased by 130%, due mainly to export prices rather than gains in productivity and production. Nowadays, terms of trade are decreasing. In the period 2012-15, terms of trade worsened by more than 15% (OECD, 2015; Reyes, 2016).

Furthermore, China's demand for commodities should continue to contract as the country rearranges its imports composition. The "new normal" in China imposes new challenges on Peru to adapt its economic structure. Based on macroeconomic scenarios for China, Peru's exports will slow down from an impressive 16% annual growth in the period 2001-10 to less than 3% up to 2030 in the baseline scenario (Figure 2.4). Under the low-investment scenario for China, mining exporters would face an even more challenging environment for job creation and investment in this sector, while manufacturing exporters would be more resilient (OECD/CAF/ECLAC, 2015).[4]

Aside from its greater vulnerability to fluctuating commodity prices and to Chinese demand for commodities, concentrated production in this sector also presents severe challenges to sustainability. These include long-term environmental impacts, lack of job creation capacity, weak links to local economic sectors and rising social conflicts (Swiss Economic Cooperation and Development [SECO], 2013). Overcoming growing dissent about mining requires a continuous relationship between communities and mining, with the industry making greater contributions at local, regional and national levels. This may be achieved by establishing and advancing environmental standards, as well as adopting technological improvements to production to monitor and reduce adverse effects, while offering the greatest opportunity for development progress. This is particularly relevant in artisanal and small-scale mining, where emissions and releases of mercury are a matter of great national concern (ECLAC/OECD, 2016).[5]

Because Peru specialises in primary products, it largely participates in the lower end of supply chains, providing inputs to other countries' production processes (forward linkages), rather than receiving production inputs from abroad (backward linkages) (OECD, 2015). Consequently, Peru participates in global supply chains more as a provider of value-added than as a recipient and is among the top providers of domestic value-added used in foreign exports among Latin American and Caribbean (LAC) countries (Blyde, 2014).[6]

Figure 2.4. **Projections for Peruvian and other Latin American exports to China, 2010-30**

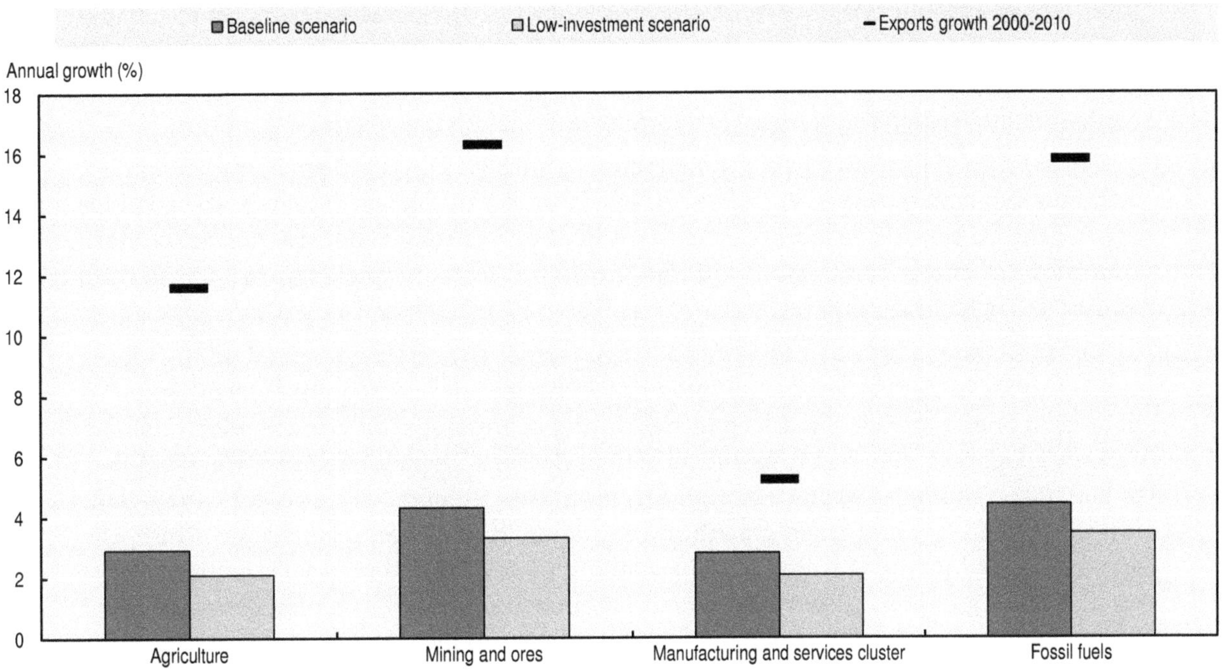

Note: Baseline scenario and low-investment scenario refer to average annual exports growth in the period 2011-30. Clusters are defined as follows: agriculture (Argentina, Brazil, Guatemala, Honduras, Nicaragua, Paraguay, Uruguay); mining and ores (Chile and Peru); manufacturing and services (El Salvador, Costa Rica, Dominican Republic, Mexico); and fossil fuels (Bolivia, Colombia, Ecuador and Venezuela).

Source: OECD/CAF/ECLAC (2015), *Latin American Economic Outlook 2016: Towards a New Partnership with China*, OECD Publishing, Paris, *http://dx.doi.org/10.1787/9789264246218-en.*

StatLink *http://dx.doi.org/10.1787/888933411226*

More accurate data are needed to analyse Peru's opportunities in global value chains. The latest input-output table data are from 2007; given recent changes in the production structure, an update is needed. Moreover, in the context of the OECD Country Programme with Peru, the inclusion of Peru in the OECD-World Trade Organization (WTO) Trade in Value-Added (TiVA) is fundamental to providing further analysis and insights into Peru's commercial relations.[7]

Productivity growth remains low. Along with a new international context in the demand for goods and services and the risks of being dependent on commodities, policy actions towards increasing economic diversification and productivity are pressing.

Opportunities to increase productivity and economic diversification

The experience of benchmark countries and international demand suggest some new products that would increase productivity and formal job creation. Instances of successful contributions to economic diversification in Peru, such as agro-industry and tourism, evidence the pre-conditions needed for greater diversification. This sub-section also highlights the recent development of two sectors: metal-mechanics and, to a lesser extent, forestry. Last is a summary of recent initiatives supporting start-ups and entrepreneurship in Peru.

Identifying promising exports

Peru has at its disposal a large set of products with unexplored potential to broaden economic diversification and boost productivity. Taking into account current global trends and domestic challenges, there are opportunities for new exports that have the potential to create formal jobs, boost productivity and produce more processed products.

Promotion of economic diversification should target industries that could profit from the latent comparative advantages of Peru's economy. Industries that exploit comparative advantages become competitive in domestic and international markets, making them sustainable beyond government support (Lin and Monga, 2010). Comparing Peru's current endowment structure to equivalent international economies is informative in identifying unexploited sectors.

In the case of Peru, international comparisons are based on OECD emerging economies, countries that have moved from middle- to high-income status in recent years and economies dependent on natural resources. The identification process builds on the benchmark countries, selected in conjunction with the Ministry of Economy and Finance (MEF) of Peru, in the OECD's *Multi-dimensional Review of Peru: Volume I. Initial Assessment* (Chapter 1).

Within those parameters, identification of unexploited sectors proceeded through three stages (Annex 2.A1). First, only export products with a revealed comparative advantage (RCA) in at least one of the benchmark countries during country-specific periods were retained. These periods corresponded to five years of high GDP per capita growth and, when applied, to periods preceding an upgrade to high-income status. Second, only products with growth rates higher than world trade growth in the period 2010-13 were considered. Third, the resulting set of products were ranked according to key dimensions, such as the level of manufacturing, exports growth rate, labour productivity, labour and capital intensities, and the probability that Peru starts exporting the selected products.[8]

Peru can explore new products to broaden economic diversification and boost productivity

The resulting set of products indicate untapped opportunities for the export of more highly processed goods, as some benchmark countries have done in recent decades. Out of the 193 identified products, 150 of them were not exported with a RCA by Peru in 2013. Of that 150, 55% are fully-processed products, 22% are semi-processed and 23% are unprocessed. They range over diverse sectors, including agricultural and forestry machinery; operation of fish hatcheries and fish farms; vegetable and animal oils and fats; cocoa, chocolate and sugar confectionery; and textile fibre preparation and weaving. The large proportion of fully-processed goods shows that product diversification can be extended towards more manufacturing goods.

Nevertheless, Peru's specialisation in unprocessed products is not unjustified, given that its capabilities make the production of unprocessed products more likely. The probability that a country starts to export a product can be estimated by measuring the proximity in the capabilities involved in the country's current export basket and those needed to export a new product (Annex 2.A1; Hidalgo and Hausmann, 2009). The probability measure for the identified products for Peru shows that unprocessed products are 0.68 standard deviations more likely to be produced by Peru than semi-processed goods. Unprocessed goods are 1 standard deviation more likely to be produced than fully-processed goods.

Yet, various semi- and fully-processed products could be exploited by Peru. The difference in RCAs among products with equal probability defines unexploited sectors. In particular, there are 12 identified products with a RCA below 1 and with a probability to be produced higher than 1 standard deviation of the average. Peru would benefit from developing a RCA in unprocessed products such as edible nuts, greasy wool or fish fillets (fresh or chilled). Among those fully- or semi-processed products, Peru could profit from the production of wine from fresh grapes, olive oil, palm oil, sugar confectionery, smoked fish, liquefied butane, electronic switch boards or crocheted textile fabrics (Figure 2.5).

Figure 2.5. **Top 35 most likely Peruvian exports by level of processing and RCA index, 2014**

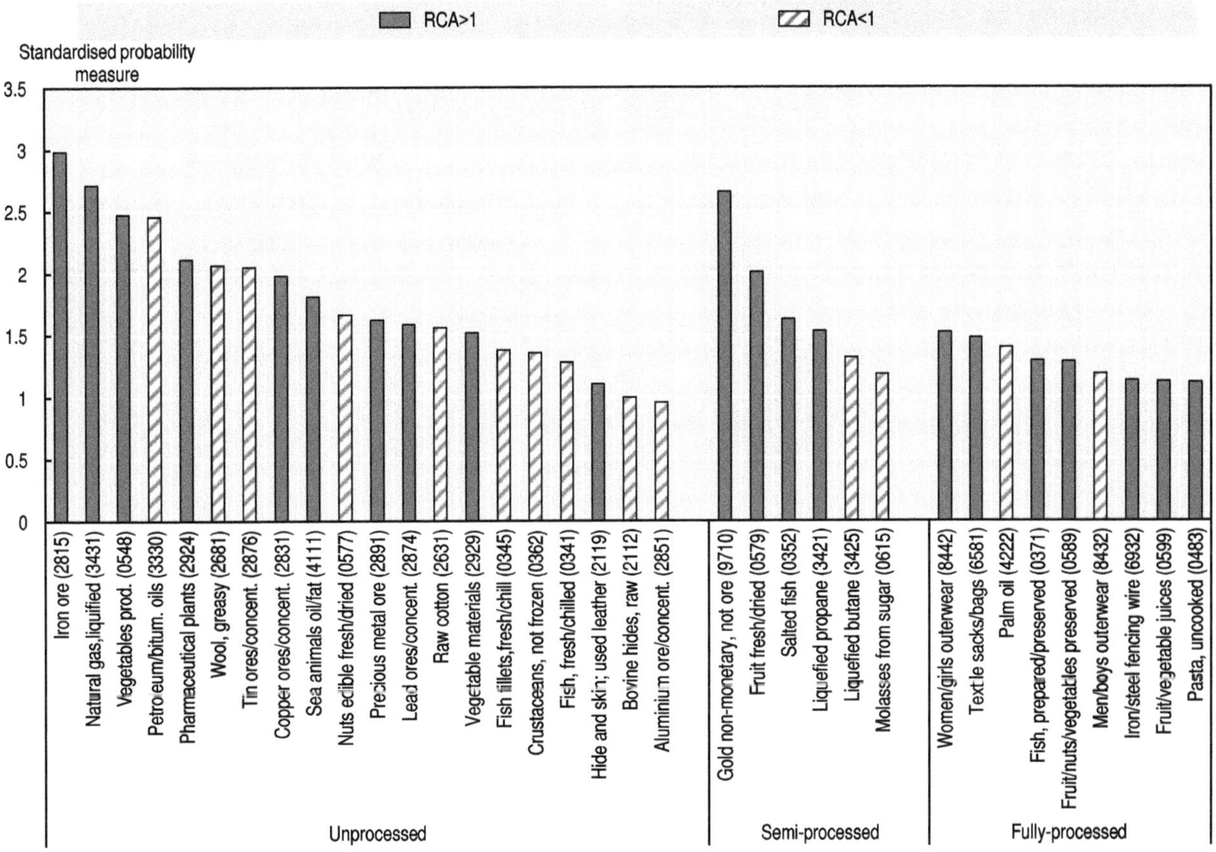

Notes: RCA (revealed comparative advantage) is an index based on Balassa (1977); values larger than 1 suggest current specialisation in a product by the country. Products are classified according to the SITC rev. 3 at the 4-digit level (in parenthesis in X axis). Density is a measure based on Hausmann and Klinger (2007), which captures a country's propensity to export a product (Annex 2.A1). Y axis = normalised values of the density measure (i.e. average set to 0 and standard deviation equal to 1). The categorisation of products according to manufacturing levels follows Rieländer and Traoré (2016).

Source: OECD calculations based on exports data from World Integrated Trade Solution (WITS)/United Nations (UN) Comtrade (database) (accessed on 1 June 2016).

StatLink http://dx.doi.org/10.1787/888933411230

Information concerning labour productivity, labour and capital intensities, and output to value-added ratio is only available for manufacturing industries, which represent 151 products (78% of the selected products) and covers mainly semi- and fully-processed products.

On average, fully-processed goods amount to USD 54 550 of value-added per worker annually, compared to USD 10 1625 for semi-processed. On average, fully-processed goods are more labour intensive than semi-processed (4.2 percentage points higher participation of wages on output), but capital participates more on output in semi-processed (by 1.1 percentage points).[9] Finally, fully-processed goods incorporate 2.89 percentage points more of aggregate value per unit of output than semi-processed.

Some new semi- and fully-processed goods could boost labour productivity and job creation in Peru. Potential products involve higher levels of labour productivity and labour intensity than Peru's manufacturing sector (origin in Figure 2.6). Particular semi- and fully-processed products with a RCA below 1 emerge: for example, apparel (woven blazers and coats), sugar confectionery, wine from fresh grapes, olive oil, and inorganic bases and metal oxides, hydroxides and peroxides.[10]

Figure 2.6. **Average value-added and labour intensity per worker for manufacturing sectors in Peru**

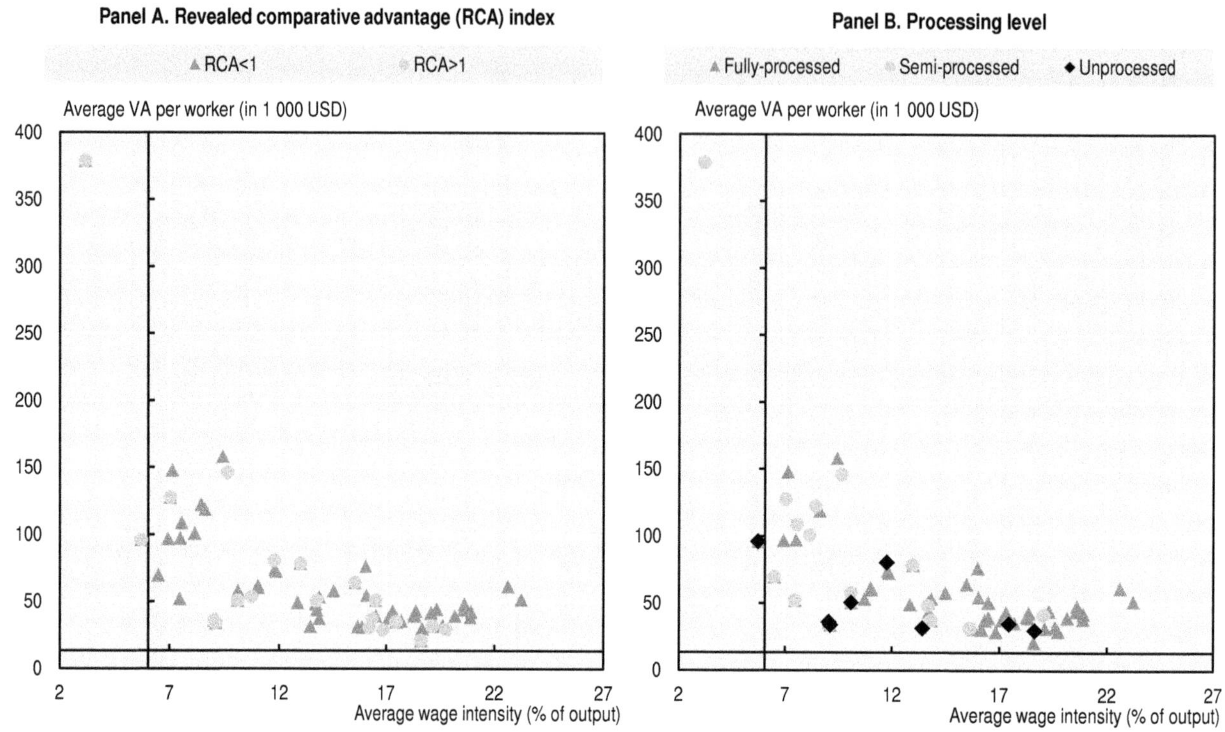

Notes: Origin = Peru's average value-added (VA) and wage intensity in the manufacturing sector in 2007 (category D, International Standard Industrial Classification [ISIC], Rev. 3). Wage intensity is the fraction of output paid in salaries and wages. For each product, the average was calculated at the 4-digit level of the ISIC classification. Calculations based on the sample of benchmark countries using the time periods for which data are available (1990 to 2010). Panel A: RCA is an index based on Balassa (1977) that measures the ratio between the contribution a product makes to the exports of a country and the same product's contribution to world trade. Values larger than 1 suggest specialisation of a product by the country. Panel B: The categorisation of products according to manufacturing levels follows the work of Rieländer and Traoré (2016), which is based on the classification of the WTO's MTN.

Source: OECD calculations based on exports data from WITS/UN Comtrade (database) and United Nations Industrial Development Organization (UNIDO) (database) (accessed on 1 June 2016).

StatLink http://dx.doi.org/10.1787/888933411241

Products identified with potential for further exploitation are heterogeneous, gathering sectors such as fish farming, the production of agricultural and forestry machinery, textile manufacturing, insulated wire and cable, and cultivating fruits and vegetables. The products also vary in their level of processing. Peru would benefit from developing a RCA in unprocessed products such as edible nuts, greasy wool or fish fillets (fresh or chilled). Among semi- or fully- processed products, Peru could profit from the production of wine from fresh grapes, olive oil, palm oil, sugar confectionery, smoked fish, liquefied butane, electronic switch boards and knitted textile fabrics.

The methodology for identifying products is only one element in determining those with potential to contribute to economic diversification. It should be complemented by other tools, analyses and considerations, such as Peru's characteristics at the sub-national level, acknowledging its territorial diversity. Furthermore, geographical constraints should be taken into account in ruling out or exploiting identified products.[11] Peru should continue efforts to design and execute diversification policies at the regional level.

Essential to exploiting these opportunities is a consideration of the tangible and intangible pre-conditions to produce more effectively in Peru – pre-conditions revealed from policies and private experiences at both the national and sub-national level. Recent successes in some sectors are informative for the development of potential sectors (see below). For instance, specific skills, targeted investment in research and development, efficient logistics services and effective co-operation with academia and international actors are some of these pre-conditions.

Products beyond commodities with lessons for greater diversification

However useful relative factor abundance is in identifying product markets, diversification goes beyond comparative advantages and involves a discovery process (Hausmann and Rodrik, 2003). This is illustrated by the incorporation of new products into Peru's export bundle (Freund and Pierola, 2010).

Although the mining sector still represents close to 60% of total exports, new products for export have emerged in the past decade, notably in agro-industry. In the period 2004-14, asparagus, avocados and grapes in particular grew 20.8% annually on average, and their participation in total exports increased by 2.09 percentage points (Figure 2.7, Panel A). However, in 2015, it still only accounted for less than 5% of total exports (Figure 2.7, Panel B).

Figure 2.7. **Export diversification in Peru**

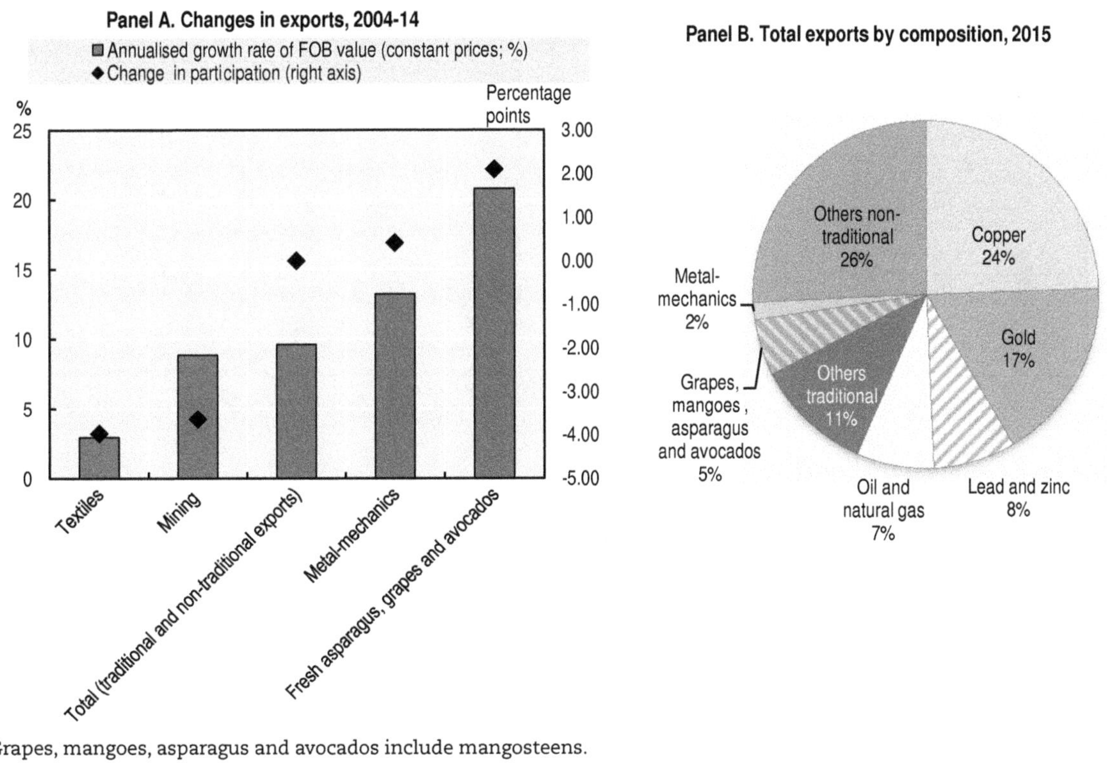

Note: Grapes, mangoes, asparagus and avocados include mangosteens.

Source: Panel A: OECD calculations based on Central Bank of Peru data on textiles, mining, metal-mechanics and total value *www.bcrp.gob.pe/estadisticas.html*; and on INEI data for avocados, asparagus and grapes *www.inei.gob.pe/media/MenuRecursivo/publicaciones_digitales/Est/Lib0774/libro.pdf* and *www.inei.gob.pe/media/MenuRecursivo/publicaciones_digitales/Est/Lib1253/compendio2015.htm*. Panel B: OECD calculations based on Superintendencia Nacional de Aduanas y de Administración Tributaria (SUNAT) data.

StatLink http://dx.doi.org/10.1787/888933411256

The success and development of two key sectors – agro-industry and tourism – and two nascent sectors – metal-mechanics and forestry – provide lessons for increased economic diversification in Peru. Among them are appropriate use of technology in different phases of production and distribution; efficient interaction between the private and public sectors; development of economies of scale through clusters; and favourable external demand.

The development of the agro-industry in Peru

The development of the agro-industry has been remarkable since the initial expansion of asparagus in the late 1980s. Mirroring that development, new products built on existing knowledge and infrastructure. Grapes and avocados, among other products, rapidly expanded as of the early 2000s. Others surging products include mandarins, mangoes, artichokes, paprika, passion fruit, citrus fruits and berries (Figure 2.8, Panel A). Expansion of agro-processing has made Peru the main exporter of asparagus for the past decade, accounting for 36% of world's exports in 2013. Peru is also the third largest exporter of avocados, the fourth largest of chillies and peppers (world's largest for Paprika), and sixth largest of grapes, mangoes, mangosteens, guavas, tangerines, mandarins, clementines and satsumas (based on FAO, 2014).

Figure 2.8. **The development of agro-products in Peru**

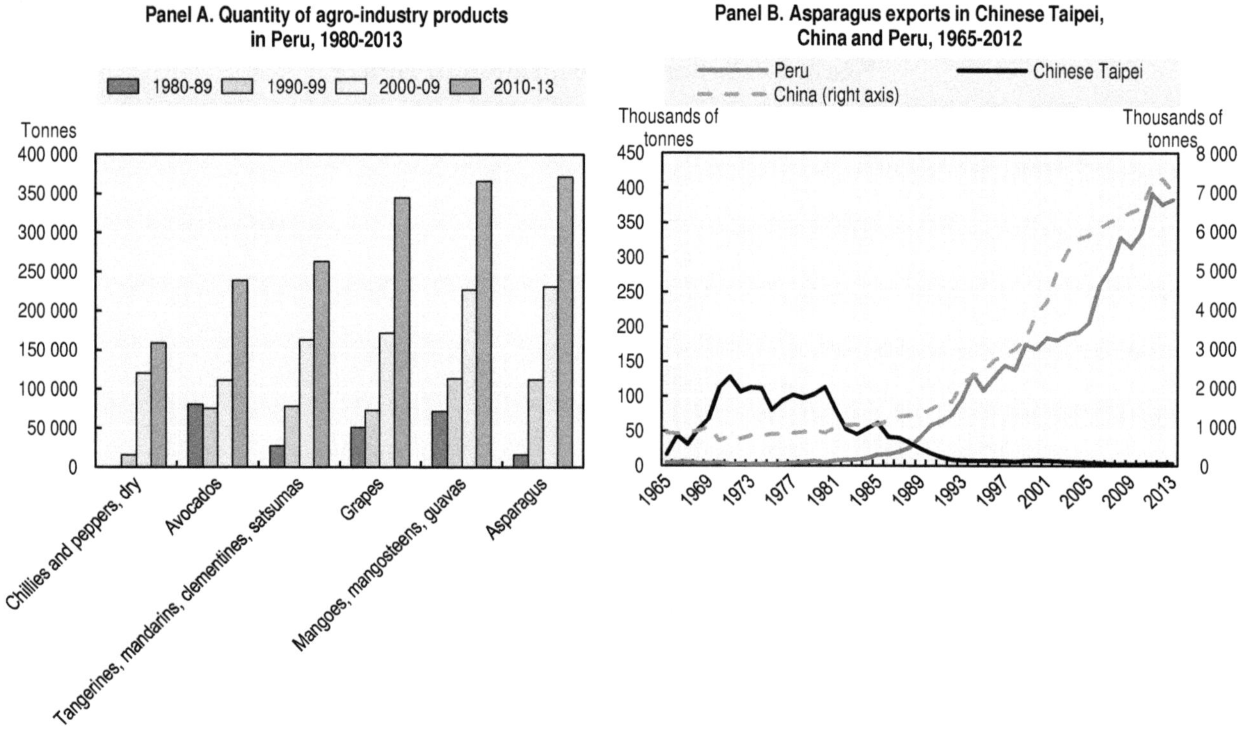

Notes: Panel A: Averages for the periods 1980-89, 1990-99, 2000-09 and 2010-13. Paprika belongs to the category chillies and peppers, dry.
Source: Food and Agriculture Organization (FAO) (2014), *FAO STAT* (database), Food and Agriculture Organization of the United Nations, Rome, *http://faostat3.fao.org/download/Q/QC/E* (accessed on 1 July 2016).

StatLink *http://dx.doi.org/10.1787/888933411269*

The emergence of the agro-industry provides valuable insights into key relationships for achieving higher productivity and economic diversification.[12] These include external factors affecting the demand and supply of these products, private partnerships with both external actors and the public sector, reforms aimed at increasing land productivity and opening markets, and the development of domestic research and areas affecting agro-processing in Peru.

Taking advantage of external conditions

A key external driver of the Peru's initial expansion of asparagus production in the 1980s was the decrease in production by Chinese Taipei, then the largest exporter. China and Peru were able to meet the unattended demand (Shimizu, 2006; Figure 2.8, Panel B). In addition, favourable temperatures in Peru yield two harvests per year versus one in the northern hemisphere. Thus, Peru can supply asparagus during northern markets' off-season. Finally, asparagus would later benefit from the rising demand in emerging and developed markets for healthy food.

Co-operating with international actors

Several partnerships and co-operations with external actors favoured the adoption of international technology standards in the production process. In the 1980s, the partnership between the U.S. Agency for International Development and the International Co-operative Agriculture Association resulted in the creation of an asparagus seed variety and the promotion of asparagus exports to the United States. Later, drip irrigation technology would be adapted from Israel (Shimizu, 2009). Some recent instances of foreign influence include imports of plastic covers from Italy to create favourable micro climates,[13] and imports of chemical fertilisers, new seed varieties and pest control mechanisms.

Favouring the interactions between the private and public sectors

Partnerships and associations between the public and private sector were fundamental in developing the agro-industry across different dimensions. The Chavimochic irrigation project was initiated under public-private association, amplifying the benefits of drip irrigation. The third stage of the Chivomochic project is currently in progress. In 2004, the Olmos irrigation project was licensed, and in 2014, it was inaugurated. Supported by public entities, private companies created associations to improve co-ordination and capacity building among these firms. Thanks to the Comisión de Promoción del Perú para la Exportación y el Turismo (PROMPERU) and the Ministry of Agriculture and Irrigation (MINAGRI), the Instituto Peruano de Espárragos was created in 1998 to raise phytosanitary standards and open new foreign markets.

Supported by the Comisión para la Promoción de Exportaciones (former PROMPERU), the creation of sectoral associations contributed to the development of new products. These include the Asociación de Productores de Uva de Mesa del Perú for grapes, Asociación de Productores de Palta Hass del Perú for avocados, and Asociación de Productores de Cítricos del Perú for citrus fruits. These institutions contributed to reaching new markets, notably Northeast Asian countries in the last years (Meade, Baldwin and Calvin, 2010).

Public reforms and initiatives to increase productivity and open markets

In addition to private initiatives, the public sector made reforms aimed at developing the agro-industry's reach to international markets. From the mid-1990s, land tenure became unrestricted, changing Peru's agrarian structure. Under the new reforms, nascent large corporations where able to integrate production and distribution processes. Furthermore, the trade agreements held with the United States were renewed in 2012, and new commercial treaties were signed with China in 2009.

PROMPERU's role to promote Peru's products and to inform on new trends in international demand has contributed to the expansion of new products and markets, in particular for micro and small firms (Carballo and Volpe Martincus, 2010).

Domestic initiatives to integrate innovation and technology

Despite the relevance of foreign expertise, some progress has been achieved at the domestic level to increase knowledge and innovation. For instance, the Asociación Civil Frío Aéreo (created in 1997) aims to improve the logistical capabilities to export fresh products and to promote research and development for effective logistics chains. In addition, the Instituto Nacional de Innovación Agraria, in co-ordination with universities, played a key role in developing fresh products, thanks to technology transfer. Owing to these initiatives, Peru could respond to European and US demand for fresh asparagus. Since 2002, exports of fresh asparagus exceeded those of processed asparagus; in 2016, they represent more than two times the exports of processed asparagus (ADEX, 2015).

Although domestic research and development remains sparse, there are useful examples. For instance, the Universidad Nacional Agraria La Molina has furnished research on the fulfilment of international quality standards and the development of new pesticides and other technologies. The success of the agro-industry has also fostered agro-engineering, as with the Universidad Privada Antenor Orrego's School of Agronomy (Carnoy and Luschei, 2008).

The development of sustainable services: the case of tourism

The expansion of tourism in Peru is relevant since it is a powerful tool for promoting economic diversification and job creation. The number of tourists has increased by 9.5% annually in the period 2005-15.[14] The tourism boom in Peru is high compared to other Latin American economies, such as Argentina, Bolivia, Chile, Ecuador and Mexico (World Bank, 2016). The resultant diversification is evident in the incorporation of 25 tourist products in 2014 and the 50 new products under development by the Ministerio de Comercio Exterior y Turismo (MINCETUR, 2014a).[15] This boom translates equally into job creation. An increase of PEN 1 million (Peruvian soles) in the final demand for travel agencies and touristic operators services creates 34 new jobs, an equal increase in the demand for restaurants and accommodation-related activities creates 50 new jobs. By contrast, only 3.5 new jobs are created in mining. Demand for tourism also increases national production considerably, due to the high participation of domestic inputs in the production process (Palomino and Pérez, 2011).[16]

The public sector has played a key role in the development of tourism. Tourism policies expanded considerably from the 1960s with the creation of the Corporación del Turismo del Perú, which later became part of MINCETUR. In the 1970s, policies were implemented to promote the formation of a professional workforce, develop tourism infrastructure and promote Peru as a destination. The creation of PROMPERU at the beginning of the 1990s contributed to diversification in tourism by highlighting Peru's archaeological heritage and natural and cultural diversity (Fuller, 2014).

PROMPERU, MINAGRI and MINCETUR policies and initiatives have also promoted Peruvian culture, such as gastronomy and craftworks, in foreign and domestic markets. In particular, Peruvian cuisine competes on par with the highest international standards, owing to 1) its geographic diversity and the variety of high-quality products from the Amazon, Andes and Pacific Ocean, and 2) its ethnic diversity (e.g. Quechua, European and Asian-Peruvian, mainly consisting in Chinese and Japanese ancestry). At the sub-national level, initiatives promoted by MINCETUR, such as "*Arequipa, una experiencia Gastrónomica*", "*La Ruta del Pisco*" and "*Turismo Gastronómico de la Quinua en Puno*", exploit the origin of gastronomy to boost tourism across regions.

MINCETUR has also advanced various initiatives to develop socially sustainable tourism, such as "*Al turista, lo nuestro*", "*De mi tierra, un producto*" and "*Turismo Rural Comunitario*" (MINCETUR, 2013). The next step is to consolidate these projects and increase community participation in that process (MINCETUR, 2014b; Asensio and Pérez, 2012; Pérez, 2008).

The potential of processed goods: the case of metal-mechanics

Metal-mechanics are indispensable inputs for major economic sectors, such as mining, construction, energy, fishing and agriculture. Furthermore, the knowledge embedded in the production of these products is valuable for the development of other high value-added industries, providing opportunities for Peru to move up from a low value-added exports basket (Hausmann, 2012).

Driven by the mining boom, metal-mechanical exports grew by 10.8% annually between 2005 and 2015, achieving USD 534 million by 2015. However, the slowdown in domestic and regional demand led to a decrease in metal-mechanical exports' participation in recent years.[17]

A key opportunity is to foster the demand for metal-mechanics beyond the mining sector. The sector currently relies on demand in development mining, hydrocarbons and infrastructure megaprojects, such as Tía María, Toquepala, Quellaveco, the Gasoducto del Sur and the refurbishment of Talara's refinery (Horizonte Minero, 2015). Increasing the use of metal-mechanics in other sectors, such as fishing and agriculture, could ensure the sustainability and growth of the sector.

The external markets put additional pressure to modernise the sector. New trade agreements – particularly with Turkey, the eighth largest exporter of steel – and China's subsidies to steelmakers deepen Peru's dependence on metal-mechanical imports (Mendes de Paula, 2011). This dependence on imports impedes the knowledge spill-overs derived from the production of metal-mechanics – knowledge highly transferable to other activities, permitting further diversification. To remain competitive, Peru requires a more extensive use of software and process automation within the industry.

The potential of the forestry

The unexploited potential of Peru's forestry industry is striking, compared to neighbour countries. Natural forests cover 53% of the country and represent the second largest naturally forested territory in Latin America. While Peru's forest products exports amounted to USD 131 million in 2014, Brazil's were USD 8 245 million, Chile's were USD 4 691 million and Uruguay's were USD 1 194 million (based on FAO, 2014). In 2014, forest products imports to Peru were 6.5 times more than domestic production and imports of forest products grew by 12% annually between 2004 and 2014 (MINAGRI, 2014).

Peruvian authorities are tackling the main challenges, such as the sector's limited access to credit, the low processing of forestry products and the difficulties in property rights for use of forested areas (MINAGRI, 2014). The Ley Forestal y de Fauna Silvestre, approved in September 2015, created the Servicio Nacional Forestal y de Fauna Silvestre (SERFOR) to provide and execute plans for the use and conservation of forestry resources, to facilitate formalities linked with the use of forestry resources and to promote the access of forestry products to financial markets. Moreover, the approved law recognises tree plantations as crops, improving access to private and public financing programmes. The importance of the forestry industry was also formally recognised in the Plan Nacional de Diversificación Productiva, which contemplates subsidies to forestry and reforms to the sector's regulations (Ministry of Production [PRODUCE], 2014).

Recent initiatives supporting start-ups and entrepreneurship

Promoting start-ups and enhancing entrepreneurship are key inputs to boost economic diversification in Peru. Recent initiatives by PRODUCE and the Council of Science, Technology and Technological Innovation (CONCYTEC) have bolstered the design and implementation of policy support to start-ups. Two key examples are StartUp Perú, part of the Innovate Perú programme from PRODUCE, and Ideas Audaces, part of the CienciActiva initiative from CONCYTEC. Both StartUp Perú and Ideas Audaces receive resources from the Fund Framework for Innovation, Science and Technology (FOMITEC). Start-up promotion is allocated 35.5% of FOMITEC's total budget of 300 million soles (close to USD 86 million). In addition, Corporación Financiera de Desarrollo (COFIDE) development bank participates in financing private initiatives to support investment funds or to select start-ups.

StartUp Perú promotes dynamic enterprises. Its introduction in 2012 marked a milestone in public policies to support start-ups in Peru, since until then, only some private sector initiatives existed (e.g. the Wayra initiative of Telefónica). StartUp Perú operates with an assigned budget from FOMITEC of PEN 50 million (close to USD 15 million), to be executed in the period 2013-19, with residual activities in 2020. In the first four calls, from 2012 to 2016, StartUp Perú evaluated 2 054 proposals and 172 start-ups and 14 incubators received support. In addition, seven incubators benefited from the programme line for strengthening ecosystem. As of 2016, StartUp Perú incorporates support for networks of angel investors and line of business accelerators (OECD, 2016b).

Ideas Audaces finances projects of the scientific and technological base in key sectors. In the first phase, it co-finances contributions to feasibility studies and prototypes with seed capital. Technically and economically viable projects move to a second phase based on growth potential, whereby Ideas Audaces provides seed capital up to PEN 2.6 million (close to USD 780 000). In its first 2014 edition, 22 projects were selected for the first phase and 4 entered the second phase of production scale; in 2015, 40 projects were selected (OECD, 2016b).

Private resource mobilisation has also been useful to promote angel investment in Peru (OECD, 2016b). For instance, Alta El Dorado entrepreneurship is a joint venture between private equity institutions Alta Ventures and El Dorado Investments. Among other programmes, Alta El Dorado has Kickstart Peru, a capital fund sponsored by COFIDE. The fund provides capital and a network of mentors for early stage development of high-impact projects to facilitate start-ups obtaining seed capital. Another example is the network of angel investors Angel Ventures Peru, established in 2014. The network has a co-investment fund and provides mentoring, consulting and other services, such as infrastructure, for entrepreneurs through a business accelerator.

Universities have become relevant in supporting start-ups in Peru. The EmprendeAhora programme, organised by the Invest Institute in conjunction with the Center for International Private Enterprise and the University of Lima, seeks to promote entrepreneurship among young people by providing scholarships to outstanding students from regional universities. Recipients benefit from a four-month training programme in business management and mentoring support to develop a business plan. In 2014, the programme attracted 130 applicants from 40 universities in 24 regions (OECD, 2016b).

Public-private networks also support corporate development in Peru. Institutions are organised into networks to promote collaboration and entrepreneurial culture. PeruEmprende brings together institutions working on entrepreneurship and innovation in the public, private and academic spheres. Fifty-three institutions participated in the 2015 "Month of

Entrepreneurship", with over 100 events in 12 cities across the country, including workshops, conferences and fairs, among others (OECD, 2016b).

However, taking advantage of these recent policies is undermined by continued bureaucratic burdens on business creation (Global Entrepreneurship Monitor Perú, 2014). In particular, bottlenecks in product market regulation (PMR) and inefficiencies in the legal framework can impede the development of start-ups in Peru.

Policy actions to increase productivity and economic diversification in Peru

The following section presents four avenues for policy action to boost productivity and economic diversification in Peru: 1) increase support for innovation and SME sustainability and reduce barriers to entrepreneurship; 2) enhanced regional integration; 3) improve management of commodity-based revenues at the sub-national level; and 4) increase fiscal revenues and implement a fairer and more efficient taxation system.

Supporting innovation and SMEs

Low levels of investment in research and development are affecting innovation outcomes in Peru. Peru's business expenditure on research and development (below 0.1% of GDP) remains significantly below the average for OECD member countries (close to 1.6% of GDP) and many other countries in Latin America (0.17% for the Latin American benchmark countries).[18] Peru also remains well below benchmark and OECD member countries in intellectual property imports and exports, figuring into the country's low contribution to global activity in research and development (OECD, 2015). One measure of innovation outcome is number of patents. Peru's patent applications per million inhabitants are below all of the benchmark countries, as well as the LAC average (Figure 2.9). While patent applications have increased in recent years from 5.7 on average in the period 2005-10 to 13.4 in 2013, this number remains well below median for OECD member countries (close to 1 194 patents in 2013) (OECD, 2011).

Figure 2.9. **Patent applications per million people in selected countries, 2013**

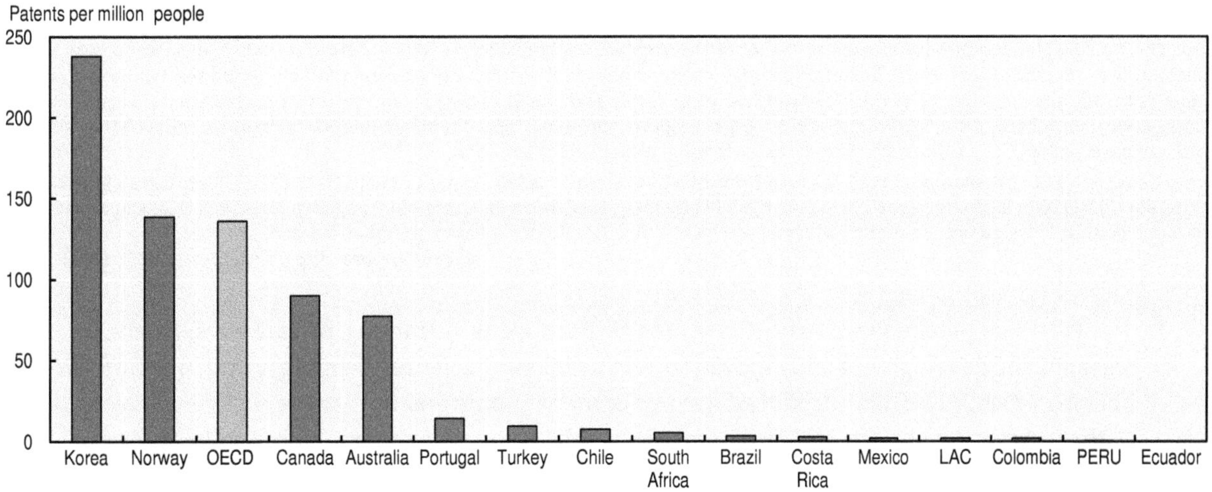

Source: Patent Cooperation Treaty, 2013 data; OECD Indicators on Patents (database), OECD, *www.oecd.org/sti/inno/oecdpatentdatabases.htm* (accessed on 1 July 2016).

StatLink http://dx.doi.org/10.1787/888933411273

Greater investment in innovation is needed to increase economic diversification and competitiveness in Peru, which in turn support higher survival rates for new product exports outside the mining sector and for micro, small and medium-sized firms (Figure 2.10).

Figure 2.10. **Survival rates of export firms in Peru, 2003-15 (%)**

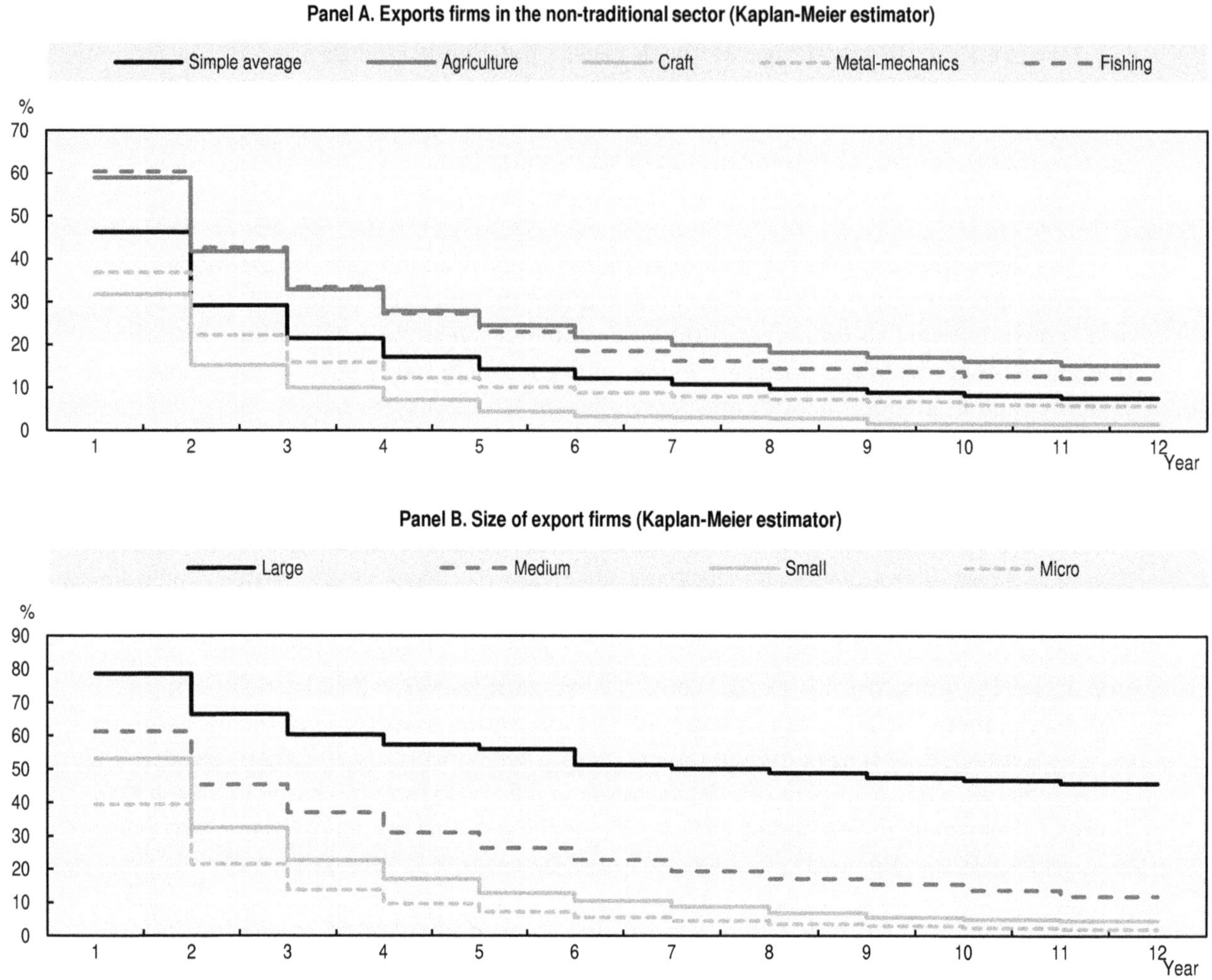

Notes: The Kaplan-Meier estimator is used to estimate the survival function from lifetime data. Estimation of year-by-year survival probabilities for exports firms. Panel A: simple average of non-traditional sectors. Agriculture and fishing are the two non-traditional sectors with the highest survival probability after five years. Craft and metal-mechanic are the two non-traditional sectors with the lowest survival probability after five years. Panel B: Large = exports value over USD 10 million. Medium = exports value USD 1-10 million. Small = exports value USD 0.1-1 million. Micro = exports value under USD 0.1 million.

Source: Panel A: OECD calculations based on data from MINCETUR and SUNAT. Panel B: MINCETUR (2015), Plan Estrategíco Nacional Exportador: PENX 2025 (National Strategic Export Plan: PENX 2025), Ministerio de Comercio Exterior y Turismo, Lima, *www.mincetur.gob.pe/newweb/Portals/0/transparencia/proyectos%20resoluciones/RM_051_2015_PLAN.pdf* based on data from SUNAT.

StatLink *http://dx.doi.org/10.1787/888933411287*

Peru has established institutions for the purpose of attracting private investment in research and development and innovation, and developing science, technology and innovation policies. CONCYTEC has introduced a series of instruments and funds to reduce bottlenecks in the innovation system and to increase business research and development. In addition, PRODUCE promotes industrial development and business innovation. PRODUCE manages two key policy instruments: the Research and Development Fund for Competitiveness, a competitive fund to co-finance projects aimed at promoting research and development for innovation; and technological innovation centres (Centros de Innovación Tecnológica [CITEs]) (OECD, 2015).

The creation of CITEs seeks to stimulate innovative and entrepreneurial behaviour in SMEs in manufacturing sectors by providing them access to the necessary knowledge, technical assistance, information and technology transfer to close productivity gaps. There are CITEs in several sectors, including agro-industry, aquaculture, leather and footwear, fisheries, mining, textiles, logistics and marketing, located across the country. The network of CITEs is co-ordinated by the Instituto Tecnológico de la Producción (ITP), a technical management entity from PRODUCE. ITP is responsible for bringing the different services of the CITEs into a harmonious and efficient relationship to serve the needs of the private sector across different regions and areas of specialisation.

Although PRODUCE foresees the creation of 44 public and private CITEs by July 2016 (37 public and 7 private), few existing public CITEs are achieving their objectives. Furthermore, some public CITEs – CITEs textile Camélidos in Cusco, Puno, Huancavelica and Arequipa; CITEs Forestal in Maynas and Pucallpa; and CITE Minero Ambiental in Madre de Dios – were only created in February 2016, too recently for informative assessment.

According to interviews with private and public actors, to achieve their main objectives, CITEs need increased technical capacity and further private sector involvement in research and development, as well as better communication with communities regarding their existence and potential benefits. The lack of information to firms regarding the main instruments to support innovation services and the absence of technology transfer are traditional inefficiencies hampering the benefits of CITEs (Cruzado and Tostes, 2015).

Tackling barriers to entrepreneurship

To promote innovation, policies should go beyond greater expenditure on research and development. As in other Latin American countries, the significant innovation gap is largely due to Peru's framework conditions, which do not make innovation a profitable form of business investment (OECD/CAF/ECLAC, 2014). In addition to the scarcity of qualified human resources (Chapter 4), barriers to entrepreneurship hinder the long-term ability of firms to accumulate in-house innovation capabilities.

Over the last decade, Peru has taken action to simplify business regulations and strengthen legal institutions in order to promote formal business practices. Several World Bank *Doing Business* indicators indicate a better performance by Peru than the LAC average, but there is room for improvement to reach OECD member country standards (OECD, 2015).

The OECD's Indicators of PMR (product market regulation) are a set of indicators that measure how policies promote or inhibit competition in areas of the product market. The three pillars are state control, barriers to trade and investment, and barriers to entrepreneurship (Barbiero et al., 2015).[19] Peru's PMR indicator was specifically developed in collaboration with the World Bank. Barriers to entrepreneurship in Peru remain above OECD member countries' average and is the most restrictive of the PMR pillars in Peru.

Among the three components of barriers to entrepreneurship, complexity of regulatory procedures and administrative burdens on start-ups (e.g. number of procedures and bodies to contact to register a company) are the most restrictive in Peru (Figure 2.11).[20] In particular, businesses operating in Peru face more complex regulatory procedures than in OECD member countries, both in licensing and permitting systems and in the general communication of rules and procedures. Sole proprietor start-up firms encounter significantly larger administrative burdens.

Figure 2.11. **Barriers to entrepreneurship index in selected countries, 2013**

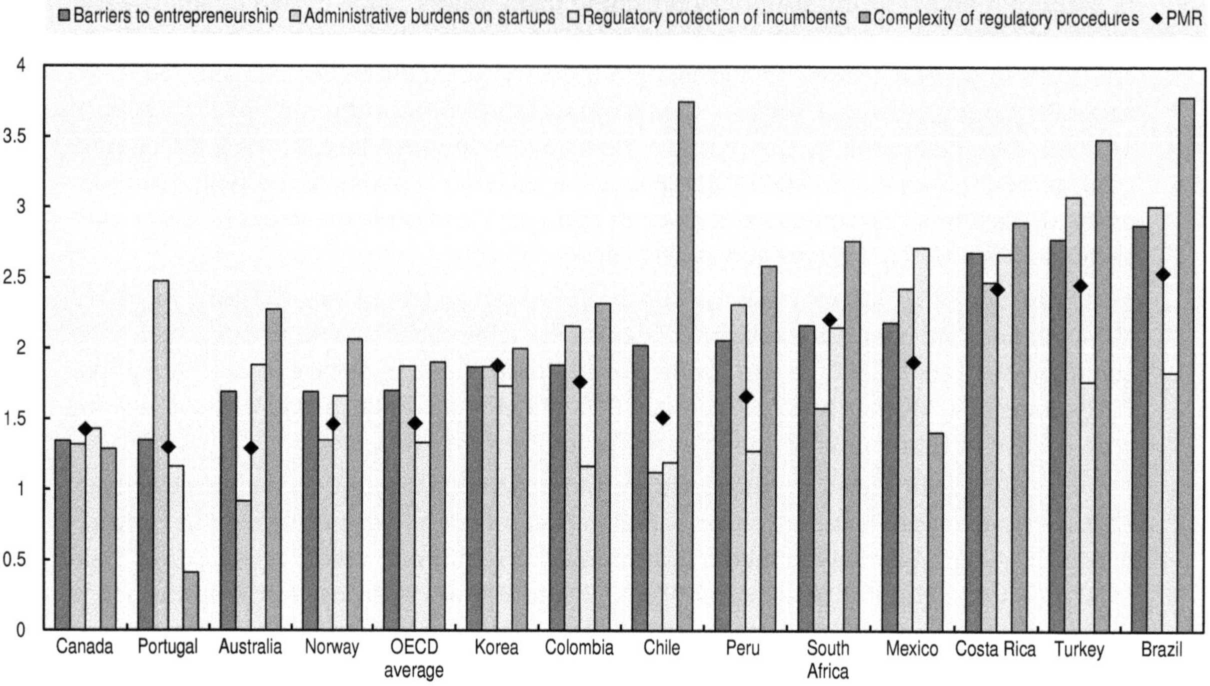

Notes: From least restrictive (0) to most restrictive (6). The figure includes OECD countries and selected benchmark economies. Barriers to entrepreneurship is one of the three components of the PMR (product market regulation) indicator. Complexity of regulatory procedures, administrative burdens on start-ups and the regulatory protection of incumbents are the three main components of the Barriers to entrepreneurship pillar. The PMR indicator for Peru was developed in collaboration with the World Bank.

Source: OECD (2013a), *OECD Product Market Regulation 2013* (database), OECD, *https://stats.oecd.org/index.aspx?DataSetCode=PMR* (accessed on 1 July 2016).

StatLink http://dx.doi.org/10.1787/888933411294

Adjustments to the legal framework in Peru are crucial to clearing these bottlenecks to entrepreneurship. In particular, the inefficiency of Peru's current bankruptcy law means that Peru's solvency regime currently takes over three years to process bankruptcies compared to 1.7 years in OECD economies (World Bank, 2015).

The informal sector accounts for over half of all labour activity in Peru (Chapter 4). In 2010, small and micro enterprises made up approximately 95% of all enterprises and employed over 9.5 million people (Torres, 2010). The government must continue to promote their proper growth and aid them in resolving hindrances to their expansion.

Increasing regional integration

Greater regional market integration with neighbour countries would allow Peru to benefit from regional economies with relatively large markets and sustainable growth. In 2012, Chile, Colombia, Mexico and Peru formed the Pacific Alliance (PA) to pursue regional integration. The PA now includes 30 observer countries, including China as of 2013.

Trade and investment flows between PA member countries are limited, representing less than 4% of total trade. In 2015, Peruvian exports to Chile, Colombia and Mexico represented only 4.1%, 2.1% and 1.2% of total trade, respectively (Reyes, 2016). This proportion remains well below intra-trade for Latin America (close to 20%), Asia (close to 45%) and the European Union (close to 60%) (OECD/CAF/ECLAC, 2015).

Peru, along with the rest of Latin American economies, should promote intra-trade of intermediate goods. Whereas the intra-trade between the United States and Canada of intermediate goods is almost 10 percentage points higher than for final goods, intra-trade of intermediate goods in Latin American economies is 4 percentage points lower than for final goods (OECD/CAF/ECLAC, 2015).

There is significant potential to strengthen intra-regional integration, underpinned by the PA's ambitious programme of trade and investment activities. Although the PA started in 2011, the formalisation of different agreements has been implemented more recently, in the past couple of years. For instance, since May 2016, there is no tariff for 92% of the products traded among PA countries, and the objective is to achieve 100% by 2030.[21] In order to promote trade across intermediate goods and foster the participation of PA countries in regional and global value chains, there is free trade of intermediate goods among these countries. They have also applied a "cumulative rules of origin", which allows products of one country to be further processed or added to products in another PA country as if they had originated in the latter country. Next steps to better take advantage of the PA as a vehicle to integrate Peru with the rest of world include the mutual recognition of standards and building in further co-operation and communication of the current benefits of this alliance.[22]

The PA will need policies to support the development of new comparative advantages in the manufacturing and service sectors in order to broaden and deepen trade flows and enable a more active role for SMEs (OECD, 2015).

The Latin American Integrated Market (Mercado Integrado Latinoamericano [MILA]) represents a key opportunity for Peru to promote investment in productive areas and attract foreign capital. Started in 2011, today, this market integrates the stock exchanges of Colombia, Lima, Mexico and Santiago. This market allows investors to access these markets through one of the registered brokers that have access to the common trading platform. It also allows companies participating in MILA to increase their capacity to raise funds. However, challenges remain to taking full advantage of this unique market. A co-ordinated approach to remove these barriers is important (International Monetary Fund [IMF], 2016), including the adoption of the highest standards in pension and financial system regulation, regulatory collaboration, and a sufficient level of legal and tax harmonisation.

In addition to trade and financial initiatives with Chile, Colombia and Mexico through the PA and MILA, Peru has moved towards greater integration with Asia-Pacific countries. Peru is a member of the Asia-Pacific Economic Cooperation (APEC), which has benefited Peru by reducing barriers and impediments to trade with the largest economies in the world, such as China (Ministry of Foreign Affairs of Peru, 2015). Peru also signed a free-trade agreement with China in 2009, which came into effect in March 2010. Along with preferential treatment to enter the Chinese market, this agreement could integrate Peru into Asian supply chains and position Peru as a business centre in South America (MINCETUR, 2015). After three years, Peru exported 312 new products (97% non-traditional) to China, created 468 new exporting companies and doubled trade between the two countries (MINCETUR, 2015).

Towards better management of commodity resources at the sub-national level

Peru's focus on commodities exports is not an isolated case, compared to OECD member countries and Latin American benchmark countries. Whereas Peru's share of commodities is higher than the OECD and Latin American averages, other countries remain more reliant on natural resources. These include OECD member countries, such as Australia and Norway, and Latin American countries, such as Colombia and Ecuador (OECD, 2015). Furthermore, some OECD member countries, such as Australia, Chile and Norway, exhibit a higher concentration of products exported than Peru. Destinations for Peru's exports are also less concentrated, compared to OECD and Latin American benchmark countries (based on WITS/ UN Comtrade, 2013).

International experience shows that countries that have managed their raw resources appropriately have seen positive benefits. The experience of OECD member countries in particular shows that commodities can be a crucial source of revenues for increasing the productivity and competitiveness of their economies (OECD, 2009). Proper management of the extraction process and the revenues raised from commodities is needed to add value in Peru's productivity.

At the national level, Peru's fiscal rule has structural (i.e. cyclically-adjusted) fiscal balance as its target to manage the volatility of commodity-based revenues (OECD, 2015). However, at the sub-national level, the volatility of international commodity prices and the uncertainty of commodity production in Peru have affected revenue streams to these authorities. Transfers of natural resources to sub-national authorities depend on canon and royalties. From the early 2000s, commodity-based regional transfers to sub-national authorities increased considerably, from less than 0.5% of GDP in 2004 to close to 1.45% of GDP in 2014. Recent decreases in commodity prices are increasing the volatility of these revenues (OECD, 2015). A key challenge, therefore, is to avoid pro-cyclicality of these funds (Jiménez and Ter-Minassian, 2016). A fiscal rule to avoid pro-cyclicality of sub-national expenditures in boom periods is needed. Linked to this, following the experiences at the national level, sub-national authorities, in co-ordination with the national government, can establish the creation of a stabilisation fund to better manage these resources.

The two main sources of commodity-based revenues for sub-national authorities, canon and royalties (Korinek, 2015), are distributed exclusively to the regional and local governments where the minerals are extracted. Canon represents half of the corporate tax from mining companies (i.e. the other half is retained by the central government), and revenue from royalties is based on the companies' profits. The fiscal transfers based on commodities per capita received by Cusco and Moquegua alone are greater than those obtained by 15 departments in Peru put together (OECD, 2015). Just 5 out of the 25 departments receive more than half of the total revenues from commodities (Figure 2.12).

In addition, these revenues have not contributed to greater productivity and inclusiveness. The concentration of these revenues in a few departments and the lack of rules regarding their expenditures have negatively affected the efficiency of municipal districts (Muñoz, 2010). Furthermore, these mining transfers have only short-term positive effects, such as an increase in temporary public employment, which responds in part to the strategic behaviour of local politicians, rather than the quality of these investments (OECD, forthcoming; Maldonado, 2015).

In addition, these fiscal revenues do not target the poorest regions, exacerbating regional disparities. Using data at the department level, the correlation between the amount of fiscal transfers per capita and the percentage of the population with at least one unmet basic need is less than -0.3. For instance, commodity-based transfers to Cusco and Moquegua are more than eight times higher than those to Amazonas, Loreto and San Martin, where over 10% of the population have at least one unmet need, compared to only 2.6% in Cusco and 1.2% in Moquegua. Revenues from FONCOMUN are not enough to compensate for the high regional heterogeneity created by revenues from natural resources. They correspond to less than half of the commodity-based transfers at the sub-national level (OECD, 2015).

Figure 2.12. **Mismatch between regional commodity transfers (2014 data) and basic needs transfers (2013 data) per capita in Peru (in PEN)**

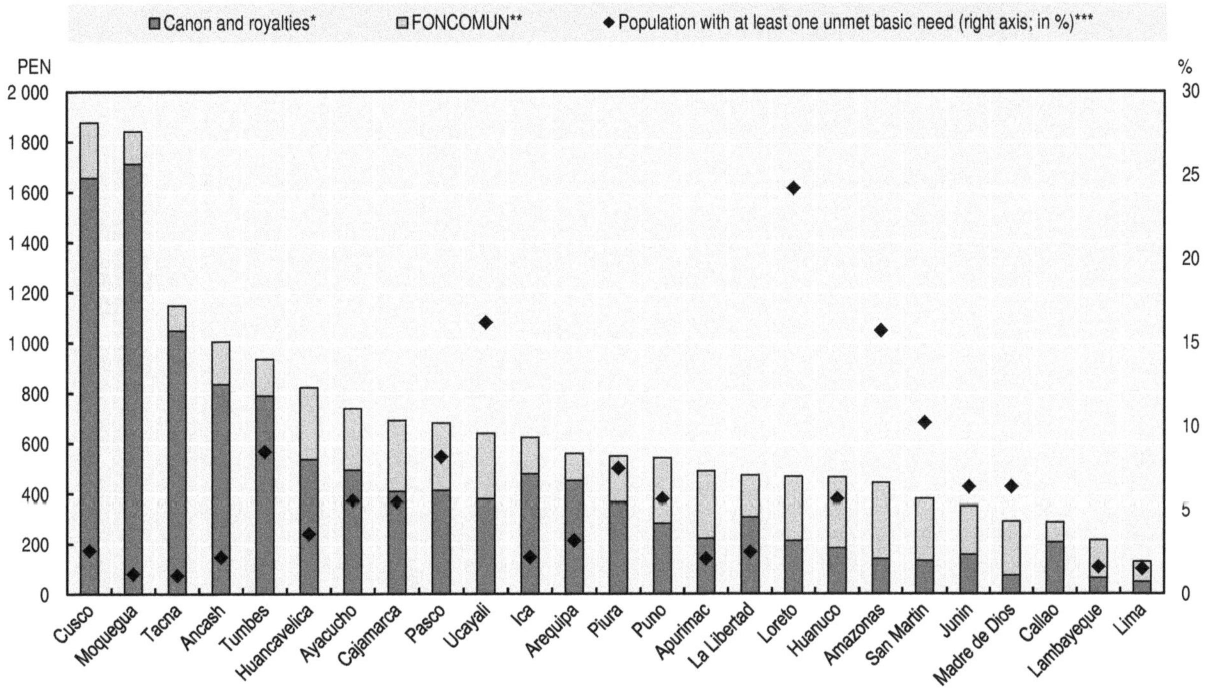

Notes: *The canon and royalties are transfers of natural resources. Canon is distributed exclusively to the sub-national governments where the minerals are extracted. Royalties are based on companies' profits and canon represents 50% of the corporate tax from mining companies. Customs are also included. **The Municipal Compensation Fund (FONCOMUM) seeks to promote investment at the municipal level with a redistributive objective. It prioritises the poorest municipalities, particularly in rural areas and marginal urban areas. ***The components of unmet basic needs are quality of the house, non-overcrowding of the house, access to sanitary services, school attendance and economic dependency. No data for Callao.

Source: Unmet basic needs data from OECD calculations based on National Households Survey, Encuesta Nacional de Hogares [ENAHO]) from the INEI, *www.inei.gob.pe/estadisticas/indice-tematico/sociales/*. Mining royalties data from SUNAT, *www.sunat.gob.pe*. Hydrocarbon royalties data from PERUPETRO S.A., *www.perupetro.com.pe/*. FONCOMUN and canon data from MEF (2015), "Consulta de Transferencias a los Gobiernos Nacional, Regional, Local y EPS", Transparencia Económica website, *http://apps5.mineco.gob.pe/transferencias/cuadros/Hoja1_1.aspx*.

StatLink http://dx.doi.org/10.1787/888933411306

A key challenge is to improve the allocation of commodity-based transfers according to the level of development of Peruvian departments and the need to increase inclusive development, competitiveness and formal job creation at the sub-national level. As with Colombia before the 2011 Royalties Reform, Peru needs to increase diversification of these revenues across the regions (OECD, 2013b) – for instance, to finance education and skills systems, infrastructure development or research and innovation policies. Prioritising and planning these investments should be carried out with a dialogue between national and sub-national governments and private actors, civil society and academia. To improve the management of these revenues, support for governance capacity at the sub-national level is also needed. This is particularly relevant, since some authorities do not follow regulatory frameworks because they lack knowledge of the complete legal process required to adopt and implement policies (Muñoz, 2005). Equalisation mechanisms to compensate for inequalities (exacerbated by commodity-based transfers) are needed among sub-national governments.

Towards greater fiscal resources with fair and efficient taxation

Although tax revenues as a share of GDP in Peru increased by more than 6.7 percentage points between 1990 and 2014 to reach 18.8% of GDP in 2014, they remain low, compared to OECD member countries, representing 34.4% of GDP and Latin American countries, representing 21.7% of GDP (Figure 2.13; OECD/ECLAC/Inter-American Center of Tax Administrations [CIAT]/Inter-American Development Bank [IDB], 2016).

Figure 2.13. **Tax revenues (% of GDP) in selected countries, 2014**

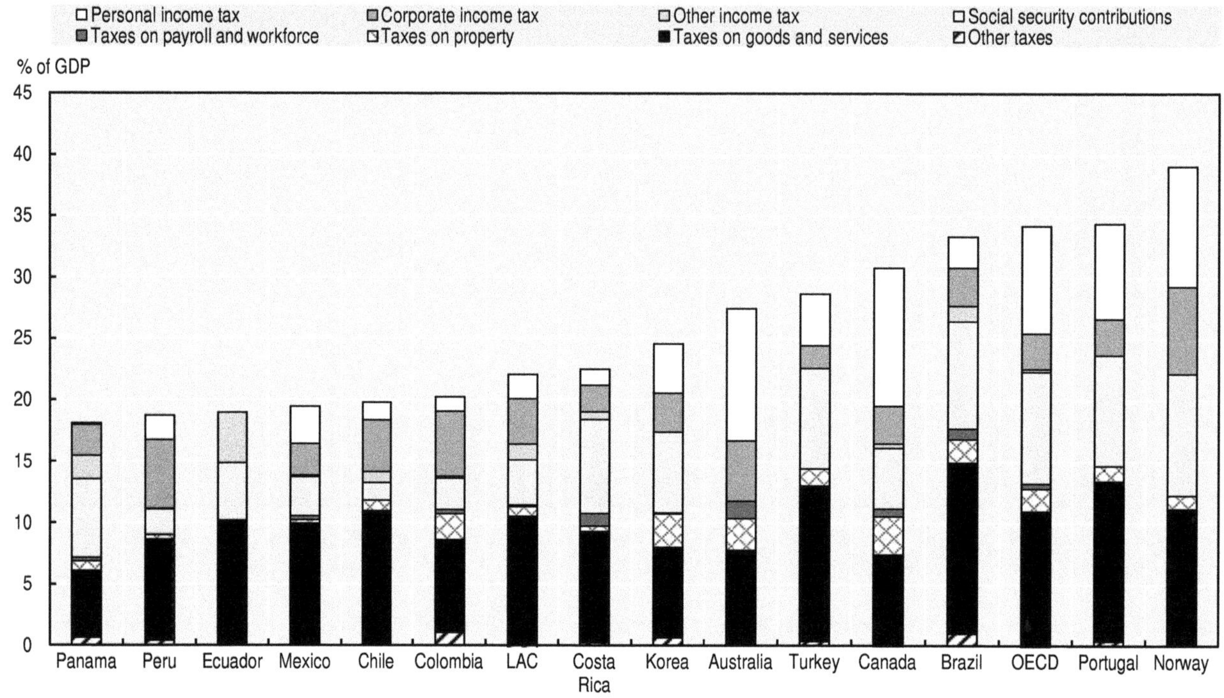

Note: 2013 data for OECD economies and OECD average, with exceptions of Chile and Mexico.

Source: OECD/ECLAC/CIAT/IDB (2016), *Revenue Statistics in Latin America and the Caribbean*, OECD Publishing, Paris *http://dx.doi.org/10.1787/rev_lat-2016-en-fr*.

StatLink *http://dx.doi.org/10.1787/888933411314*

Peru must improve its tax policy to finance the investment necessary to increase productivity, achieve economic diversification and sustain socioeconomic progress. The current tax system does not raise sufficient revenues to finance needed research and development and innovation; transport infrastructure and logistics (Chapter 3); and education and skills (Chapter 4; OECD, 2016a). Tax reforms should take into account the synergies and trade-offs of policies targeted at each issue so as to achieve win-win policies that increase productivity and reduce inequalities (OECD, 2016c). Furthermore, to ensure the fiscal legitimacy to support tax reforms, Peru should continue improving its public governance and investments, by improving for instance the prioritisation and implementation of a strategic development plan and the management of commodity-based revenues.

Contrary to most OECD economies, Peru's tax structure is characterised by a high dependence on indirect taxation that limits redistribution effects and hampers entrepreneurship. In 2014, taxes on goods and services (indirect taxes) represented nearly 44% of all taxes. While comparable to the average for Latin American economies (49.5%), this share is high, compared to the OECD member country average (32.7%). A key component of taxes on goods and services is the Value Added Tax (VAT), from which revenues increased 5.5 percentage points from 1990 to 2014.

The limited share of the most progressive tax does not offset the non-progressive VAT (Barreix, Bès and Roca, 2011; Jaramillo, 2014). Direct taxes, personal income taxes in particular, remain low. While personal income taxes represent close to 25% of total taxes in OECD economies on average, they represent only 11% in Peru, a slightly higher proportion than in Latin American countries (OECD/ECLAC/CIAT/IDB, 2016). Moreover, personal income taxes as a share of GDP represent close to 7 percentage points less than in OECD economies. The absence of an inheritance tax also undermines the progressiveness of the taxation system.

Taxes and social transfers do little to reduce income inequalities in Peru. While, in Peru, inequalities (measured by the Gini index) decline by only 1 percentage point after taxes and transfers, they decline by 2.2 percentage points in LAC economies and more than 15 percentage points in OECD economies (based on OECD, 2016d, for OECD economies; and Lustig, 2016, for Latin American economies).

To increase the tax base to finance broad-based policies to boost productivity and improve progressiveness, reforms should reduce elusion and evasion (with better institutional capacity to address the challenges), decrease generous tax exemptions and gradually increase the marginal personal income tax rate. As in other emerging markets, base erosion and profit shifting (BEPS) has major significance for Peru due to the country's heavy reliance on corporate income tax, particularly from multinational enterprises. Peru's further involvement in OECD work on BEPS would help to minimise it.[23]

Creating better planning and implementation frameworks to boost economic diversification and productivity

Implementing policies that tackle barriers to greater productivity and economic diversification requires a better institutional framework for the strategic development agenda. The role of the centre of government (CoG) can be strengthened by increasing leadership, co-ordination and long-term implementation of that agenda (OECD, 2016e). A key aspect is to execute, through public investment and other implementation policies, the prioritisation and planning of policies highlighted in the development agenda. Also identified are actions to increase the capacity of sub-national authorities in the design and implementation of their regional, provincial and district plans and to improve the co-ordination with the national government.

Towards the design and implementation of a development strategy

One of the four objectives of the National Accord (Acuerdo Nacional) is to promote competitiveness in Peru.[24] The National Accord started in 2002 and is the set of state policies for sustainable development, developed and approved on the basis of dialogue and consensus after a process of workshops and consultations at the national level. Party to the accord are the government, political parties with representation in the Congress and organisations representing civil society at the national level.

In recent years, Peru has proposed many policies to promote economic diversification and productivity. Several ministries and public-sector entities have presented valuable analyses on current socioeconomic challenges and set out objectives for the medium term. Most include a component on productivity and economic diversification policies. Examples are the Plan Bicentenario: El Perú hacia el 2021 (and its Plan Estratégico de Desarrollo

Nacional Actualizado); the Agenda de Competitividad 2014-2018; the National Plan for Productive Diversification; the National Strategic Export Plan (PENX); the National Strategy on Development and Social Inclusion: Incluir para Crecer; and Plan Estratégico Nacional de Turismo (PENTUR) 2008-2018.

The Plan Bicentenario: El Perú hacia el 2021 is the National Strategic Development Plan (Plan Estratégico de Desarrollo Nacional), launched in 2011 by the National Centre for Strategic Planning (CEPLAN) as part of the Presidency of the Council of Ministers (PCM) and with the participation of different ministries, sub-national authorities, the private sector and civil society (CEPLAN, 2011). An updated version of this plan was released in October 2015, renamed Plan Estratégico de Desarrollo Nacional Actualizado: Perú hacia el 2021 (CEPLAN, 2015). This updated version presents scenarios and targets for the Peruvian economy in 2021. Annex 2.A2 outlines components of this plan.

The formulation of strategic development plans, at both the sectoral and territorial level, takes as guidelines the objectives of the National Accord and the framework of the Plan Bicentenario (Figure 2.14). These strategic development plans suppose the defining of development plans at the horizontal level, among different sectoral ministries, and at the vertical level, among different levels of government, following the general principles highlighted in the Plan Bicentenario. These plans should also contribute to improving the quality of public investment by enabling prioritisation of projects requiring public investment.

At the horizontal level, the PENX, led by the Ministry of Trade and Tourism, and the National Plan for Productive Diversification, led by PRODUCE, are among the key plans to boost productivity, competitiveness and economic diversification in Peru. In addition, the National Competitiveness and Formalisation Council (Consejo Nacional de Competitividad y Formalización [CNCF]) produces the Agenda de Competitividad 2014-2018 with short- and medium-term measures to increase competitiveness towards Peru's successful immersion into the global market. Annex 2.A2 describes the objectives and topics of these plans.

Examples of other national sectoral plans on policies affecting productivity and economic diversification include the National Strategy on Development and Social Inclusion: Incluir para Crecer; the National Strategic Plan of Tourism 2008-2018, complemented by the National Plan of Tourism Quality; and the Development Plan of Logistics Services on Transport (Chapter 3).

While all these plans and agendas aim to tackle the main challenges in Peru, the country will need better co-ordination among public institutions to determine priorities and a better connection between the budgeting process and these agendas to adopt and implement reforms for inclusive development (Figure 2.14; OECD, 2016e). Peru should strengthen the CoG by better integrating and co-ordinating the PCM and MEF in the prioritisation process.

In particular, Peru lags behind benchmark countries in the co-ordination of public policies. Despite efforts to increase dialogue among different institutions in recent years, the lack of collaboration and co-ordination among ministries and within the administration is an obstacle to effective policy making and implementation. On a scale of 0 (very little co-ordination) to 4 (strong co-ordination), perception of co-ordination and collaboration between ministries and with administration in Peru scores 1 – below averages for both Latin America (2) and OECD member countries (2.5) (Institutional Profiles Database [IPD], 2012). This poor performance can be explained by a number of factors, such as weak prioritisation and implementation phases for policies involving several ministries, a direct consequence of which is the lack of trust in institutions and of fiscal legitimacy. Several institutions in Peru suffer from lack of public confidence. In particular, compared to benchmark countries, few citizens in Peru trust the national government (OECD, 2015).

Figure 2.14. **Strategic and development plans in Peru at different levels of government**

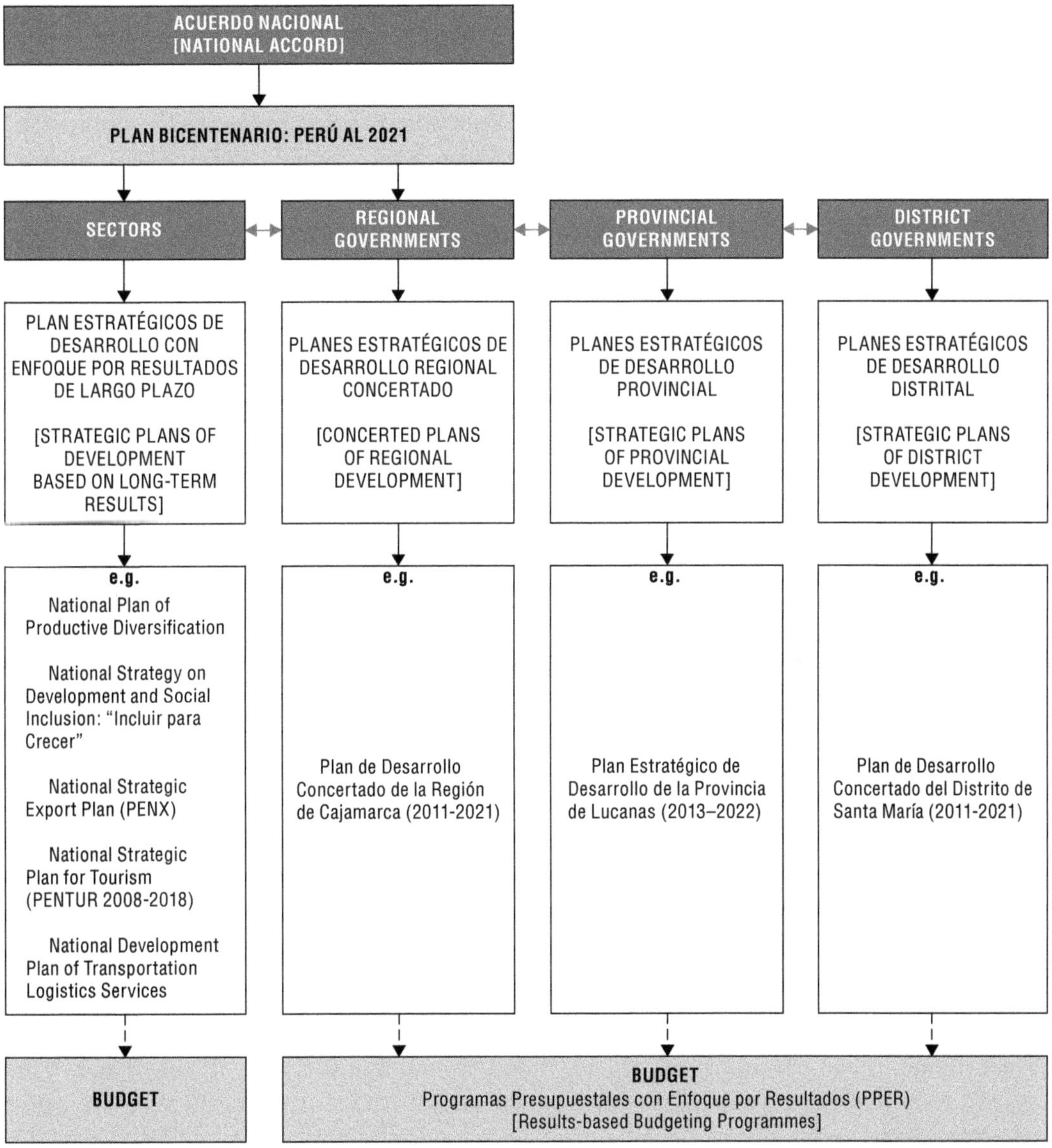

Source: OECD based on National Accord, *http://acuerdonacional.pe/* (accessed on 1 July 2016).; CEPLAN (2015), Plan Estratégico de Desarrollo Nacional Actualizado: Perú hacia el 2021, Centro Nacional de Planeamiento Estratégico, Lima; MINCETUR (2015), Plan Estrategíco Nacional Exportador: PENX 2025 (National Strategic Export Plan: PENX 2025), Ministerio de Comercio Exterior y Turismo, Lima, *www.mincetur.gob.pe/newweb/Portals/0/transparencia/proyectos%20 resoluciones/RM_051_2015_PLAN.pdf*; and PRODUCE (2014), Plan Nacional de Diversificación Productiva, Ministerio de la Producción, Lima.

Moreover, these plans are not binding, in terms of the implementation of regulatory or investment policies to achieve the objectives highlighted in the National Strategic Development Plan. These plans are also not linked with the two policy frameworks – the Multi-Annual Investment Plan and the Presupuesto por Resultados (results-based budgeting) – set by the MEF to increase coherence in the delivery of public policy, nor are they place-based.

Consequently, the CoG faces challenges related to leadership, co-ordination and long-term implementation of policies. The CoG is composed of the PCM, including CEPLAN, and the MEF. To increase the effectiveness of public policies, a country's CoG needs to offer vision, leadership and innovation. This is especially difficult in Peru, as the country faces high levels of political and public-sector fragmentation. In addition, the lack of enforcement of a National Development Plan in the long term negatively affects both strategic policy-making capacity and service-delivery capacity. In that context, there is a lack of co-ordination of public policies in the medium and long term, and there is a high turnover of representatives in one of the main CoGs. In the period 2000-15, there were 20 different Presidents of the Council of Ministers, representing close to 6 appointments per presidential mandate. This high turnover owes primarily to political and corruption scandals (even those originating outside the PCM).

To provide further leadership, co-ordination and long-term implementation of policies, the CoG should improve the planning and prioritisation of polices while improving the implementation of the objectives. First, the strategic plan defined by the CoG must highlight the priorities to increase inclusive development. Given better co-ordination and leadership with the ministries, other plans and agendas should follow those priorities at the sectoral level. Second, the priorities should be binding at the implementation level, including the budget and changes in the regulatory framework. Regarding the former, the National System of Public Investment (SNIP) should be aligned with the priorities and policies defined in the plan. Linking strategic planning with the fiscal framework would create a greater incentive to produce coherent and actionable plans and to develop a more strategic approach to public investment.

Towards greater capacity and co-ordination in the design and implementation of the development agenda at the sub-national level

Strategic planning at the sub-national level needs greater consistency with national planning. The National Strategic Development Plan establishes a framework for national policy priorities, and Concerted Regional Development Plans provide a complementary framework for priority setting at a regional level (Figure 2.15 above).[25] However, national policies and priorities are not necessarily reflected or considered in sub-national planning (OECD, forthcoming; OECD, 2015).

To improve co-ordination between levels of government, an institutional framework for inter-governmental commissions was put in place as of 2007, but its implementation remains poor. Composed of representatives from national ministries and sub-national governments, these commissions are intended to manage the decentralisation process across different sectoral policies. However, by the end of 2015, only three such commissions were considered active by the Decentralisation Bureau: health, labour and education. The lack of implementation is partly due to lack of agreement about the mechanisms to elect representatives of local governments (OECD, forthcoming).

In addition, the poorest municipalities have limited capacity to execute an effective development agenda. Local governments lack the human resources and experience to fulfil their roles, resulting in poor management of municipal public services. Some authorities do not follow regulatory frameworks because they lack knowledge of the complete legal process required to adopt and implement policies (Muñoz, 2005). Sub-national authorities require effective support from the central government to improve the efficiency of expenditures from regional transfers (OECD, 2015). The central government should also consider implementing more asymmetric, place-based decentralisation (OECD, forthcoming). Currently, small municipalities have the same requirements as bigger ones, without the same capabilities, nor necessarily the same types of issues.

As such, Peru should establish more effective and strategic institutional support capacity that can facilitate a partnership-based approach to regional development between departments and the national government. There are two options to achieve this outcome. A deconcentrated agency of the PCM and MEF can work in partnership at a macro-regional level, or regional development agencies (RDAs) can be constituted as a partnership between departments and the national government (OECD, forthcoming).

Last, regional planning should be better integrated with the fiscal framework. While regional plans provide a platform to strengthen regional priorities in the design and execution of national sectoral policies, they are not totally integrated nor efficiently linked to the fiscal frameworks. The MEF (through the RDA or deconcentrated agency) could be required to work in partnership with departments to develop medium-term capital investment programmes that deliver on strategic priorities identified in Regional Concerted Development Plans (OECD, forthcoming). In addition, an established process to monitor the implementation of the Concerted Regional Development, aligned with department's budget, would favour the execution of these plans.

Conclusions and policy recommendations

This chapter highlights opportunities and policy actions to boost economic productivity and diversification in Peru. In particular, sectors with potential for greater exploitation were identified based on international experiences and recent trends in international trade demand. Agro-industry, tourism and, more recently, metal-mechanics and forestry reveal underlying factors for successful economic diversification: appropriate co-operation with international actors, effective interactions between private and public sectors, domestic initiatives to integrate innovation and technology, and structural reforms.

A series of policy actions will promote further economic diversification and productivity, such as improving the quality of education for all Peruvians, supporting innovation and development of SMEs, tackling barriers to entrepreneurship, promoting greater regional integration, improving the management of commodity-based resources, and increasing tax revenues to finance effective broad-based policies.

To achieve these policy actions, Peru needs to improve the institutional framework in the design and implementation of a development agenda. In particular, the CoG needs to improve the co-ordination, leadership and implementation of long-term policies. Based on policy priorities presented in the National Development Plan, policies should be executed effectively at and among the national and sub-national levels.

Box 2.1 summarises the main policy recommendations and requirements for each area covered in this chapter.

These recommendations were informed by the three future-state scenarios outlined in Chapter 1. The chapter concludes with an assessment of their implications to incentives, trade-offs and prioritisation of policy reforms.

Box 2.1. Main policy recommendations to increase economic diversification and productivity in Peru

1. *Identify new products and sectors to contribute to further economic diversification and productivity*

1.1 Determine main pre-conditions for the development of new sectors

- Improve data to evaluate Peru's potential benefit in global value chains (updated input-output table and inclusion of Peru in TiVA data).
- Make technical assessments to determine future new sectors, taking into consideration comparative advantages, international and domestic demand and potential spill-overs (formal job creation and productivity).
- Increase the effectiveness in the dialogue with academia, sub-national authorities, local communities, international actors and the private sector in the identification of new sectors and the pre-conditions for their development (e.g. effective investment in research and development, specific skills and efficient logistics services).

2. *Promote education, innovation, entrepreneurship and regional market integration*

2.1 Improve the quality of education for all Peruvians

- Continue the implementation of incentive mechanisms (e.g. remuneration based on performance) to improve the quality of teachers and of the full-time school model.
- Implement the Ley Universitaria and in particular the objectives fixed to SUNEDU (Superintendencia Nacional de Educación Superior Universitaria).
- Continue to increase investment in school infrastructure, in particular in remote areas.

2.2 Increase investment in innovation

- Increase investment in research and development; identify further areas of work shared between the private and public sectors.
- Focus on the most relevant CITEs; improve the technical capacity, technology transfer and further involvement of the private sector in the CITEs.
- Evaluate the benefits of recent start-up initiatives.

2.3 Eliminate existing barriers to entrepreneurship

- Reduce the complexity of regulatory procedures by making more efficient licence and permit systems and by improving the communication of rules and procedures.
- Eliminate administrative burdens on start-ups, in particular for sole proprietor firms.

2.4 Continue to promote regional integration

- Take advantage of and better communicate recent advancements in aspects of the Pacific Alliance, such as tariffs and cumulative rule of origin.
- Continue efforts towards greater financial market integration (e.g. MILA) by increasing standardisation and harmonisation in tax, legal and procedural rules.

3. *Improve the use of commodity-based resources and enhance domestic resource mobilisation*

3.1 Improve the use of commodity-based resources at the sub-national level

- Consider a fiscal rule for sub-national commodity-based transfers to avoid pro-cyclicality of expenditures; consider the establishment of a stabilisation fund to manage these revenues.
- Strengthen equalisation mechanisms to help compensate for inequalities between sub-national governments, which are exacerbated by commodity-based transfers.
- Improve allocation system of these resources to invest effectively in areas contributing to inclusive development at the sub-national level.
- Support sub-national authorities with further technical capacity in the management of these resources.

Box 2.1. **Main policy recommendations to increase economic diversification and productivity in Peru** *(cont.)*

3.2 Increase fiscal resources to finance broad-based policies

- Promote a higher dependence on direct taxation (personal income taxes) with a more redistributive and efficient taxation principle.
- Gradually increase the tax base, the progressivity of personal income tax revenues and reduce elusion and evasion levels.

4. Develop an effective strategy to increase productivity and economic diversification

4.1 Design and implement a unique National Strategic Development Plan

- Strengthen the role of the Centre of Government (CoG) by improving leadership and increasing co-operation and co-ordination between ministries and agencies.
- Strengthen CoG effectiveness by better integrating and co-ordinating the PCM and MEF to improve the planning and prioritisation of polices.
- Make binding strategic plan policies, both in budgeting (including SNIP) and adherence to the regulatory framework.
- Monitor the outcomes and objectives of the plan periodically.

4.2 Improve prioritisation and execution of sub-national development plans

- Ensure that objectives and guidelines presented in the National Strategic Plan are considered and reflected in the planning at the sub-national level.
- Support capacity to sub-national authorities in the design and implementation of sub-national plans; consider implementation of a more asymmetric, place-based decentralisation.
- Facilitate a partnership based approach to regional development by considering the creation of a deconcentrated agency of the PCM and MEF or RDAs constituted as a partnership between departments and the national government.
- Develop medium-term capital investment programmes that deliver on strategic priorities identified in Regional Concerted Development Plans.
- Monitor the implementation of Concerted Regional Development Plans to ensure alignment with the department's budget.

In "Scenario 1: A new commodity super cycle", the commodity boom would provide opportunities for diversification of the Peruvian economy. Peru could focus on diversifying in areas linked to the mining sectors, such as metal-mechanics. New demand for commodities and food products by China's expanding middle class would consolidate ongoing efforts to diversify and expand Peruvian agro-industry. With mining and extraction industries thriving, improvements in the allocation and use of commodity-based transfers across departments in Peru would be particularly important to increase competitiveness and economic diversification.

"Scenario 2: Increasing technology and mechanisation" could position Peru as a hub for technological innovation in the region. At the regional level, CITEs would play an important role in disseminating and co-ordinating the diffusion of technology and in adapting new technology to the Peruvian context based other countries' experience, as was done, for instance, with asparagus. Increasing investment in research and development and removing barriers to start-ups with more efficient license and permit systems would be policy priorities.

Trade and financial regional integration would be especially important both to increase Peru's participation in global value chains and to raise funds from external investors.

In "Scenario 3: Rising expectations of the middle class", good management of broad-based policies affecting productivity, such as education and skills, innovation, and infrastructure, would be increasingly important to consolidate the middle class and respond to its expectations. Improving the redistributive quality and efficiency of the tax system will also be important to underpin fiscal legitimacy by ensuring that Peru's development is inclusive and benefits all.

ANNEX 2.A1

Methodology to identify new potential sectors in Peru

The initial list of new potential sectors in Peru included 1 034 products at the four-digit level of the Standard International Trade Classification revision 3 from the *WITS/UN Comtrade* database. The selection process then unfolded in three stages.

First, only export products with a RCA by at least one of the benchmark countries during country-specific periods were retained. Only products exported with a RCA were considered as they are a stronger predictor of development than marginal exports (Rieländer and Traoré, 2016). The analysis used a 5-year period for each benchmark country. These intervals were defined by periods of high GDP per capita growth and, when applied, periods preceding an upgrade to high-income status. This last case is particularly relevant due to the current MIT challenge Peru is facing.

The countries, periods and reasons for inclusion are the following: Australia (1994-98), Canada (1997-2001) and Norway (1994-98) due to the prominence of natural resources sectors in their economies; Portugal (1992-96) as one of the OECD member countries to move from middle- to high-income status in recent years (1996) and exhibiting high GDP per capita growth before achieving high-income status; Korea (1991-95) due to its remarkable transition towards an open, high-income economy, distinguished by high-tech exports; Brazil (2008-12), Chile (2003-07), Colombia (2009-13) and Mexico (2001-05) as they experienced high GDP per capita growth in these years, while relying on commodities exports; Turkey (2007-11) as one of the few OECD emerging economies to have experienced a high, five-year-long GDP per capita growth in the 2000s; Costa Rica (2003-07) as successful in attracting foreign investment and tourism; and Panama (2007-14) as a Latin American economy exhibiting one of the highest GDP per capita growth in the past years.

Second, only products with an increasing international demand were included. To select promising products and to avoid identifying irrelevant products in world trade, this analysis only considered products whose compound annual growth rates in the period 2010-13 were higher than world trade growth.

Under these criteria, 193 products were identified. Products were ranked according to five dimensions: 1) annual exports growth rate in the last decade in world trade in the period 2003-13; 2) labour productivity, measured as value-added per worker; 3) labour intensities; 4) capital intensities, measured as participation of labour and capital used in output; 5) output to value-added ratio; and 6) probability that Peru starts exporting the selected products, given Peru's current exports. Data regarding the dimensions on value-added, labour and capital intensities were derived from UNIDO at the 4-digit level of ISIC (INDSTAT4), which only provides information regarding the manufacturing sector.

Measuring the probability to export selected products based on benchmark country exports

The probability that Peru starts exporting a new product can be estimated by measuring the "proximity" in the capabilities involved in Peru's current export basket and those needed to export a new product (Hidalgo and Hausmann, 2009). Following this analysis, the proximity between a pair of goods can be approximated by the percentage of countries that export both products with a RCA out of the total number of countries that export one of them in a given year.

However, the resulting conditional probabilities increase when the product in the conditional is scarcer. Thus, exporting goods that are specific to a country (e.g. ostrich eggs to Australia) imply a conditional probability equal to 1 for the event of exporting the rest of products exported by the country (Hausmann and Klinger, 2007). This problem can be avoided by taking the minimum of the two conditional probabilities formed by each pair of goods (equations 1 and 2) (Hausmann and Klinger, 2007). This measure is called proximity ($\varphi_{i,j}$). Conditional probabilities were calculated using 2013 data for all countries.

$$\varphi_{i,j} = min\{P(x_i \mid x_j), P(x_j \mid x_i)\} \quad (1)$$

Where,

$$x_{i,c} = \begin{cases} 1 \text{ if country } c \text{ has a RCA index} > 1 \text{ in product } x_i \text{ in 2013} \\ 0 \quad \text{otherwise} \end{cases} \quad (2)$$

Finally, the probability that Peru starts exporting each potential product given its current exports may be calculated in two alternative ways. The traditional approach adds up all the capabilities available to Peru for producing the new good, adjusted by the total number of capabilities related to the new good. That is, the sum of all the proximities between the potential good and the goods produced with comparative advantage by Peru divided by the sum of all proximities associated with the new good, known as the measure of density (Hausmann and Klinger, 2007; equation 3). The alternative approach is an estimator of the highest proximity ($\varphi_{i,j}$) of those linking the new product and the set of products exported by Peru with a RCA (equation 4).

$$Density_{i,peru} = \frac{\sum_j \varphi_{i,j} x_{j,\,Peru}}{\sum_j \varphi_{i,j}} \quad (3)$$

$$Max\ Proximity_{i,peru} = \max_{s \in S} \{\varphi_{i,s}\}\ ;\ where\ S = \{s \mid x_{s,peru} = 1\} \quad (4)$$

Where j represents the set of all possible products and S represents the set of products for which Peru has a RCA.

The measure of density is informative regarding the probability that Peru starts exporting each potential product given its current exports. Within the selected set, products currently exported by Peru with a RCA index greater than 1 have, on average, values of density 1.1 standard deviations larger than those without a RCA. Such difference of means – significant to 1% confidence – argues in favour of density's predictive power of RCAs.

This analysis is useful to determine the feasibility of the new exports given Peru's exports structure, while taking as a starting point international experiences from benchmark countries (OECD, 2015). This methodology should be considered as an input among others to determine possible ways to promote economic diversification in Peru.

ANNEX 2.A2

Overview of main national plans and agendas to boost economic diversification and productivity

This annex presents the main topics covered in the following five plans and agendas: 1) the Plan Bicentenario: El Perú hacia el 2021; 2) the Plan Estratégico de Desarrollo Nacional Actualizado: Perú hacia el 2021; 3) the PENX; 4) the National Plan for Productive Diversification; and 5) the Agenda de Competitividad 2014-2018.

The Plan Bicentenario: El Perú hacia el 2021 is the National Development Strategic Plan (Plan Estratégico de Desarrollo Nacional), launched in 2011 by CEPLAN (CEPLAN, 2011) as a long-term plan covering national development policies to 2021. As highlighted in the plan, it is not an action plan but rather an orientation plan, requiring a multi-annual programme to implement it. Although all six strategic axes of the plan affect policies to boost productivity and economic diversification, the strategic axe on "economy, competitiveness and employment" specifically touches on several objectives to improve these policies, some of which affect sectoral policies in areas such as agro-industry, tourism and gastronomy, and mining.

The Plan Estratégico de Desarrollo Nacional Actualizado: Perú hacia el 2021 (CEPLAN, 2015) is an updated version of the Plan Bicentenario, released in October 2015. It presents scenarios and targets for the Peruvian economy in 2021. In particular, it presents specific key objectives to increase the diversification of productivity and to boost the manufacturing sector with improved technology, qualified workers and lower informality. The objectives cover participation in global value chains, strengthening technical and management skills, labour conditions to improve formalisation, macroeconomic stability, financial development, doing business and innovation. The key indicator targeted is to achieve a GDP per capita of USD 12 852 in 2021 at the constant prices of 2005. This target presupposes that the Peruvian economy will have tackled the MIT in 2021. Also included are other quantitative targets, such as the economic complexity index, changes in traditional exports, higher education, informality, sovereign ratings, access to finance, doing business, and exports in high-tech.

The trade promotion strategy at the national level is raised in the PENX. The main target of this plan is to foster competitiveness, diversification and value-added on goods and services exports. Components of the PENX were defined by a joint public and private agenda directed to promote the development of exports and trade facilitation, among other objectives. In its latest version, the Plan Estratégico Nacional Exportador 2025's main objective is to internationalise Peruvian firms within a ten-year horizon (MINCETUR, 2015). Focusing on firms, the plan brings policy objectives related to instruments supporting entrepreneurship under four key pillars: market diversification; competitiveness and sustainability of the exports; trade facilitation and efficiency in the international logistics chain; and capacity building to create an "export culture".

The main objective of the National Productive Diversification Plan (Plan Nacional de Diversificacion Productiva) is to promote new engines of economic growth by improving economic diversification and economic sophistication. The plan emphasises reduced dependence on a natural resources, greater productivity, increased formal jobs and sustainable economic growth as fundamental in that direction. Similar to the GDP per capita targets indicated by the Plan Estratégico de Desarrollo Nacional Actualizado: Perú hacia el 2021, the plan would allow Peru to tackle the MIT and to reach a GDP per capita of USD 17 000, adjusted by PPPs, by 2021.

The National Productive Diversification Plan comprises 3 key axes and 11 action lines. The first axe is to promote productive diversification, and its main lines of action are integration into global value chains, attracting foreign direct investment, and innovative entrepreneurship. The second axe is to simplify administrative barriers and to promote adequate regulations. The third axe is to expand productivity, and its main lines of action are to extend knowledge and technology. Fundamental is the development of CITEs and other initiatives to enhance the productivity of micro, small and medium-sized enterprises (MSMEs) (analysis below). Others aspects include implementation of a national innovation policy, the national quality policy (Instituto Nacional de Calidad), development and promotion of modern industrial parks, and reduction in financing costs for MSMEs. One year into the plan, several concrete measures have already been implemented, including expansion of the network of CITEs, creation of the National Quality Institute, tax reform to promote research and development, and design of several industrial parks.The three axes also address horizontal policies linked to health, education, infrastructure and state modernisation.

In addition to the mentioned National Strategic Plans, the CNCF developed the Agenda de Competitividad 2014-2018 (MEF/CNC, 2014). The CNCF was created in 2002 as a co-ordinating committee on policies related to competitiveness and recently formalisation was included as a key component in its agenda.The board of directors includes representatives from the public and private sectors and is supported by a technical secretariat attached to the MEF. Since its creation, the CNCF has promoted inter-sectorial and inter-governmental co-ordination and provided accountability and monitoring for previous work. Notably, the CNCF endeavours to form integrated teams with representatives from the private and public sectors and different levels of government to address the thematic areas included in the agenda.

The main objective of this agenda is to boost competitiveness in Peru towards increasing job formalisation and well-being in the population. The main targets in the period 2014-18 are to increase labour productivity by 15%, reduce informality by 5% and reduce logistics costs from 32% to 23% of product value. For each of the following areas, there are specific goals and policy actions to achieve them: productive and business development; science, technology and innovation; internationalisation of firms; infrastructure; logistics and transportation (Chapter 3); information, technology and communications; human capital; business facilitation; and natural resources and energy.

Notes

1. Furthermore, at regional level, the limited impact of labour productivity convergence on poverty has been explained by the fact that poorer people are employed in sectors where convergence across departments has been slower (such as agriculture), and there is very little labour reallocation towards converging sectors (such as manufacturing) (Lacovone, Sánchez-Bayardo and Sharma, 2015).
2. Based on data from Superintendencia Nacional de Aduanas y de Administración Tributaria (SUNAT), *http://ww2.mincetur.gob.pe/comercio-exterior/reportes-estadisticos/exportaciones/* (accessed on 1 July 2016).
3. These include asparagus, grapes, mangoes, avocados, paprika and calcium-related products. Metal-mechanical products include, for example, mechanical and electrical apparels and their components, and components of automotive, air and water vehicles.
4. Two scenarios for China's economy up to 2030 were modelled based on the projections analysis for China 2030 in investment and GDP growth (World Bank-Development Research Centre of the State Council [DRC], 2013): a normal-pace transition (baseline scenario) and a high-pace transition (low-investment scenario). The high-pace transition scenario shows a lower GDP growth, especially evident in the period 2021-30. None of these scenarios assume specific external or internal shocks to China's economy, only different trajectories for China's transition from a middle-income, investment-driven economy towards a high-income, consumption-based one (OECD/CAF/ECLAC, 2015).
5. The Operational Framework on Public-Private Collaboration for Resource-based Value Creation being developed as part of the OECD Policy Dialogue on Natural Resource-Based Development (included in the OECD Country Programme with Peru) is a reference to help Peru address these challenges.
6. LAC countries are Argentina, Brazil, Chile, Colombia, Costa Rica, Ecuador, El Salvador, Guatemala, Mexico, Panama, Peru, Uruguay and Venezuela.
7. The OECD Initiative on Global Value Chains, Production Transformation and Development is another OECD platform that could help Peru to promote development through greater participation in and upgrading of global value chains.
8. The RCA index, based on Balassa (1977), measures the ratio between the contribution a product makes to the exports of a country and the same product's contribution to world trade. Values larger than 1 suggest specialisation of a product by the country. Density is a measure based on Hausmann and Klinger (2007), which captures a country's propensity to export a product. The measure reflects the closeness between the capabilities needed to export a new product and the capabilities already incorporated in a country's export basket (Annex 2.A1).
9. Some semi-processed goods are characterised as commodity-related products, with high labour productivity but little job creation.
10. Furthermore, within the identified products, exploratory regressions do not show an association between Peru's RCAs and labour (or capital) intensities, value-added to output ratio or value-added per worker, showing potential to increase economic diversification with productivity and job creation.
11. Twenty-three percent of the identified products are currently exported for values less than USD 10 000, which suggests geographical constrains for their production. In this regard, the National Productive Diversification Plan privileges the use of regional studies to delineate region-specific agendas to address each of the plan's objectives. Similarly, another study identifies opportunities in five regions: north, centre, south, jungle and Lima (Consorcio Cluster Development, Gaia and D'ávila Quevedo, 2013).
12. For instance, measured as kg per acre, in 2013, Peru more than doubled the world's average production of asparagus and grapes, and was a quarter higher for avocados (based on FAO, 2014).
13. Based on discussions and interviews with economic actors of this sector.
14. Compound annual growth rate, 2005-15.
15. However, tourism revenues are largely concentrated in Lima (65% of the aggregate value of the restaurants and hotels sector in 2012), and only a few sites capture most visitors. Machu Picchu represents 32.5% of places visited in Peru in 2015. Based on data provided by the Directorate-General for Research and Studies about Tourism and Crafts of the Ministry of Trade and Tourism (MINCETUR).
16. Based on the input-output table of 2007.
17. OECD calculations based on data provided by the Central Bank of Peru (Banco de la Reserva del Perú), webpage, *www.bcrp.gob.pe/estadisticas.html* (accessed on 1 July 2016); the INEI, webpage, *www.inei.gob.pe/estadisticas/indice-tematico/economia/* (accessed on 1 July 2016); and ADEX Inteligencia Comercial

(2015), Exportaciones News, Dic 2015, Asociación de Exportadores, Lima, *www.adexperu.org.pe/index.php/exportaciones-news*.

18. Based on OECD Main Science and Technology Indicators (database), *www.oecd.org/sti/msti* (accessed on 1 July 2016); and Red de Indicadores de Ciencia y Tecnología –Iberoamericana e Interamericana (accessed on 1 July 2016).
19. *www.oecd.org/eco/growth/indicatorsofproductmarketregulationhomepage.htm* for more information.
20. The third component is the regulatory protection of incumbents through legal barriers to entry and antitrust exemptions.
21. Only a few agriculture products are not included.
22. Other key challenges are linked to logistics process and transport infrastructure (Chapter 3).
23. *www.oecd.org/tax/beps/* for further information.
24. *http://acuerdonacional.pe/* for further information on the National Accord (Acuerdo Nacional).
25. *www.ceplan.gob.pe/planes/planes-desarrollo-regional-concertado* for Concerted Regional Development Plans in Peru.

References

ADEX Inteligencia Comercial (2015), *Exportaciones News*, Dic 2015, Asociación de Exportadores, Lima, *www.adexperu.org.pe/index.php/exportaciones-news*.

Asensio, R. and B. Pérez (eds.) (2012), "Retóricas de turismo y desarrollo en los Andes. La red de turismo rural comunitario Pacha Paqareq, Perú", in *¿El turismo es cosa de pobres? Patrimonio cultural, pueblos indígenas y nuevas formas de turismo en América Latina*, PASOS Revista de turismo y patrimonio cultural, Tenerife.

Balassa, B. (1977), "'Revealed' comparative advantages revisited: An analysis of relative exports shares of the industrial countries, 1953-1971", *The Manchester School*, Vol. 45/4, John Wiley & Sons Ltd. and the University of Manchester, Manchester, pp. 327-344, *http://dx.doi.org/10.1111/j.1467-9957.1977.tb00701.x*.

Barbiero, O. et al. (2015), "The 2013 update of the OECD's database on product market regulation: Policy insights for OECD and non-OECD countries", *OECD Economics Department Working Papers*, No. 1200, OECD Publishing, Paris, *http://dx.doi.org/10.1787/5js3f5d3n2vl-en*.

Barreix A., M. Bès and J. Roca (2011), "El IVA Personalizado: Aumentando la recaudación y compensando a los más pobres", *Documentos* No. 8/2011, Instituto de Estudios Fiscales, Madrid, *www.ief.es/documentos/recursos/publicaciones/documentos_trabajo/2011_08.pdf*.

Blyde, J.S. (ed.) (2014), *Synchronized Factories: Latin America and the Caribbean in the Era of Global Value Chains*, Springer-IDB, New York.

Carballo, J. and C. Volpe Martincus (2010), "Is export promotion effective in developing countries? Firm-level evidence on the intensive and the extensive margins of exports", *IDB Working Paper Series*, No. IDB-WP-201, Inter-American Development Bank, Washington, D.C., *http://dx.doi.org/10.1016/j.jinteco.2008.05.002*.

Carnoy, M. and T. Luschei (2008), "Skill acquisition in 'high tech' export agriculture: a case study of lifelong learning in Peru's asparagus industry", *Journal of Education and Work*, Vol. 21, No. 1, Routledge, New York, pp. 1-23, *http://dx.doi.org/10.1080/13639080801956982*.

CEPLAN (2015), *Plan Estratégico de Desarrollo Nacional Actualizado: Perú hacia el 2021*, Centro Nacional de Planeamiento Estratégico, Lima.

CEPLAN (2011), *Plan Bicentenario: El Perú Hacia el 2021*, Centro Nacional de Planeamiento Estratégico, Lima.

Conference Board (2016), *Total Economy Database* (database), The Conference Board, New York, *www.conference-board.org/data/economydatabase/* (accessed on 1 July 2016).

Consorcio Cluster Development, Gaia, M. and J. D'ávila Quevedo (2013), *Elaboración de un mapeo de clusters en el Perú*, Consorcio Cluster Development for Consejo Nacional de la Competitividad, Lima, *www.cnc.gob.pe/images/upload/paginaweb/archivo/25/Informe%20Final%20Mapeo%20Clusters.pdf*.

Cruzado, E. C. and M. L. Tostes (2015), "Evaluación del modelo de gestión de los Centros de Innovación Tecnológica: El rol de la Oficina Técnica de los Centros de Innovación Tecnológica en el período 2006 a 2012", ALTEC Brasil 2015. Available at *www.altec2015.org/anais/altec/papers/248.pdf*.

ECLAC/OECD (2016), *Environmental Performance Reviews: Peru, Highlights and recommendations*, OECD/Economic Commission for Latin America and the Caribbean, United Nations/OECD, printed at the UN, Santiago.

FAO (2014), FAO STAT (database), Food and Agriculture Organization of the United Nations, Rome, *http://faostat3.fao.org/download/Q/QC/E* (accessed on 1 July 2016).

Freund, C. and M.D. Pierola (2010), "Export Entrepreneurs: Evidence from Peru", *Policy Research Working Paper Series*, No. 5407, World Bank, Washington, D.C.

Fuller, N. (2014), "Políticas públicas de turismo en el Perú" *(Tourism's Public Policies in Peru)*, updated version of "El turismo en el Perú", *in Turismo y cultura. Entre el entuasismo y el recelo (Tourism and Culture: Between Enthusiasm and Suspicion)*, Fondo Editorial de la Pontificia Universidad Católica del Perú, Lima.

Global Entrepreneurship Monitor Perú (2014), Global Entrepreneurship Research Association, London, *www.gemconsortium.org* (consulted March 2016).

Hausmann, R. (2012), *The Atlas of Economic Complexity*, Puritan Press, Cambridge.

Hausmann, R. and B. Klinger (2007), "The structure of the product space and the evolution of comparative advantage", *Center for International Development at Harvard University Working Papers*, No. 146, Cambridge.

Hausmann, R. and D. Rodrik (2003), "Economic development as self-discovery", *Journal of Development Economics*, Vol. 72(2), Elsevier, Amsterdam, pp. 603-633, *http://dx.doi.org/10.1016/S0304-3878(03)00124-X*.

Hidalgo, C. and R. Hausmann (2009), "The building blocks of economic complexity", *Proceedings of the National Academy of Sciences 106 (6)*, pp. 10570-10575, *http://dx.doi.org/10.1073/pnas.0900943106*.

Horizonte Minero (2015), "Las nuevas exigencias de la metalmecánica", *Horizonte Minero Magazine*, Lima, *www.horizonteminero.com/2015/05/21/las-nuevas-exigencias-de-la-metalmecanica/* (accessed on 1 July 2016).

IMF (2016), "Financial Integration in Latin America", *IMF Policy Papers*, International Monetary Fund, Washington, D.C.

INEI (2016), Insitutito Nacional de Estadística e Informática, website, Lima, *www.inei.gob.pe* (accessed on 1 July 2016).

IPD (2012), "2012 governance data", *Institutional Profiles Database* (database), *www.cepii.fr/institutions/EN/ipd.asp* (accessed on 1 July 2016).

Jaramillo, M. (2014), "The incidence of social spending and taxes in Peru", *Public Finance Review*, Vol. 42(3), SAGE Publications, Thousand Oaks, pp. 391-412, *http://dx.doi.org/10.1177/1091142113496134*.

Jiménez, J.P. and T. Ter-Minassian (2016), "Política fiscal y ciclo en América Latina: el rol de los gobiernos subnacionales", *Serie Macroeconomía del Desarrollo*, ECLAC, Santiago, No. 173, available at *http://hdl.handle.net/11362/40252*.

Kaldewei, C. and J. Weller (2013), "Empleo, crecimiento sostenible e igualdad", [Employment, sustainable growth and equity], *Macroeconomía del Desarrollo*, No. 145, ECLAC, Santiago.

Korinek, J. (2015), "Managing the minerals sector: Implications for trade from Peru and Colombia", *OECD Trade Policy Papers*, No. 186, OECD Publishing, Paris, *http://dx.doi.org/10.1787/5jrp6wrc2r7l-en*.

Lacovone L., L. Sánchez-Bayardo and S. Sharma (2015), "Regional Productivity Convergence in Peru", *World Bank Policy Research Working Paper*, No. 7499, World Bank, Washington, D.C., available at *http://ssrn.com/abstract=2692342*.

Lin, J. and C. Monga (2010), "Growth Identification and Facilitation. The Role of the State in the Dynamics of Structural Change", *Policy Research Working Paper*, No. 5313, World Bank, Washington, D.C.

Lustig, N. (2016), "The impact of taxes and social spending on inequality and poverty in Argentina (2011), Bolivia (2009), Brazil (2009), Chile (2013), Colombia (2010), Costa Rica (2010), Ecuador (2011), El Salvador (2011), Guatemala (2011), Honduras (2011), Mexico (2010), Peru (2009) and Uruguay (2009): An overview", *CEQ Working Paper*, No. 47, CEQ Institute, Tulane University, New Orleans.

Maldonado, S. (2015), "The Political Effects of Resource Booms: Political Outcomes, Clientelism and Public Goods Provision in Peru", Mimeo, University of California, Berkeley, *https://stanislaomaldonadodotorg1.files.wordpress.com/2015/05/resourcecurse-and-political-support-042915.pdf*.

Meade, B., K. Baldwin and L. Calvin (2010), "Peru: an emerging exporter of fruits and vegetables", Report from the Economic Research Service, No. FTS-345-01, United States Department of Agriculture, Washington, D.C., *www.ers.usda.gov/media/134648/fts34501.pdf*.

MEF/CNC (2014), *La Agenda de Competitividad 2014-2018*, Rumbo al Bicentenario, Ministerio de Economía y Finanzas/Consejo Nacional de la Competitividad, Lima.

Mendes de Paula, G. (2011), "Development of the Latin American metal-mechanical industry", 1er Congreso Mexicano de la Industria Siderúrgica, *www.canacero.org.mx/Es/assets/19-estudio-ila-fa-germano-mendes.pdf*.

MINAGRI (2014), *Presente y Futuro del Sector Forestal Peruano: el Caso de las Concesiones y las Plantaciones Forestales* (Present and Future of the Peruvian Forest Sector: The Case of Concessions and Forest Plantations), Ministerio de Agricultura y Riego, *www.bcrp.gob.pe/docs/Publicaciones/Seminarios/2014/forestal/forestal-2014-munoz.pdf*.

MINCETUR (2015), *Plan Estrategíco Nacional Exportador: PENX 2025* (National Strategic Export Plan: PENX 2025), Ministerio de Comercio Exterior y Turismo, Lima, *www.mincetur.gob.pe/newweb/Portals/0/transparencia/proyectos%20resoluciones/RM_051_2015_PLAN.pdf*.

MINCETUR (2014a), *Agenda: Desarrollo e Innovación de Productos Turísticos en Regiones 2015-2016* (Agenda: Development and Innovation of Tourism Products in Regions 2015-2016), Ministerio de Comercio Exterior y Turismo, Lima.

MINCETUR (2014b), *Informe de Evaluación Anual del Plan Estratégico Institucional 2012-2016* (Annual Evaluation Report of the Institutional Strategic Plan 2012-2016), Ministerio de Comercio Exterior y Turismo, Lima.

MINCETUR (2013), *PENTUR: Plan Estratégico Nacional de Turismo 2012-2021. 'Consolidando un Turismo Sostenible'* (PENTUR: National Strategic Plan of Tourism 2012-2021. 'Consolidating a Sustainable Tourism'), Ministerio de Comercio Exterior y Turismo, Lima.

Ministry of Foreign Affairs of Peru (2015), *APEC Action Plans*, Lima, available at *www.acuerdoscomerciales.gob.pe/index.php?option=com_content&view=category&layout=blog&id=156&Itemid=174*.

Muñoz, P. (2010), "¿La Política Importa? Los Determinantes Políticos de la Eficiencia del Gasto Municipal", Censorcio de Investigacíon Económicas y Sociales, Asociación Servicios Educativos Rurales, Lima.

Muñoz, P. (2005), *El Diseño Institucional Municipal 1980-2004 y sus Implicancias para las Zonas Rurales*, Asociación Servicios Educativos Rurales, Lima.

Observatorio Turístico del Perú (n.d.), *Base de datos turísticos del Perú* (database), Lima, *http://observatorioturisticodelperu.com/badatur/turismo-en-numeros* (accessed on 1 July 2016).

OECD (forthcoming), *OECD Territorial Reviews: Peru 2016*, OECD Publishing, Paris.

OECD (2016a), "Avanzando hacia una mejor educación en Perú / Moving towards a better education in Peru", *Making Development Happen*, No. 3, OECD Development Centre, OECD Publishing, Paris, *www.oecd.org/dev/Avanzando-hacia-una-mejor-educacion-en-Peru.pdf*.

OECD (2016b), "Startup in Latin America 2016: Building an Innovative Future", *OECD Development Centre Studies* (forthcoming), OECD Publishing, Paris.

OECD (2016c), *The Productivity-Inclusiveness Nexus*, OECD Publishing, Paris. *http://dx.doi.org/10.1787/9789264258303-en*.

OECD (2016d), *OECD Income Distribution Database* (database), OECD, for OECD economies, *http://stats.oecd.org/Index.aspx?DataSetCode=IDD* (accessed on 1 July 2016);

OECD (2016e), "Peru: Implementing integrated governance for inclusive growth", *OECD Public Governance Reviews* (forthcoming), OECD Publishing, Paris.

OECD (2015), *Multi-dimensional Review of Peru: Volume 1. Initial Assessment*, OECD Publishing, Paris, *http://dx.doi.org/10.1787/9789264243279-en*.

OECD (2013a), *OECD Product Market Regulation 2013* (database), OECD, *https://stats.oecd.org/index.aspx?DataSetCode=PMR* (accessed on 1 July 2016).

OECD (2013b), *OECD Economic Surveys: Colombia 2013: Economic Assessment*, OECD Publishing, Paris, *http://dx.doi.org/10.1787/eco_surveys-col-2013-en*.

OECD (2011), *OECD Indicators on Patents* (database), OECD, *www.oecd.org/sti/inno/oecdpatentdatabases.htm* (accessed on 1 July 2016).

OECD (2009), *Natural Resources and Pro-Poor Growth: The Economics and Politics*, DAC Guidelines and Reference Series, OECD Publishing, Paris, *http://dx.doi.org/10.1787/9789264060258-en*.

OECD/CAF/ECLAC (2015), *Latin American Economic Outlook 2016: Towards a New Partnership with China*, OECD Publishing, Paris, *http://dx.doi.org/10.1787/9789264246218-en*.

OECD/CAF/ECLAC (2014), *Latin American Economic Outlook 2015: Education, Skills and Innovation for Development*, OECD Publishing, Paris, *http://dx.doi.org/10.1787/leo-2015-en*.

OECD/ECLAC/CIAT/IDB (2016), *Revenue Statistics in Latin America and the Caribbean 2016*, OECD Publishing, Paris, *http://dx.doi.org/10.1787/rev_lat_car-2016-en-fr*.

Palomino, V. and J. Pérez (2011), "Teoría y Aplicaciones de la Tabla Insumo-Producto a la Planeación Estratégica" (Theory and Applications of the Input-Output Table for Strategic Planning), *Documentos de Trabajo*, No. 4, Centro Nacional de Planeación Estratégica, Lima.

Pérez, B. (2008), "El patrimonio inmaterial en proyectos de desarrollo territorial en comunidades indígenas de Los Andes peruanos" (Intangible heritage in territorial development projects in indigenous communities of the Peruvian Andes), *Revista Electrónica de Patrimonio Histórico*, No. 3, Universidad de Granada, Granada, pp. 138-162, *http://revistaseug.ugr.es/index.php/erph/article/view/3346/3358*.

PRODUCE (2014), *Plan Nacional de Diversificación Productiva*, Ministerio de la Producción, Lima.

Reyes, G. (2016), "Condicionantes económicas y sociales de Perú y de países de la Alianza Pacifico", *Universidad del Rosario Working Paper*, Escuela de Administración, Bogotá (unpublished).

Rieländer, J. and B. Traoré (2016), "Explaining diversification in exports across higher manufacturing content –what is the role of commodities?", *Journal of International Commerce, Economics and Policy*, Vol. 2, No. 2, World Scientific Publishing Company, Singapore.

SECO (2013), *Peru Country Strategy 2013-2016*, Swiss Economic Cooperation and Development, Berne, *www.eda.admin.ch/content/dam/countries/countries-content/peru/en/Strategie-SECO-Peru-2013-16_en.pdf*.

Shimizu, T. (2009), "Structural changes in asparagus production and exports from Peru", *Discussion Paper*, No. 201, Institute of Developing Economies, Chiba City.

Shimizu, T. (2006), "Expansion of asparagus production and exports in Peru", *Discussion Paper*, No. 73, Institute of Developing Economies, Chiba City.

Torres, D. (2010), *APEC Forum on Human Resources Development 2010: Peruvian Economy Report*, General Directorate of Micro and Small Enterprises and Cooperatives, Ministry of Production of Peru, Lima, *http://buenaspracticas.stps.gob.mx/buenaspracticas/pdf_2011/11_Economy_Report_Peru.pdf*.

UNIDO (2016), *UNIDO Industrial Statistics* (database), United Nations Industrial Development Organization, *www.unido.org/resources/statistics/statistical-databases*.html (accessed on 1 June 2016).

Vostroknutova, E. et al. (2015), *Peru Building on Success: Boosting Productivity for Faster Growth*, World Bank Group, Washington, D.C., available at: *http://documents.worldbank.org/curated/en/2015/10/25122535/peru-building-success-boosting-productivity-faster-growth*.

WITS/UN Comtrade (2013), *WITS/UN Comtrade* (database), World Integrated Trade Solution/United Nations Comtrade, *https://wits.worldbank.org* (accessed on 1 June 2016).

World Bank (2016), "International tourism, number of arrivals", *World Development Indicators* (database), World Bank, Washington, D.C., *http://data.worldbank.org/indicator/ST.INT.ARVL*. (accessed on 1 July 2016).

World Bank (2015), "Peru", *Doing Business – Measuring Business Regulations* (database), World Bank, Washington, D.C., *www.doingbusiness.org/data/exploreeconomies/peru* (accessed on 1 July 2016).

World Bank-DRC (2013), *China 2030: Building a Modern, Harmonious, and Creative Society*, World Bank/Development Research Centre of the State Council, People's Republic of China, Washington, D.C., *www.worldbank.org/content/dam/Worldbank/document/China-2030-complete.pdf*.

Chapter 3

Improving transport connectivity in Peru

Several indicators on transport costs, logistics performance and transport infrastructure show Peru lagging behind OECD members and some benchmark countries in transport connectivity. Improving transport policies nationally and in urban centres, in alignment with the national development strategy, can have a significant impact on inclusive development and quality of life in the country. This chapter provides background in transport connectivity and performance indicators in Peru. It then focusses on the need for a national transport plan to define transport policy priorities and the particular importance of developing a National Policy for Urban and Metropolitan Mobility. This chapter also studies connectivity needs in urban centres, focusing on the Lima-Callao metropolitan area, and highlights the benefits of governance by a world-standard metropolitan transport authority, as well as the necessary actions to harness benefits from being a port city. Finally, the chapter concludes with the main recommendations to improve connectivity in Peru and test them against the scenarios set out in Chapter 1.

Greater connectivity is fundamental to reducing transport costs and boosting productivity, competitiveness and quality of life in Peru. Good transport connectivity can make Peru more efficient and facilitate reaching sustainable and inclusive development goals. Improving connectivity requires going beyond transport infrastructure provision, recognising the need for policies and strategies that focus on increasing efficiency and reducing the costs of transport, including time, financial cost and negative environmental and social impacts. The development of a strategy for improving connectivity is particularly relevant for Peru, where transport costs are high, compared to OECD member countries, and transport is considered one of the main bottlenecks to development. Better logistics in transport and adopting a multi-modal approach that shifts focus from roads (e.g. developing railways, ports and waterways) are central to this strategy. Also key are improvements in the institutional framework related to the design and implementation of transport policies at national and sub-national levels.

This chapter analyses transport policy in Peru in light of international progress in designing more effective policies and realising higher social and economic value from transport investment. It provides recommendations for incorporating a more comprehensive vision of connectivity into Peru's transport planning and appraisal framework – recommendations informed by analysis of countries with long experience with a more progressive vision for connectivity and those newly adopting the significant changes involved.

This chapter presents the concept of connectivity and the transport performance indicators in Peru compared to OECD member countries and benchmark countries. It then highlights the need for a national transport plan to define policy priorities in alignment with the country's wider priorities for economic development and enhanced quality of life. Improving investment criteria and logistics data through the creation of a logistics observatory will be fundamental in the design and implementation of a successful plan. Main items for the development of National Urban and Metropolitan mobility policy are identified. These include setting objectives for the sector, and creating national frameworks for improving local transport planning and strengthening local capacity to invest in urban mobility. Lima-Callao provides a case study for urban connectivity in Peru, indicating a need to establish a unique mobility authority and the necessary conditions for its success. The chapter concludes with main recommendations to improve connectivity in Peru towards becoming a high-income country.

Enhancing connectivity beyond transport infrastructure to increase competitiveness and inclusiveness in Peru

Peru needs to adopt a comprehensive vision of connectivity, setting transport strategies in references to economic and well-being objectives rather than infrastructure development exclusively.

The relevance of connectivity has increased in recent decades and is now key in transport policy in most OECD economies and some emerging economies. Connectivity goes beyond transport infrastructure delivery and has as key purpose the reduction of transport costs, including time, financial cost and negative environmental and social impacts. Its impact is particularly relevant for Peru, whose transport outcomes show important gaps, compared to OECD economies and some Latin American economies.

Connectivity: going beyond transport infrastructure

Rather than an end in itself, transport should be considered a mean for achieving explicit development objectives, such as economic growth, equity and employment. The focus of transport improvements has gradually shifted in OECD economies, from enhancing physical structures and increasing traffic volumes to creating adequate access to jobs, services and consumption. This evolution has been informed by constant interactions between policy makers, academia and civil society.

Re-examining the rationale behind transport policy and investment has been a recurrent theme in many European countries in past decades. Among the most important triggers is a rapid rise in evidence of the downsides: congestion, pollution, and an imperfect correlation between transport infrastructure provision and economic prosperity. Countries outside Europe increasingly join these efforts as they too encounter limitations in their transport policies, rising costs and failure to trigger economic and social benefits. Progress has not been linear and its shape and pace has varied across countries. However, more rigorous scrutiny of the relationship between transport, the economy and the wider living environment has resulted in a growing consensus on the need for a more progressive vision for guiding transport policy and investment. In the case of Peru, the time is ripe for building on international experience and moving towards a more progressive view of connectivity.

Adopting a multi-modal approach and moving away from an overriding focus on road infrastructure investment have been central to this increasingly widespread evolution in transport policy and its capacity to improve connectivity. Added traffic generated by road expansion (induced demand) in the United Kingdom in the early 1990s – and experienced elsewhere with the same result – was an important inducement to the change in thinking (Standing Advisory Committee for Trunk Road Assessment [SACTRA], 1994). Clearly, a "predict and provide" transport policy focussed on estimating traffic demand and providing additional road capacity yielded no benefit: no ease in congestion; no improved accessibility. Policy documents in the United Kingdom and elsewhere increasingly agree on certain central principles of effective transport policy (Department of the Environment, Transport and the Regions [DETR], 1998). First, trains, buses, walking and cycling should have a central priority because of their capacity to provide less carbon- and space-intensive mobility and their potential role in providing access for all. Second, the price of travel should reflect the costs of congestion and pollution.[1] Thus, road use and parking charges have become important policy tools. Third, better maintenance and management have to be the priority for the road network, and new road construction should be assessed against alternative policies or measures, including demand management measures and investment in alternative modes. Adequately evaluating policies, programmes and projects according to these criteria is a challenge, but the desirability of the principles is increasingly being adopted by countries.

Recent performance in transport outcomes in Peru

Better connectivity can make the Peruvian economy more efficient and promote productivity and competitiveness. After controlling for other variables affecting economic growth, there is a significant association between improved logistics and transport infrastructure performance on the one hand and productivity gains and sophistication of exports on the other (OECD/Development Bank of Latin America [CAF]/Economic Commission for Latin America and the Caribbean [ECLAC], 2013). This is particularly relevant in economies like Peru's where, due to the composition of Peruvian exports, high transport costs have a negative impact on its competitiveness.[2] The World Bank's Logistics Performance Index (LPI) compares logistics and transport infrastructure performance through six components: customs, infrastructure, ease of arranging shipments, quality of logistics services, tracking and tracing, and timeliness.[3] The LPI scores countries between 1 and 5. Countries which improve their score by 1 in the LPI improve their labour productivity by 35% on average, the productivity gain Peru would enjoy if it achieved the same LPI as Canada (OECD, 2015a).

Despite some recent improvements, logistics and transport infrastructure performance remains below most benchmark and OECD economies. Figure 3.1, Panel A shows the differences for the six LPI categories between the best-performing OECD country and Peru, Latin America, the seven biggest Latin American economies, and the OECD average. The largest gaps occur in infrastructure (the quality of trade and transport infrastructure), tracking and tracing (ability to track and trace consignments), and timeliness (frequency with which shipments reach consignees within scheduled or expected delivery times). Peru performs below the OECD average and the seven biggest Latin American economies for these three indicators. Furthermore, Peru's overall logistics performance is below most of the benchmark countries and OECD economies (Figure 3.1, Panel B). The Peruvian gap is equivalent to 2.5 times the gap for OECD countries.

Other indicators confirm that high transport and logistics costs in Peru are affecting trade and competitiveness. Domestic transport cost per distance remains high, compared to other Latin American economies, according to *Trading Across Borders* data.[4] Furthermore, total logistics costs represent a high proportion of total costs for some agricultural exports: 50% for onions, 38% of quinoa, 33% for grapes, 26% for cacao and 21% for coffee (World Bank, 2016). Moreover, in three successful cases of non-traditional Peruvian exports (i.e. high-quality cotton apparel, table grapes and mining equipment), transport infrastructure and logistics constraints represent key obstacles for further development (Vostroknutova et al., 2015). More generally, the ratio of freight costs to tariffs for trade in Peru is higher than in OECD member countries and benchmark countries, based on costs of trade with the United States (Figure 3.2). In 2015, the ratio for Peru was more than 20 times the OECD average. Finally, while Peru is ranked 69 out of 140 countries in the Global Competitiveness Index from the World Economic Forum, transport infrastructure alone is ranked at 94 out of the same 140 countries.[5] Reducing transport costs would allow Peru to diversify its economy, as it would significantly lower prices and, thus, promote the competitiveness of many of its tradable goods.

Transport infrastructure in Peru provides insufficient multi-modality, making ineffective its contribution to connectivity. The strong focus on road transport over other modes affects complementarities among modes of transport. For instance, while the country's rail network has stagnated at around 2 000 km in the past decade, the road network increased by nearly

80% in the same period to close to 150 000 km. Furthermore, the quality of ports, rails and roads remains below that of most benchmark countries. For instance, paved roads represent less than 15% of total roads (OECD, 2015a). Peru not only needs to invest in new transport infrastructure, it must also improve its existing infrastructure. Getting the balance right between investing in new construction and maintaining existing infrastructure is essential, since the overall cost of preserving a poorly maintained road is three to seven times more than for one perfectly maintained (OECD/ECLAC, 2012).

Figure 3.1. **Logistics performance gap to the best-performing OECD country, 2016**

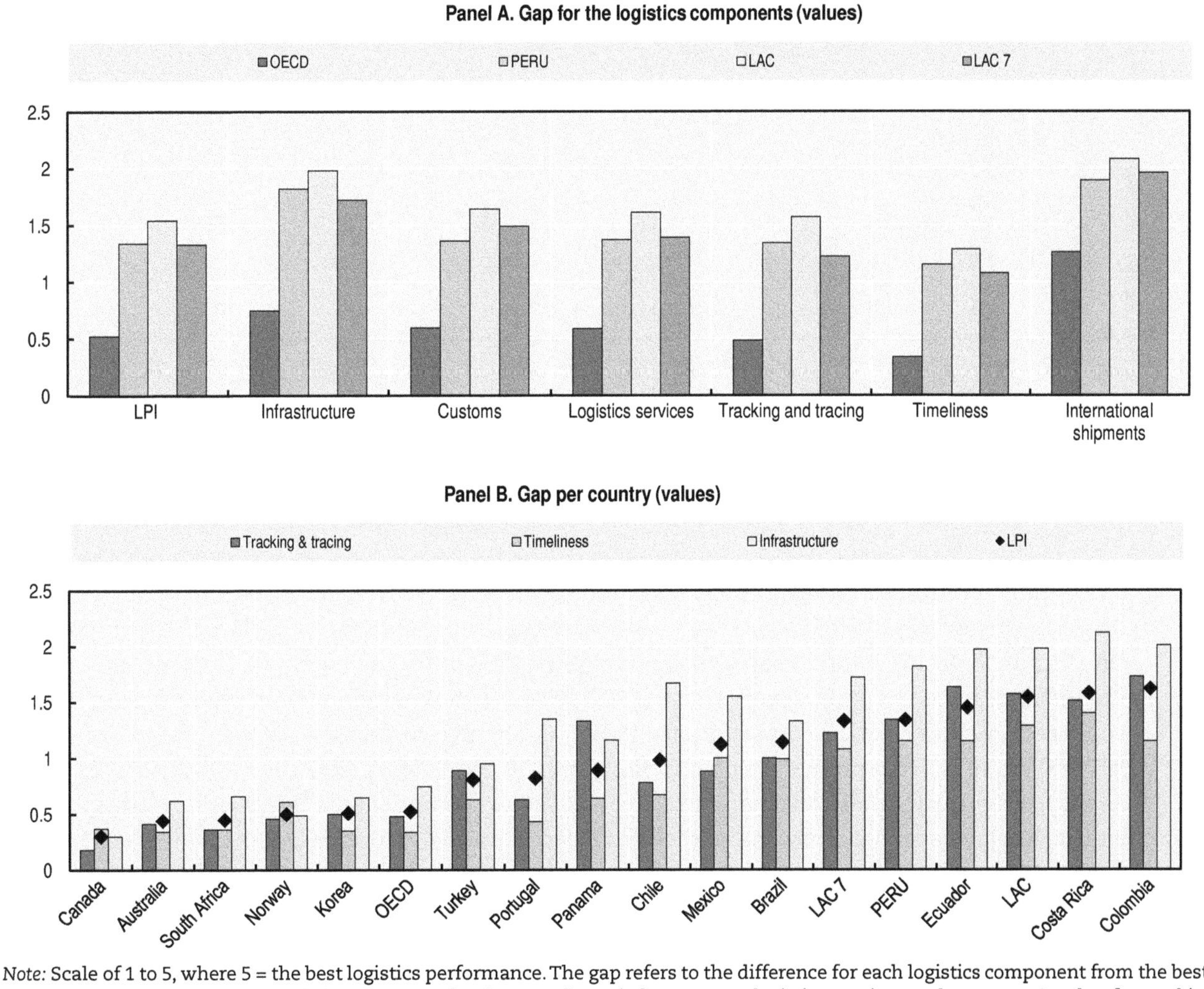

Note: Scale of 1 to 5, where 5 = the best logistics performance. The gap refers to the difference for each logistics component from the best-performing OECD country, these being Germany for the overall LPI, infrastructure, logistics services and customs; Sweden for tracking and tracing; and Luxembourg for international shipments and timeliness. LAC 7 refers to the seven largest economies in Latin America and the Caribbean (LAC) as measured by gross domestic product (GDP): Argentina, Brazil, Chile, Colombia, Mexico, Peru and Venezuela.

Source: Based on World Bank 2016 data (LPI), *http://lpi.worldbank.org/*.

StatLink http://dx.doi.org/10.1787/888933411321

In addition to a poor multi-modal framework for transport infrastructure, trade facilitation – measured as port efficiency, the customs and regulatory environment, and electronic business usage – should continue improving in Peru. Peru operates single-window facilities for foreign trade (*Ventanillas Únicas de Comercio Exterior*), and in recent years, it has streamlined border procedures and improved co-operation with neighbouring and third countries, according to the 2015 OECD Trade Facilitation Indicators, which cover the full spectrum of border procedures (Elorza, 2012).[6] However, areas where Peru lags behind other Latin American economies include external and internal co-operation among the country's various border agencies, and the simplification and harmonisation of documents. Improving these would boost both trade and productivity in Peru. The country should take advantage of the OECD Trade Facilitation Indicators to guide policy making.

Figure 3.2. **Ratio of freight costs to tariffs, 2012-15**

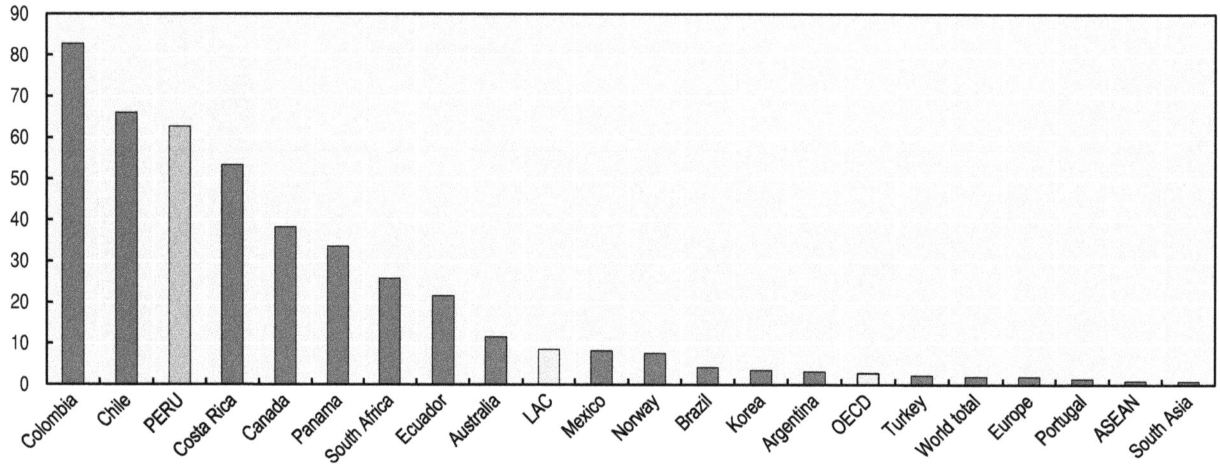

Note: Calculations based on imports from the US market. This figure shows the ratio of freight cost to tariffs on imports to the United States. ASEAN = Association of Southeast Asian Nations. LAC consists of 21 countries. Values are calculated as the median among 2012-15 values.
Source: Based on data from United States Department of Commerce, Bureau of the Census (2016).

StatLink http://dx.doi.org/10.1787/888933411332

Finally, to improve tracking and tracing and timeliness – two key bottlenecks in the LPI for Peru – better use of available ICT can reduce transaction and logistics costs by lowering the cost of accessing information and encouraging efficient use of existing infrastructure. For instance, port gate management using ICT systems to schedule pick-up and delivery could reduce congestion at port terminals. There is a positive correlation between access to ICT and logistics performance after controlling for GDP per capita (OECD/CAF/ECLAC, 2013). As with other Latin American economies, in Peru, the availability of the latest technologies and technology absorption by companies are lower than in OECD member countries. The use of ICT remains well below the benchmark countries too (OECD, 2015a).

Creating a national transport strategy aligned with the development agenda

The shift towards setting transport strategies according to overall economic and well-being objectives emphasises the need to integrate transport policies into wider strategies from other areas, such as environment, economic diversification and competitiveness, labour market, and education and skills. In addition, careful study of the factors influencing trip lengths and modal choice has stressed the importance of integrating spatial and transport development in regional and urban environments. Experiences of OECD member countries are useful in that context. For instance, the Netherlands has issued national guidelines linking spatial planning and infrastructure in regions and urban agglomerations since the 1960s, with a growing focus on development of economic clusters. French law introduced urban transport plans as a key tool for all agglomerations of over 100 000 population to link urban planning and transport infrastructure development in 1982.

In Peru, the transport strategy is articulated through different transport plans. In 2014, to improve connectivity, as a factor determinant of productivity and economic diversification, the Ministry of Transport and Communications (MTC) conducted the Development Plan of Logistics Services on Transport (Plan de Desarrollo de los Servicios Logísticos de Transporte). The plan proposes medium- to long-term measures for strengthening domestic logistics and taking advantage of the existing opportunities in international markets. Twenty logistics corridors were prioritised based the main productive activities identified as demanding logistics transportation services. In addition, the MTC set out key plans to increase multi-modality in Peru: Plan Nacional de Desarrollo Portuario for the development of ports and Plan Nacional de Desarrollo Ferroviario for the development of railways.

Peru should set a transport plan according to the guidelines and objectives of the National Strategic Development Plan (Chapter 2). While the transport plans highlighted above assess indispensable logistics corridors in Peru based on interactions with local communities and technical evaluation, as well as investment projects to increase multi-modality, several bottlenecks affect the design and implementation of these plans. The logistics corridors and transport infrastructure projects lack adequate links to a national strategic agenda. Prioritisation and planning defined in a development agenda should be the basis for a transport strategy in Peru. Indeed, the Programa de Inversiones 2011-2016 Gestión Estratégica – Corredores Logísticos only makes reference to the Plan Bicentenario 2021 domestic trade analysis (and not to policies to boost exports) and does not conduct a specific criteria to match development objectives with the transport framework.[7] In addition, the investments needed for the implementation of these plans are not binding and not necessarily included in the budget for results (*presupuesto por resultados*) or in the national framework for public investment – Sistema Nacional de Inversión Pública (SNIP). As broadly highlighted in Chapter 2, there is a need to better match project execution with design and prioritisation.

Consequently, defining transport strategies to realise outcomes for the economy and the population, rather than for infrastructure development exclusively is key. With this frame of reference, increasing connectivity in Peru means developing a national strategy focused on reducing time and financial transport costs, as well as negative environmental and social externalities, and promoting multi-modality.

Going beyond infrastructure requires the following key actions. First, designing a national transport plan is crucial to defining transport policy priorities, which should be derived from a national infrastructure assessment process. The United Kingdom provides a well-developed methodology for developing a strategic plan over a 25 to 30 year time horizon. Transport, in this case, is embedded in a wider framework covering digital and communications, energy, water and drainage, flood defences and waste. Cross-cutting elements such as funding and financing, costs, sustainability, governance, evaluation and performance measures are taken into account. A comprehensive process is carried out by the National Infrastructure Commission for identifying future needs and understanding key issues, including the following: the infrastructure baseline, key drivers of infrastructure (economic growth, productivity and technology), modelling and analysis, the consultation process with industry, central and local government and prioritisation of options according to their costs and their alignment with national priorities. Further revisions of models and methodologies, as well as public consultation processes, are carried out before the final version is approved by Parliament and adopted by the government (National Infrastructure Commission, 2016).

Second, priorities set by the plan should be reflected in investment projects and policy decision frameworks. This is in particular relevant in Peru, since the transport sector represents the highest investment needs, accounting for 36% of the total infrastructure gap which requires investments close to 8.3% of GDP annually for the period 2016-25 (Asociación para el Fomento de la Infraestructura Nacional [AFIN], 2015). In addition, better maintenance and management have to be the priority for the existing transport infrastructure and new transport modes.

Effective cost-benefit analysis embedded in a wider framework for assessment and prioritisation

Cost-benefit analysis (CBA) is a useful tool for prioritising transport investments. Public investment projects in Peru are subject to CBA and procurement is through competitive tenders. Recent improvements in the information available and technologies used for tracking public investment have increased transparency. All direct public investment projects are subject to the SNIP, with rules defined and under the rectory of the Ministry of Economy and Finance (MEF). All projects costing more than PEN 20 million (Peruvian soles) require feasibility studies, including CBA, and the approval of the project by the SNIP.

While a useful tool, CBA has limitations that should be taken into consideration. For instance, CBA is better suited to comparing similar projects (e.g. establishing priorities between investments in similar road schemes). It can only be one part of the analysis in establishing priorities between projects with very different financial characteristics or strategic functions (e.g. in choosing between a road and a rail investment or between a road to relieve congestion and a road to promote rural development). Different policy objectives cannot always be measured by the same yardstick. Distributional concerns will require additional analysis, as two projects with very similar net present values can have very different distributional effects across the population. Good practice in OECD member countries that make regular use of CBA in the transport sector includes a summary appraisal table that highlights the key results of assessment and potential trade-offs, to make the outcome of analysis transparent for decision makers. Typically, the results of CBA, in terms of internal rate of return and cost-benefit ratio will be presented alongside additional relevant analysis, e.g. presenting greenhouse gas emissions (in tons and possibly also valued in monetary terms), impacts on air quality, a description of potential distributional equity impacts and/or the relation of the project to any other issues relevant to the political agenda. Consequently, the purpose of CBA is to make the results of analysis understandable for decision makers rather than making the decision for them.

Reliance on international experiences for improving and making better use of CBA is valuable to Peru. The recent French appraisal system and the United Kingdom's project valuation framework are useful examples that emphasise multi-criteria analysis, rather than focus on a unique objective (see Box 3.1). Note that, in the United Kingdom, summary appraisal tables deliberately avoid trying to produce a single quantitative indicator of the overall value of the project across all economic and policy dimensions, whereas, in France, greater use is made of multi-criteria analysis to produce a single quantitative indicator.

Box 3.1. **Cost-benefit analysis: French appraisal system and United Kingdom project valuation framework**

The French appraisal system for transport public projects has traditionally been shared between cost-benefit and multi-criteria analysis. In 2007, the reforms following the Grenelle Round Table on environment dialogues, composed of firms, trade unions, environmental groups, and national and local government, shifted the system towards multi-criteria analyses, which uses a comprehensive approach by ranking project impacts under three lines converging in sustainable development: economy, social effects and environment (Ministry of Ecology of France, 2008). Some new indicators have been developed, both qualitative and quantitative, correlating to the proposed categories. Nevertheless, the implementation of the agreed criteria has remained limited, and some categories are double-counting (OECD/ITF, 2011). In this environment, feedback from all sectors has been emphasised as future improvement in this new comprehensive approach.

United Kingdom's project valuation framework aims to harmonise three distinct spheres: public opinion, economic appraisal, and political process and agenda. The rules for appraisal are owned by the Department of Transport and summarised in internet-based Transport Analysis Guidance "WebTAG", which provides information on the role of transport modelling and appraisal techniques. Following a report from an expert committee to the Department of Transport, SACTRA (1999), the CBA framework in the United Kingdom was expanded to include three potential sources of benefit – agglomeration economies, enhanced competition and improved labour market supply impacts – that, if ignored, could make the results of assessment inaccurate (OECD/ITF, 2011). It is not appropriate to incorporate any standard mark-up to the benefits arising from transport investments to account for these factors, as impacts vary very much from project to project; in some case, it may increase benefits 25% and, in others, zero. For types of projects that might unlock significant additional benefits of these kinds, additional modelling is undertaken with analysis to pinpoint exactly how these benefits will be delivered.

Source: OECD/ITF (2011), *Improving the Practice of Transport Project Appraisal*, OECD Publishing, Paris, *http://dx.doi.org/10.1787/9789282103081-en*.

The framework for private-sector involvement is improving

Similar to other Latin American countries, Peru has renegotiated several concession contracts in transport infrastructure. Flaws in the design of concession contracts have caused excessive costs in Latin America (OECD/ECLAC, 2012). In the case of Peru, out of a sample of 15 national road concession contracts signed from 1994 to 2010, 11 were renegotiated at least once, amounting to a total of 53 changes, over USD 300 million in additional costs and 9 years extension over the concessions' terms (Figure 3.3; Bitran, Nieto-Parra and Robledo, 2013). Although roads have been more likely in terms of concessions and changes in the contracts, other transport modes have also been observed to experience a large number of contract changes. From 1999 to mid-2016, there have been 50 changes in 12 road concession contracts, 17 changes in 3 airport concession contracts, 17 changes in 4 rail/metro concession contracts and 6 changes in 4 port concession contracts.[8]

Weaknesses in the prioritisation and planning phases can also cause inefficiencies in public-private partnership projects. *Ex ante* feasibility studies and value-for-money evaluations could help solve difficulties at these stages. However, the institutional framework supporting value-for-money analysis in Peru remains weak.

Figure 3.3. **Initial and renegotiated costs of concession contracts in Chile, Colombia and Peru (1993-2010)**

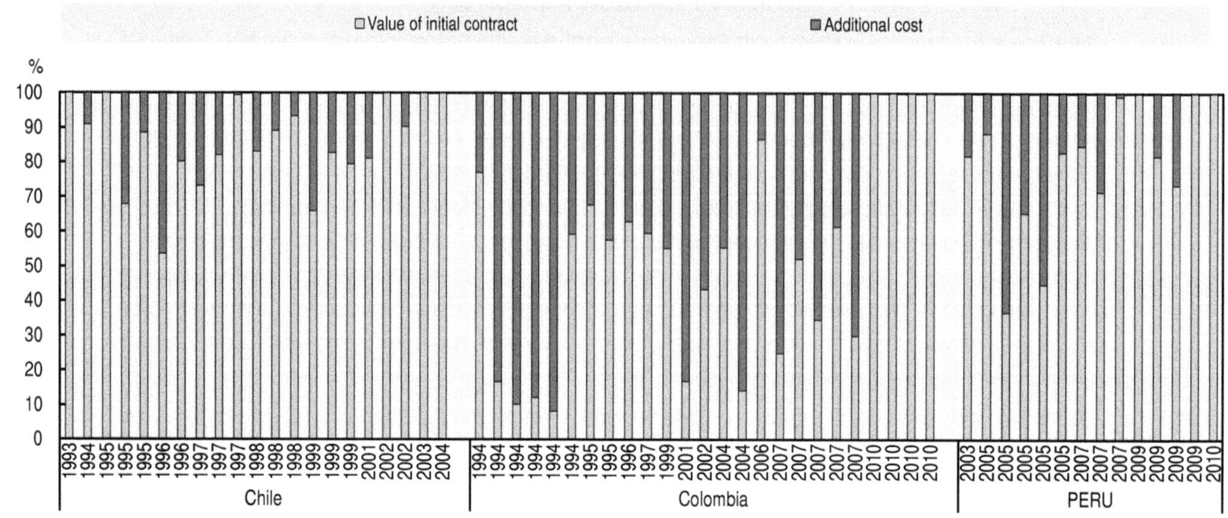

Note: X-axis = the year in which the concession contract was initially signed.

Source: Bitran, E., S. Nieto-Parra and J.S. Robledo (2013), "Opening the black box of contract renegotiations: An analysis of road concessions in Chile, Colombia and Peru", *OECD Development Centre Working Papers*, No. 317, OECD Publishing, Paris, *http://dx.doi.org/10.1787/5k46n3wwxxq3-en*.

StatLink http://dx.doi.org/10.1787/888933411344

Recent efforts to increase efficiencies in the processes of environmental and land licensing should improve the timing and certainty of concession contracts. Similar efforts should be carried out to increase effectiveness in the consultation with local communities for future public-private partnerships.

Poor past performance highlights the need to better account for the risks associated with public-private partnerships in the fiscal framework. While ProInversion's selection process has improved its efficacy in recent years, these partnerships must be included in the reporting of fiscal risks to limit the chances of unexpected costs from renegotiations.

Finally, at the sub-national level, the institutional framework for public-private partnerships remains weak and the technical capacity to achieve is poor. It is crucial to create mechanisms at the national level to support sub-national authorities in the design and implementation of public-private partnerships to avoid delays and renegotiation of contracts at the sub-national level.

Towards the creation of a logistics observatory in Peru

Logistics observatories have been widely used across countries to provide the needed data for analysis of freight transport and for facilitating dialogue for policy making. In 2009, the Netherlands established the Dutch Institute for Advanced Logistics to spur research and innovation in logistics through the collaboration of the private sector, public sector, think tanks and academia (OECD/International Transport Forum [ITF], 2016). France has also created national and regional logistics observatories focusing on specific sub-sector issues, such as formation on costs, prices and taxes in the sector or cross-border transport systems. In Latin America, the Inter-American Development Bank has developed a regional observatory, reporting key indicators for each country, and some countries are developing national observatories, including Chile and Mexico (OECD/ITF, 2015a; OECD, 2016).

A logistics observatory in Peru would help to strengthen decision making, increase the quality and reliability of data and promote dialogue among stakeholders. A logistics observatory in Peru could collect pool data and disseminate high-quality data on the Peruvian logistics sector, alongside their analyses. These data and analyses could inform dialogue between the public and private sectors on opportunities and challenges facing the logistics sector. Ultimately, the observatory could provide key inputs for the development and monitoring of a strong logistics strategy and/or efficient regulations and reforms to improve performance.

To provide high-quality data, a logistics observatory in Peru should develop robust statistical and analytical methodologies in collaboration with international and national experts. To evaluate the impact of the logistics sector on social and economic development, the observatory needs to be able to access and disseminate meaningful sectoral, operational, financial and duration data. Developing key indicators to track the competitiveness of logistics in Peru is equally fundamental. The use of internationally comparable data and international standard indicators would reveal progress or gaps against a chosen set of benchmarks (OECD/ITF, 2016).

The data provided by the logistics observatory need to be translated into visible and useful analysis, which allows for proper monitoring and policy design. The observatory should have a research and analysis programme, accompanied by a clear and ambitious communications plan to disseminate results. As an example, Chile's logistics observatory uses quarterly information bulleting to present main supply chain data, with the objective of presenting in near real time the current state of logistics in Chile (OECD/ITF, 2016).

The observatory must have the tools and the means to obtain and disseminate results. These include the legal right, technical ability and resources to acquire, store and disseminate all necessary data elements. Similarly, based on international comparisons (Kauppila, 2014), the observatory requires a well-defined business plan delimiting its functions, accompanied by strong independent governance, leadership and support from government and international agencies (OECD/ITF, 2016). Close involvement of the private sector is also important, both to ensure a focus on business-relevant indicators and to facilitate collection of key data.

Developing a national policy for urban and metropolitan transport

While urban transport responsibilities tend to be assigned to local governments worldwide, national guidance for urban mobility is increasingly acknowledged as key to more homogenous and widespread improvements in urban centres and enhanced local capacity to carry out responsibilities. In Peru, whether urban transport policies favour public transport or private vehicles over the next decades will importantly determine vehicle fleet growth in the country (Figure 3.4, Panel A and B). This, in turn, will translate into important differences in the environmental impacts of transport. Implementation of urban transport policies favouring public transport would bring significant CO_2 mitigation potential (compared to a business-as-usual scenario or one in which urbanisation is increasingly supportive of private vehicle use) (Figure 3.5). This highlights the importance to support, at a national level, sustainable urban transport policies as a common objective for the country.

National urban mobility policies have been developed by countries with diverse administrative structures, levels of economic development and cultural environments. Different countries have opted for diverse leading agencies and institutional configurations for developing national urban mobility policies. In Brazil and Mexico, for example, new ministries have been created (or transformed in the case of Mexico) for leading urban policy at the national level. Brazil created the Ministry of Cities in 2003 and, in Mexico, the Ministry of Agrarian Reform was transformed into the Ministry of Territorial, Agrarian and Urban Development in 2013 (Secretaría de Desarrollo Agrario, Territorial y Urbano). Other countries have assigned responsibility for developing national mobility policies to existing ministries, e.g. Colombia (Ministry of Transport through the Sustainable Urban Mobility Unit, in co-ordination with the National Planning Department); France (Ministry of Ecology, Sustainable Development and Territorial Management, MEDAD), India (Ministry of Urban Development of India); and the United Kingdom (Department for Transport).

Figure 3.4. **Influence of car-oriented vs. public transport-oriented transport policies on car and motorcycle ownership in Peruvian cities, 2010-50**

Car and motorcycle ownership per 1 000 inhabitants in cities with over 500 000 inhabitants

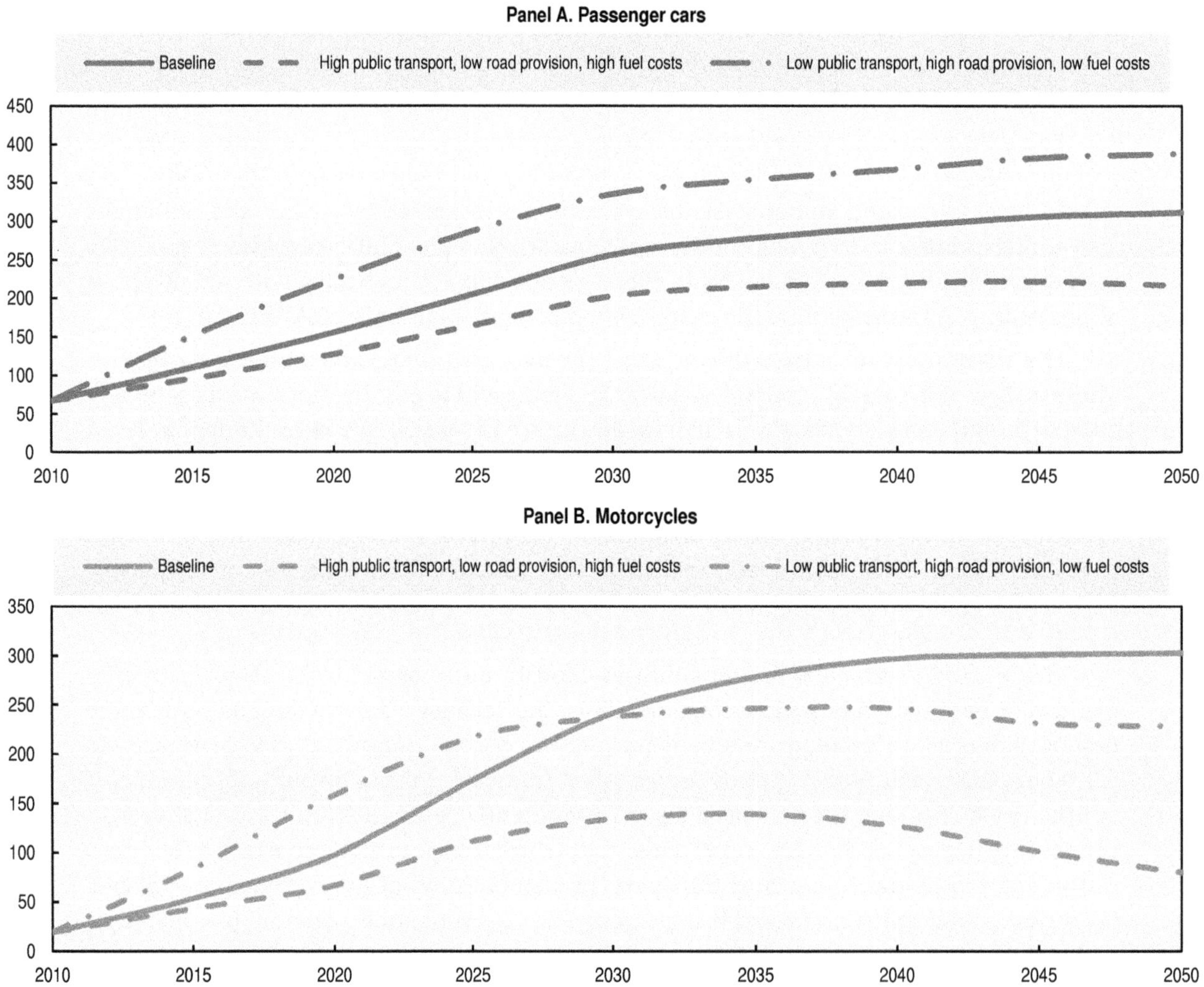

Source: OECD calculations based on OECD/ITF (2015), *ITF Transport Outlook 2015*, OECD Publishing, Paris, *http://dx.doi.org/10.1787/9789282107782*

StatLink *http://dx.doi.org/10.1787/888933411353*

The Ministry of Housing, Construction and Sanitation (MVCS), in close co-ordination with the MTC, would be an adequate institution for developing the national urban mobility policy for Peru. However, a starting point would be to strengthen its technical capacity and secure adequate funding. In Peru, no national entity has formally been assigned responsibility over urban mobility issues. The MTC has a role in the planning, management and administration of local road infrastructure through the Special Programme for Decentralised Transport Infrastructure (Proyecto Especial de Infraestructura de Transporte Descentralizado). However, this role has been limited to projects in rural areas. The Ministry of Housing, Construction and Sanitation is in charge of urban development and issued the National Urban Development Plan 2006-2015 (MVCS, 2006). The plan does not develop guidelines for urban mobility, but it does acknowledge connectivity as a key pillar to be addressed by urban development policies. In addition, the programmes and actions by this ministry in the areas of public space, territorial development, housing and urban services have naturally led to addressing accessibility improvement in cities. Consequently, national support for improving urban mobility has been added as one of the elements addressed in its City Programme (Programa Nuestras Ciudades). The important link between urban development, housing and mobility, plus the fact that support has already been initiated through the MVCS, suggests this institution to lead national urban mobility policy in Peru.[9]

Figure 3.5. **Influence of car-oriented vs. public transport-oriented transport policies on CO_2 emissions in Peruvian cities, 2010-50**

Cities over 500 000 inhabitants

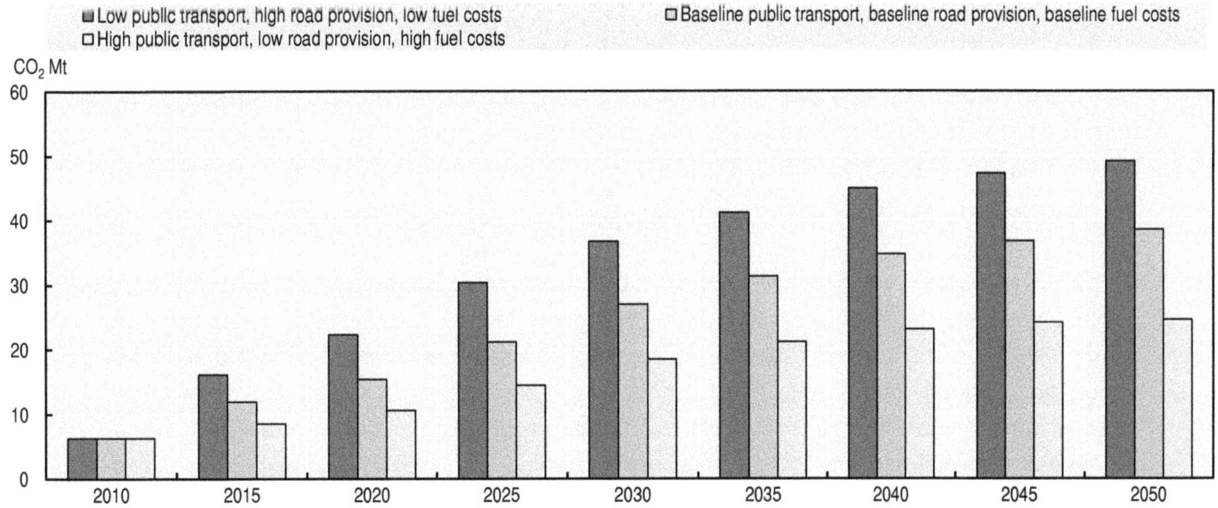

Note: Mt = millions of metric tonnes.

Source: OECD/ITF (2015b), *ITF Transport Outlook 2015*, OECD Publishing, Paris, *http://dx.doi.org/10.1787/9789282107782-en*

StatLink *http://dx.doi.org/10.1787/888933411360*

The MVCS could focus on actions that have been useful for improving urban mobility in other countries. While actions taken by agencies leading national urban mobility policies can take many forms, three elements have proven particularly valuable: 1) developing specific objectives, targets and guidelines for the sector that translate the general principle of developing sustainable and inclusive mobility into operational goals; 2) supporting better urban mobility planning and investment prioritisation through frameworks that promote the development of urban mobility master plans; and 3) advancing programmes that strengthen the capacity of urban authorities to fund projects.

The remainder of this section focuses on these three elements and provides lessons and recommendations. The recommendations build on the experiences of France and the United Kingdom, which have mature institutional frameworks developed in various decades of focus on urban mobility issues. They also draw relevant insight from emerging economies in the region, including Brazil, Colombia and Mexico, which have only more recently engaged in developing national urban mobility policies. Adapted to the Peruvian context, these experiences are useful in the design and implementation of urban transport policies in Peru.

Developing objectives, targets and guidelines for urban mobility

In the context of cities unlocking the benefits of public transport, walking and cycling is central to adopting a comprehensive vision for mobility policy and investment decisions. Cities have characteristics that make it possible to attain multi-modal mobility. First, higher density of demand in urban centres increases the scope for reliance on public transport modes, mass transit in particular.[10] Second, high densities can also contribute significantly to shortening the average distance of trips, making cycling and walking more attractive. Third, as motorisation grows and road space becomes scarce, congestion tends to limit the benefits of private transport, particularly cars, for travel in cities (Aguilar Jaber and Glocker, 2015).

Realising this potential and attaining higher shares of walking, cycling and public transport can bring cities substantial economic, environmental and social benefits. Public transport generates less pollution and carbon emissions per unit of mobility delivered than cars and motorcycles (Figure 3.5); it also provides social benefits for mobility-disadvantaged residents and improves the liveability of cities (Cervero, 2011; ITF, 2013). Furthermore, both public transport and non-motorised modes can deliver mobility using less space than the same mobility demand met by cars and motorcycles, reducing pressures on road infrastructure capacity.

Four principles should improve urban mobility with an eye to unlocking the benefits of public transport, walking and cycling. First, prioritise financial resources and road space for public transport, walking and cycling. Give priority to pedestrians, followed by cyclist, public transport, freight vehicles and, lastly, motorcycles and cars. Second, create integrated transport systems. Urban transport planning should ensure seamless connections between the different transport modes and put special emphasis on the physical, operation and tariff integration of all public transport modes. Third, implement effective transport demand management by using policy tools such as parking policies and road pricing schemes to ration the use of cars and motorcycles in cities. Finally, integrate land use and transport policy. Co-ordinating transport and land-use planning is central to achieving urban development that favours non-motorised and public transport.

Developing explicit documents for setting objectives, targets, and guidelines for urban mobility, aligned with the four principles above, will be a solid step for the MVCS. Reflecting them in the legal framework will also be important. Having explicit documentation for guiding the urban transport sector has been key for countries with different levels of development, such as Brazil, Colombia, France, India, Mexico and the United Kingdom.

Developing appropriate objectives and guidelines for urban mobility is important to respond to citizen complaints in Peru. Citizens listed public transport as the second greatest problem limiting quality of life in Lima (after insecurity). In addition, 77% of citizens interviewed consider tackling vehicle emissions a priority to address pollution in the city, which is seen as the third greatest problem hampering quality of life (Lima Cómo Vamos, 2014).

Towards a solid framework for urban mobility master plans

The process of developing mobility master plans can significantly strengthen the planning capacity of urban authorities. A mobility master plan identifies the challenges faced by an urban area and sets out a roadmap to guide the city on a sustainable course regarding its land use and transport system (GIZ, 2013). Having a solid strategy provides certainty on the links between the city's objectives and investment decisions. For these reasons, countries with national governments that have engaged in developing national urban mobility policies have focused on creating frameworks promoting the development and use of urban mobility master plans to advance their policy objectives, as have all countries selected for analysis in this section (Brazil, Colombia, France, India, Mexico and the United Kingdom) (Certu, 2012; GIZ, 2013; IUT, 2014).

The MVCS could build on the current programme for urban mobility studies to create a national framework for urban mobility master plans. The ministry recently started to support cities by financing urban mobility studies as part of the City Programme (Programa Nuestras Ciudades). Studies have been developed for Huaral, Tacna, Conglomerado Cañete and Huancayo.

To achieve significant progress in leading the urban sector towards more sustainable and inclusive mobility, the programme would have to evolve into a national strategy. In that context, the current studies should be transformed into comprehensive mobility master plans. Elements identified as essential to comprehensive mobility master plans according to the International Union of Public Transport (Union Internationale des Transports Publics [UITP]), based on international experience, are useful for that purpose (Box 3.2). Diagnostic of the challenges (currently included in the studies) is one of many other elements needed for developing this planning tool. In addition, transport proposals must be followed by an implementation plan linked to a funding strategy and a framework for reporting and monitoring progress. Indicators used for the reporting and monitoring process should be aligned with both national objectives and particular goals set for the city. It is also important that alternative scenarios are studied before arriving at the preferred plan for land-use patterns and the transport system.

Peru should also go from pilot projects to a nation-wide framework that is flexible but adapted to local conditions. International experience has shown that strong binding mechanisms for widespread development and use of urban mobility master plans are needed. Accordingly, many national governments have made development of urban master plans compulsory by law for urban areas with a population above a certain threshold. Urban mobility master plans have also been made central to the eligibility criteria for cities to get national funds. The leading agency should guarantee conformity with minimum quality standards and alignment with the regional and local development plans (*planes concertados regionales y locales*). Leading agencies in many countries have issued specific documents for guiding local administrations in the process of developing these tools. Financial and human resources allocated to this must be considered.

A framework developed by the MVCS should also make sure that the development of mobility master plans contributes to enhancing local capacities and involves local actors. Private consultants and non-governmental organisations can certainly bring important expertise. However, the development of these planning tools without significant involvement from local government staff, as is the case in the current programme, is a lost opportunity to build technical capacity within urban authorities. Improvements in human capital and further local financial resources will be necessary. In addition, making the development of urban mobility master plans a participatory process is essential for having comprehensive tools developed with an interdisciplinary approach. It helps with avoiding the exclusion of vulnerable groups, as well as building a shared vision for future projects and actions. This can effectively reduce forthcoming protests and discontent (GIZ, 2013).

Box 3.2. **Developing successful mobility master plans**

UITP action points are sets of recommendations in specific fields of public transport policy. As part of this work, the institution has analysed international experience in developing integrated mobility plans and identified the following elements as essential to include:

- Vision – long-term political vision of the city/region, including the future role of sustainable mobility.
- Context – detail regarding the transport geography of the area, the integration with land use and other policy areas, including plans for growth.
- Challenges and strategic policies – outline of the challenges to overcome with clear goals and objectives, supported by an analysis of future scenarios. Policies are also developed to support the achievement of these goals and objectives through the delivery of the strategy.
- Transport proposals – sustainable multi modal transport proposals to deliver on objectives and overcome future challenges.
- Expected outcomes – analysis of the impact of proposals on delivering objectives.
- Implementation plan – short-, medium- and long-term plan for delivery.
- Costs and resourcing – identification of funding sources for the strategy.
- Monitoring and reporting – framework of indicators and targets to measure the strategy's performance.

Source: OECD (2015b), *OECD Territorial Reviews: Valle de México*, Mexico, OECD Publishing, Paris, *http://dx.doi.org/10.1787/9789264245174-en*.

Advancing a similar planning framework would be highly beneficial for Peru and would contribute to better managing current efforts to increase public participation in government decisions. Peru has introduced a participatory budget instrument (*presupuesto participativo*) whereby the MEF assigns certain funds to regional and local governments that must be spent on projects agreed through a participatory process. The process has proven challenging, especially in ensuring that final decisions over the use of the funds correspond to priorities of urban areas and are the result of an effective participatory process. Building a framework for urban mobility master plans could substantially help advance participatory initiatives. Simpler additional consultation for specific funds would be needed, given the previous participatory process already undertaken for developing the urban mobility master plan. Also, decisions for participatory funds would focus on previously identified options included in the roadmap set by the master plan, improving correspondence between investments and priorities.

Advancing programmes to enhance the local financial capacity of cities

National programmes supporting investment in urban mobility enhance local financial capacity and incentivise better urban planning. As concentration of the population in urban centres increases, cities face important investment needs for building transport infrastructure. Consequently, the creation of national programmes to support urban mobility investment projects financially has also become a component of national urban transport policies. Financial support is sometimes awarded through grants, loans or a combination of both. Various countries have established different proportions of national and local contributions. Colombia and Mexico, for instance, require a quota of private investment for the project to be approved. When appropriately designed, national programmes can widen local financial capacity to implement transport projects that deliver on sustainable and inclusive mobility goals and advance national economic and well-being objectives. In addition, they can set out a national framework for improving the planning and evaluation capacities of local governments (GIZ/EMBARQ, 2013).

Developing a programme(s) to support urban transport investment in Peru will require leadership from the MVCS, supported by other relevant national agencies. The creation of such a programme(s) will require support from the executive and legislative bodies in charge of budget allocation. In addition, the proposed programme should be aligned with the objectives and guidelines set by other relevant entities, such as the MTC, the MEF and the Ministry of Environment.

While proposed at a national level, the scope of programmes must address the heterogeneous conditions and needs of Peruvian cities. Programmes analysed in Brazil, France and Mexico, for example, focus on supporting mass transit systems, recognising its higher capacity and importance to transit-oriented development.[11] As shown by the category of cities eligible for this type of programme, the focus on mass transit is tailored to medium and large cities with a population of over 500 000. Since 50% of Peru's urban population lives in urban centres below 500 000, it will be important to develop other solutions for smaller cities. A current programme explicitly targeted at cities of different sizes is Colombia's Urban Transport National Programme. Support for mass transit systems has been central to the eligibility of projects supported through this programme in the case of larger cities with a population above 600 000. In parallel, this programme also provides financial support to cities with a population of between 250 000 and 600 000 that are focussed on other types of solutions. A wide range of actions are supported, including the development of technical studies for developing integrated transport systems, road infrastructure enhancement, construction and improvement of public transport access facilities, and traffic management implementation (GIZ/EMBARQ, 2013).

Peru should build on previous experience in the region to enrich the programme(s) developed. Experience in various cities of the region and in Lima emphasize the role of Bus Rapid Transit (BRT) and other bus corridor projects in reforming the current system of concessions and the regulatory framework for bus services.[12] It would, therefore, be valuable for national programme(s) to require that a well-set strategy for advancing regulatory reform is integrated into the rationale and plans submitted when applying for funds to be applied for these projects. In addition, regional experiences illustrate that programmes should not privilege certain types of projects (e.g. BRT vs. metro). Instead, these programmes, together with urban mobility master plans, should foster the creation of a multi-modal strategy that is well suited to long-term mobility needs and that takes advantage of the characteristics of different modes and projects. Projects approved should also foster good integration between mass transit corridors and feeder services, as well as adequate incorporation of transport services into the urban environment.

Making support from programmes a condition of urban mobility master plans is a good strategy to incentivise better planning and evaluation by local authorities. The link is well established in the *Major Schemes Programme* in England. In addition, as funding approval is subject to the submission of project evaluations by local entities, introducing specific requirements for these is important to incentivise development of better appraisal methodologies. Methodologies required to be used by local authorities increasingly incorporate a wider range of economic, social and environmental costs and benefits, which are not always monetised and are instead often included as qualitative factors (Owen, Carrigan and Hidalgo, 2012). Peru could benefit from an improved project evaluation methodology to strengthen that of SNIP, which has limitations for capturing social and environmental benefits. This should be done in co-operation with the MEF.

Consolidating the technical and financial capacity of the MVCS and developing the three actions outlined in this section would be a solid step in building a national urban transport policy in Peru. In parallel, however, the overall institutional framework will need to be adjusted to address the importance of metropolitan governance of urban mobility, since the expansion of urban areas beyond administrative boundaries makes it increasingly difficult to provide well-functioning transport services and spatially coherent policies. The development of analysis and data collection for functional urban areas (the effective commuting area of an urban centre) is needed (OECD, forthcoming).

Improving transport connectivity in the Lima-Callao metropolitan area

Hosting Peru's capital city and main port, and being the centre of economic and cultural activity, the metropolitan area of Lima-Callao and its performance is essential to the country's development. Lima itself concentrates 50% of GDP. The metropolitan region includes the two regional jurisdictions: Lima (43 districts) and Callao (7 districts). Lima-Callao reached 9.8 million inhabitants in 2015, representing 32% of Peru's total population and over 40% of Peru's total urban population (INEI, n.d). Its location has strategic advantages as both a gateway for Latin American trade and a competitive alternative to the Panama Canal ports for trans-shipment, especially on the Asia-Latin America route.

Port traffic in Callao has been growing rapidly. Container throughput between 1995 and 2014 grew by 650%, making it the sixth largest port in Latin America in Twenty-Foot Equivalent Units (TEUs). More than 60% of Peru's foreign trade goes through Callao (Mesquita Moreira, 2013). In 2013, containers handled at the port represented close to 85% of all container traffic in Peru (author's calculations based on World Bank, 2014).

Deficient transport services and restricted connectivity hinder Lima-Callao's potential for economic development and improvement of citizen well-being. As the population and economic activity have grown, mobility needs have increased. The number of motorised trips in the metropolitan area increased by 10 million between 1989 and 2012 (Figure 3.6, Panel A), corresponding to an increase from an average of 1.1 daily motorised trips per inhabitant to almost 2. Including walking, in 2012, the metropolitan area reached 22.3 million yearly trips (2.4 per person daily). While total trips increased by 4.2% yearly between 2004 and 2012, the population increased by 2.1% yearly during the same period (Municipalidad Metropolitana de Lima, 2014).

The urban mobility system of Lima-Callao is struggling to meet mobility demand and ensure reliable, safe, clean and accessible transport services. Increasing congestion is perceived as an important problem by the population. Average travel time for the average trip in the metropolitan area increased almost 20% between 2004 and 2012, from 31 to 37 minutes. Working trips reported higher than average travel times and have increased from 40 minutes on average in 2004 to 45 minutes on average in 2012 (Municipalidad Metropolitana de Lima, 2014). Lima-Callao also has high levels of pollution, which puts at risk the health of the population (Transitemos, 2015). Between 70% and 80% of the pollution in Lima is estimated to be caused by vehicles (Barbero, 2006). Another major concern is the high and increasing number of deaths due to transport accidents. Lima concentrates about 62% of the national accidents and reports an average of 590 deaths, 180 injuries and 30 permanently disabled yearly as a consequence of transport accidents (Transitemos, 2015).

Figure 3.6. **Transport in Lima-Callao**

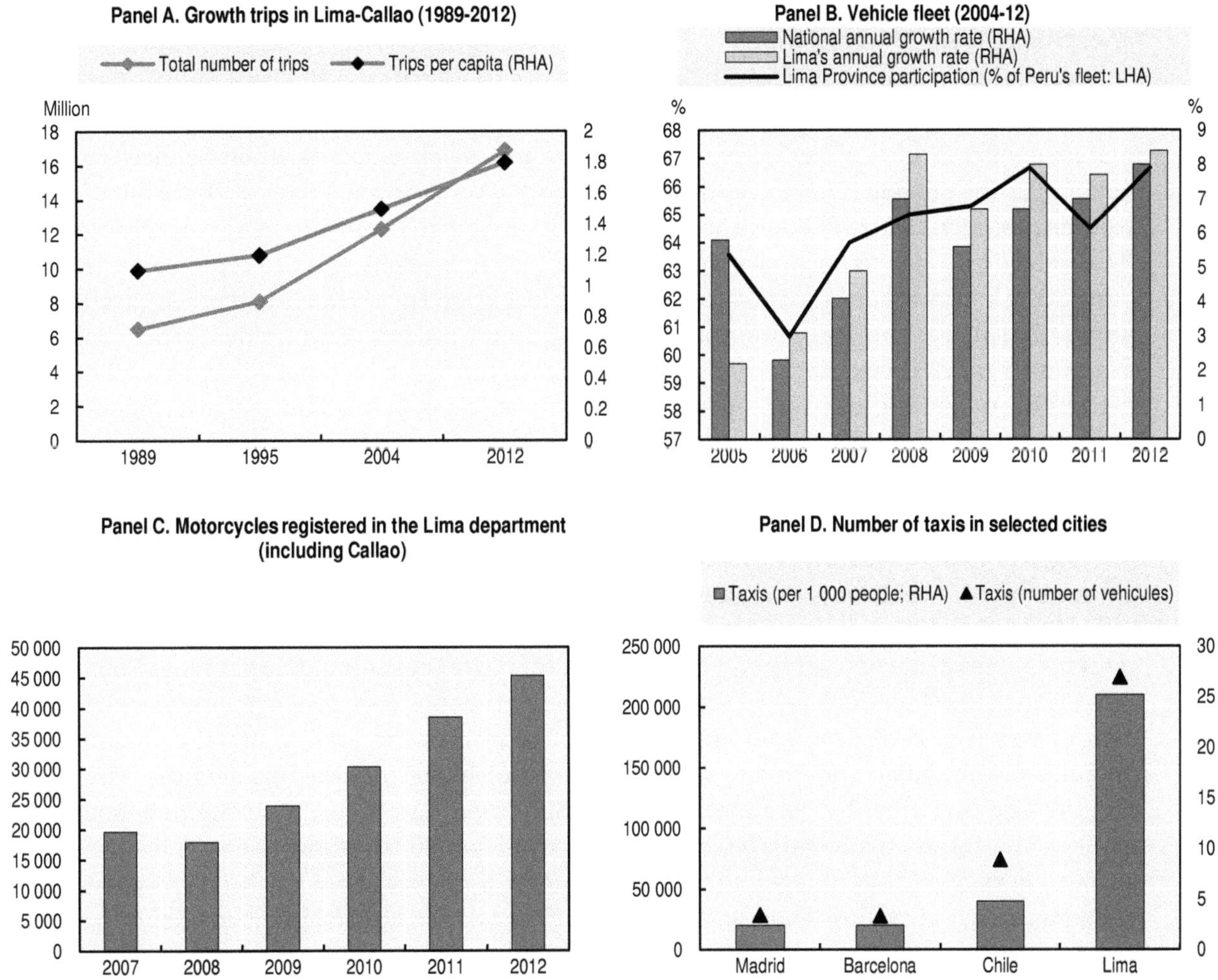

Source: Based on Municipalidad Metropolitana de Lima (2014), PLAN Lima y Callao 2035, Lima, Peru, available at: *www.transitemos.org/aprende-de-movilidad/plam-lima-y-callao-2035/*; Centro Investigacion Desarrollo Asesoria Transporte Terrestre (CIDATT) (2015), "Informalidad laboral y competitividad del transporte urbano", presentation given to the OECD delegation, Lima, December 2016; and MTC (2015), "Parque de Motocicletas Inscritas Según Departamento, 2007-2012", Ministerio de Transporte y Comunicaciones - Oficina General de Planeamiento y Presupuesto con datos de la Superintendencia Nacional de los Registros Públicos, Peru, 2015.

StatLink *http://dx.doi.org/10.1787/888933411378*

The accelerated growth of the vehicle fleet is a major challenge, especially in a context of limited traffic management capacity. The vehicle fleet in the department of Lima (including Callao) reached almost 1.45 million in 2013, representing 60% of the total vehicle fleet in the country (Lima Cómo Vamos, 2013). Although the resulting motorisation level (160 vehicles per 1 000 population) is relatively low compared to other capitals of the region (e.g. 233, in Bogotá, and 247 in Santiago), growth of the vehicle fleet has been rapid, putting pressure on the city. The growth rate of the vehicle fleet in Lima and Callao has been higher than that of the country in recent years (Figure 3.6, Panel B). While still a small number, growth in motorcycles has accelerated in recent years (Figure 3.6, Panel C). Traffic management systems, including traffic light management, are limited and inefficient, which creates important bottlenecks and congestion. The situation is exacerbated by inadequate driver behaviour and lax implementation of traffic rules (Ardila-Gómez, 2012). Taxis and moto-taxis in particular are over dimensioned and under regulated in Lima-Callao. In 2013, there were 230 000 taxis, of which only 40% were registered (Citylab, 2014). In contrast to the private vehicle fleet, taxis per 1 000 population in 2010 represented a high proportion, compared to other cities (Figure 3.6, Panel D).

The deficient capacity and quality of public transport and the poor walking and cycling facilities are key conditions for the rapid growth of private vehicles and taxis and severely hinders quality of life for a majority of the population. Most public transport services in Lima-Callao are provided by semi-formal small-capacity vehicles (microbuses), the result of a decree passed in 1991 to liberalise public transport services in Peru with the aim of solving the shortage of public transport services. The new system brought significant problems as many of the informal enterprises were formalised and bigger concessionaires were replaced by multiple small enterprises (Municipalidad Metropolitana de Lima, 2014). In this model, the government grants concessions to enterprises, which in turn contract other enterprises who own bus fleets, diluting even further responsibility for services. In addition, the government has not regulated minimum quality and safety standards for services.

The existing model also brought indiscriminate granting of concessions, yielding an over-dimensioned fleet with routes that overlap in many cases, while leaving service shortages in many areas. The bus fleet in Lima-Callao is about 34 200 vehicles, of which the oversupply of vehicles is calculated at approximately 17 800 (CIDATT, 2015). Moreover, fare collection is not centralised. Therefore, service providers compete with each other for passengers, creating real safety and quality concerns. The recent implementation of Bus Rapid Transit (BRT) services, called *Metropolitano*, and other bus corridors with preferential right of way (e.g. *el corridor azul*) are an attempt to reform the system by rebalancing the roles of the public and private sector in favour of higher quality bus services. The city has also implemented two metro lines. While important steps, both the new bus services and the metro remain too marginal to meet public transport needs and have not been developed as an integrated transport system. Similarly, there has been marginal implementation of cycling lanes, and existing cycling and walking facilities are deficient in ensuring user safety.

In addition to underinvestment in public and non-motorised transport, allocation of road space and the transport pricing framework favour car and motorcycle travel. Parking fees are low, safety and environmental standards regulation for cars and motorcycles is lax and the place given to walking and cycling facilities in the road infrastructure of the metropolis is scant. Such policy and pricing does not reflect the social costs of travel by the different modes (e.g. pricing does not cover the congestion and pollution generated by cars and motorcycles). In addition, given that public transport and walking account for 60% of trips (Municipalidad Metropolitana de Lima, 2014), the current model does not prioritise modes used by the majority of the population and on which the most vulnerable in the population in particular rely (Figure 3.7). Underinvestment in walking and cycling facilities and public transport, accompanied by under-priced motorcycle and car travel and the preponderance of road space given to these modes, have accelerated vehicle ownership and reliance in taxis. Under present conditions, this trend will only intensify as incomes continue to grow.

The metropolitan area will face a growing challenge and increasing pressure to manage congestion and pollution, while those reliant on public transport and walking will continue to endure poor-quality mobility, restricted accessibility and significant safety threats.

Figure 3.7. **Share of transport modes by level of household income**

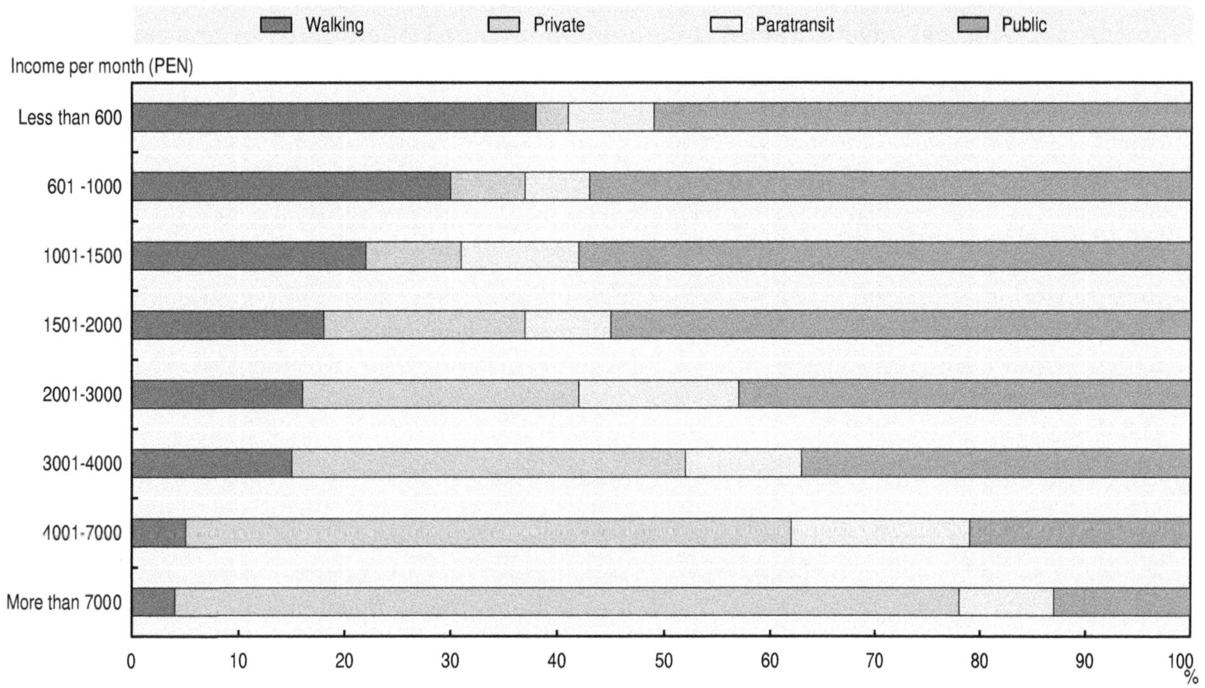

Source: Based on Dextre, J. and P. Avellaneda (2014), *Movilidad en Zonas Urbanas*, Fundación Transitemos/Fondo Editorial, Pontivicia Universidad Católica del Perú, Lima, available at *www.fondoeditorial.pucp.edu.pe/libros-impresos/109-movilidad-en-zonas-urbanas-.html#.V6yx53xTHIU*.

StatLink http://dx.doi.org/10.1787/888933411384

The implementation of projects and policies to address these mobility challenges is severely limited by the lack of metropolitan vision and deficient co-ordination between levels of government. The institutional set-up for managing and planning transport in Lima and Callao is complex, as it involves multiple agencies and co-ordination among them has been limited or non-existent (Box 3.3). The lack of co-ordination for implementing better traffic management has restricted the capacity to improve travel behaviour. The municipality of Callao recently introduced technologies to improve surveillance of traffic offences. However, implementation does not cover the metropolitan area, which has created a series of unintended ill effects.[13]

The lack of metropolitan strategy has also limited initiatives to reform the bus system, such as the implementation of the *Metropolitano* and the *corredor azul*. Re-grouping small and semi-formal bus providers into more professional enterprises subject to higher quality standards and providing services through high-capacity, cleaner buses was central to the municipality of Lima implementing the *Metropolitano* and other new bus corridors. However, there has been a lack of co-operation from the municipality of Callao in avoiding that the semi-formal services concessioned by this government compete with the *Metropolitano* and the new corridors. The resulting reduced demand represents a financial strain on the new system. In addition, semi-formal buses running in the same corridors increase congestion, which in turn reduces the competitiveness of the complementary bus corridors (those that have preferential right of way but not confined lanes). Finally, due to the lack of co-operation between the two municipalities there is no plan to extend BRT services or build new bus corridors towards a metropolitan-scale network that can effectively serve trips from origin to destination.

Box 3.3. **Principal governmental stakeholders involved in planning, management and investment for transport in Lima and Callao**

Municipalidad Metropolitana de Lima

- Urban Transport Department (Gerencia de Transporte Urbano) – responsible for conducting traffic and transport studies, and for regulation and inspection of transport services.
- Protransporte – responsible for implementation, management and regulation of the BRT corridor (Metropolitano).
- Department for the Promotion of Private Investment (Gerencia de Promoción de la Inversión Privada) – responsible for carrying out the process of promoting private investment and strategic alliances with the national government, regional governments, local governments, private investment and civil society in order to promote private investment in assets, companies, projects, services, public infrastructure and public services.
- Metropolitan Fund for Investment – public agency (órgano descentralizado) in the metropolitan municipality of Lima created to provide resources for financing the Programme for Investment and Urban Works and supervise compliance with contracts involving local private investment.
- Toll Management Company – responsible for road maintenance, road works and management services responsible for road maintenance, road works and management services. This is a private company contracted by the municipality of Lima.

Municipalidad Provincial del Callao

- Urban Transport Department (Gerencia General de Transporte Urbano) – responsible for conducting traffic and transport studies, and for regulation and inspection of transport services.
- Department for Urban Development (Gerencia General de Desarrollo Urbano) – responsible for formulating and evaluating specific urban plans, conduct and supervise authorizations, certifications, awards and settlements concerning urban development.
- Municipal Fund for Investments in Callao – municipal company (descentralizado) that performs all activities related to the execution of public works in Callao.

National Government

- MTC (Ministry of Transport and Communications)
- Department for Surface Transport (Dirección General de Transporte Terrestre) – responsible for regulating and setting standards for transport services and road safety.
- Planning and Budgeting Office (Oficina General de Planeamiento y Presupuesto) – responsible for planning and programming national transport investments.
- Authority for Electric Massive Transport in Lima and Callao (Autoridad Autónoma del Sistema Eléctrico de Transporte Masivo de Lima y Callao) – special project of the MTC, attached to the Vice Ministry of Transport. It is responsible for outreach activities, planning, implementation and management of the Lima Metro Railway Infrastructure.
- OSITRAN – public body (órgano descentralizado) linked to the Presidency's Council of Ministers. It is responsible for supervision of the metro concession.

Source: Base on Transitemos (2015), "Autoridad Unica de Transporte y Movilidad para Lima Metropolitana y provincias conurbadas", presentation given to the OECD delegation.

The national government also plays an important role, having invested in the two metro lines and with another four lines already in the pipeline. However, without adequate co-ordination with local governments, the metro is not well integrated (physically, operationally or in terms of tariff) with the *Metropolitano* or the new bus corridors. Metro lines have not been planned according to local urban and transport plans or origin-destination surveys either. Supervision of the metro system was assigned to OSITRAN (Box 3.3). While this organisation has a high technical capacity for supervising infrastructure contracts, it has limited capacity for adequately supervising the metro concessions, as it requires capacity to supervise service quality (which goes beyond the role assigned to this institution).

Mobility challenges in the Lima-Callao metropolitan area are further aggravated by traffic flows generated by the port. The metropolitan area of Lima-Callao and the port have been growing fast but independently. As a consequence, relevant public and private institutions have not worked on a strategy for ensuring port benefits to the local economy while reducing the negative impacts of port activities on the city. Due to the reliance of the Peruvian logistics on trucking, business brought by the port contributes significantly to road congestion, pollution and road safety issues. Ninety-five percent of Peruvian trade is moved through roads, and 100% of goods coming in and out of the port of Callao do so by truck (APM Terminal [APMT], the main container terminal operator in Callao). Between 2 730 and 5 460 trucks were estimated to have entered or left the port of Callao every day in 2014, which figures only account for container-related traffic (based on 2014 data from Containerisation International, 2015).

In turn, transport inefficiencies in the city hinder the port's competitiveness and limit benefits of investments made for port expansion. The location and potential of the port of Callao attracted DP World and APMT, which committed to extensive investments to make it a world-class port. DP World has completed the first phase of a USD 300 million development of the southern dock (Muelle Sur), which is now able to host simultaneously two ships with a capacity of 8 000 TEUs. Each of the ship emplacements are 350 m long and 16 m deep, enabling the terminal to host even larger ships in the future.[14] Investments have also translated into important enhancements of the terminal's handling capacity, which had been very limited. The terminal's yard now has a handling capacity of 850 000 TEUs per year and will reach 1.35 million TEUs per year when all upgrades are completed. APMT launched a very large development project of the northern docks (Muelle Norte), planning to invest USD 750 million in five phases up to 2022. By the end of the project, the terminal will be able to process 2.9 million TEUs per year (compared to 0.8 million TEU before the operator took over in 2011) and 9.9 million t of non-containerized cargo. It will be able to receive ships up to 16 m deep (compared to the maximum 11 m allowed today) and will be prepared with all the necessary equipment to ensure world-class productivity for container and other types of cargo. Enhancements already carried out at both terminals have enabled the port to reach good efficiency standards.[15]

Among the ten largest Latin American countries for maritime trade, Peru is the sixth fastest in terms of container ship turnaround time. Callao, specifically, ranks fourth among the ten largest ports on the continent, according to this port efficiency indicator (Figures 3.8, Panels A and B). The number of container moves per crane per hour is around 30 at DP World and 26 at APMT, a high performance that would not have been possible without the acquisition of state-of-the art ship-to-shore cranes. The truck turnaround time within APMT is below 30 minutes, which is also considered fast. Between 2011 and 2014, the costs of shipping a container went from USD 435 to USD 238 at Muelle Norte, which is partly due to recent investments (Maersk, 2014). This enabled the operator to increase the number of vessels calling at the port by 59% and increase container volumes passing through the port by 21%.

Figure 3.8. **Average days per container ship turnaround in 2014**

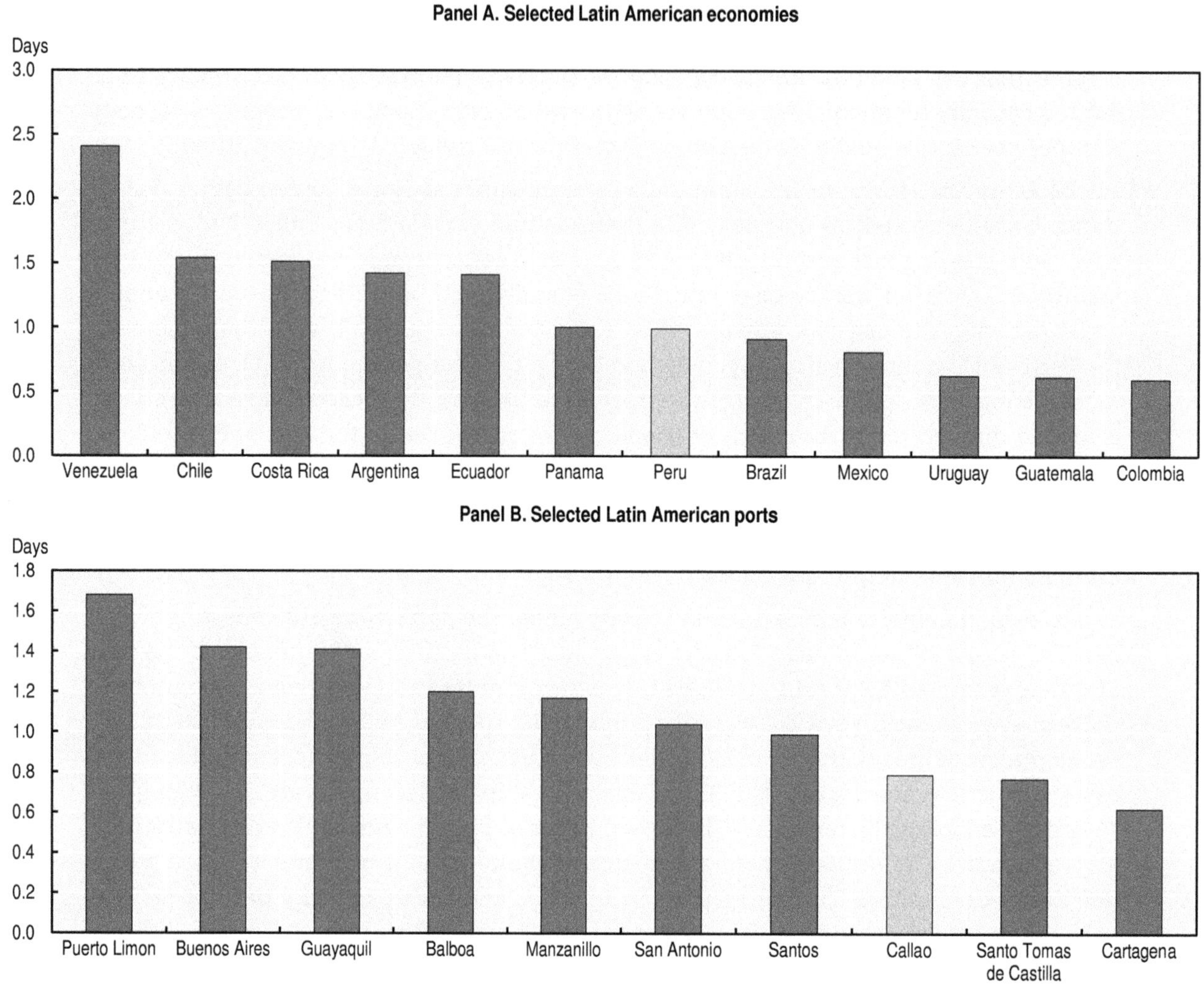

Source: OECD/ITF (2015c), "The Impact of Mega-Ships", *International Transport Forum Policy Papers*, No. 10, OECD Publishing, Paris, *http://dx.doi.org/10.1787/5jlwvzcm3j9v-en*.

StatLink *http://dx.doi.org/10.1787/888933411393*

The already well-advanced modernisation process can indeed explain a large part of the increase in cargo traffic over the last few years. However, improvements in port competitiveness are limited by the density of passenger traffic, which challenges efficient logistics throughout the urban area. Other than impacts on urban quality of life, congestion has important consequences to the city's productivity, making it more timely and costly for trucks to reach the port area. Overall, the social costs of congestion in Lima are estimated at USD 7 billion per year, of which an important part are lost business opportunities (MTC/GIZ, 2015).

Congestion and security around the port gates remain the most important bottleneck, with significant impacts on surrounding communities. Time is critical in logistics services. Each additional day spent in transit by cargo corresponds to an additional cost of between

0.6% to 2.1% of value (Hummels and Schaur, 2013). APMT estimates considerable time is lost at the port gates, with consequences to logistics efficiency and the surrounding communities. Overall, 90% of cargo traded at the port comes or leaves from off-docks in Callao and the surrounding area.

The total truck turnaround time from Callao to the port and back averages six hours, within which only 30 minutes are spent at the terminal. It is difficult to estimate precisely what part of the remaining 5.5 hours are spent in congestion, but APMT's typically experiences queues of 350 to 400 trucks at the terminal gates, which stretch back over 1 km along the two lanes available to trucks. The terminal typically has three shifts per day over which traffic volume is almost evenly distributed, meaning that congestion is a steady state. This bottleneck is, in large part, due to inefficient traffic management and the lack of infrastructure for truck parking around the port. It produces other negative consequences besides. Trucks stuck on roads surrounding the port are vulnerable to theft, burdening cargo owners, trucking companies and employees with additional risk. Other than reducing the port's competitiveness in terms of turnaround times, truck congestion around the port's gates is also responsible for the degradation of the urban environment, as it generates pollution, noise and visual disturbance and obstructs passenger mobility.

Towards a mobility authority for Lima-Callao

Establishing metropolitan mobility authorities is increasingly common, and the many success stories show the potential benefits possible for Lima-Callao. Internationally, mechanisms for the co-ordination of metropolitan mobility planning and policy come in many forms. Indonesia employs informal metropolitan-wide co-ordination forums; Mexico employs more formal metropolitan commissions, but without a legally binding obligation to co-operate. Although simple to implement, these mechanisms have often proved limited by the need for consensus in order to pursue their programme of work, with consequent long delays. They also tend to be particularly sensitive to changes in administration. By contrast, formal metropolitan-wide authorities with transferred responsibilities, capacities and funds generally deliver more solid and long-term improvements (Aguilar and Glocker, 2015). In some cases, metropolitan mobility bodies are implemented as part of a wider metropolitan governance structure. Transport for London (TfL), for example, was created through the Greater London Authority (GLA) Act with the purpose of facilitating GLA's transport responsibilities. In other cases, although without a wider metropolitan governance structure, metropolitan-scale transport planning and regulation is nonetheless recognised and dedicated authorities have been created for this purpose (e.g. Syndicat des transports d'Île-de-France [STIF]).

Voluntary co-operation between municipalities denominated *mancomunidades* are the only existing mechanism in Peru that could foster co-ordination between municipalities in different jurisdictions within a single metropolitan area. Nonetheless and particularly for mobility, stronger mechanisms for ensuring planning and policy making at the metropolitan level is needed. The possibility of setting up a unique authority in charge of mobility for the Lima-Callao metropolitan area is increasingly acknowledged by the government and supported by civil society and international institutions. The significant benefits of metropolitan mobility authorities in other countries make a solid case for Lima-Callao to engage in the institutional and legal reforms necessary to develop this type of authority (Annex 3.A1 describes some of the most successful cases worldwide). Similar to the STIF, the initiative currently being studied for Lima-Callao is a separate, dedicated metropolitan authority for transport and mobility without a wider metropolitan government.

Creating essential conditions for the success of the mobility authority for Lima-Callao

International experiences in creating metropolitan mobility authorities demonstrate solid improvements in mobility, given five conditions central to success. These conditions can be summarised: 1) the capacity of the authority to set integral mobility strategies; 2) an institutional arrangement for co-ordination with metropolitan-wide land-use and housing strategies; 3) building internal financial and technical capacity; 4) gaining legal authority and political support; and 5) once established, ensuring ability to deliver public value. The three latter conditions have been highlighted in work carried out by the World Bank as key to creating long-term sustainability and effectiveness (Kumar and Agarwal, 2013). Creating these conditions should be a priority in setting up an authority for Lima-Callao.

Table 3.1 summarises international experiences in establishing these five conditions.

Table 3.1. **International experiences for achieving a successful mobility authority in Lima-Callao**

Secure capacity to develop integral strategies
International examples: The TfL (London), Urban Development Planning Authority Curitiba (URBS) (Curitiba) and Land Transport Authority (LTA) (Singapore) have responsibility over all public transport modes, plus cycling and walking facilities. They also have capacity for setting transport demand management strategies, such as parking, road pricing schemes (e.g. congestion charges and low-emission zones [TfL and LTA]) and the vehicle quota system for controlling vehicle ownership (e.g. LTA). Both TfL and LTA have responsibility over road safety and freight regulation.
Recommendation for Lima-Callao: The metropolitan mobility authority for Lima-Callao will need to have capacity to plan and manage public transport policies, investment and regulation at the metropolitan level but also, to implement effective transport demand management policies. Granting it with authority and responsibility over walking and cycling policies, as well as over road safety and traffic management should also be considered.
Develop an institutional arrangement that guarantees integrated land- use and transport planning
International examples: Transport planning by TfL is carried out within a wider metropolitan integrated planning framework, co-ordinating it with spatial and economic development strategies. In Curitiba, close co-operation between the metropolitan authorities responsible for mobility (URBS) and land-use planning (Instituto de Pesquisa e Planejamento Urbano de Curitiba [IPPUC]) has been key for the creation of the Integrated Transport Network and its development within a transit-oriented development scheme.
Recommendation for Lima-Callao: The transport and mobility authority for Lima-Callao will need to be embedded in an institutional configuration in which long-term land use planning and regulation at the metropolitan scale is guaranteed.
Build internal financial and technical capacity
International examples: Successful urban transport authorities have been distinguished by a highly qualified team. The size of the staff can vary, depending on the responsibilities performed and whether personnel working for subsidiary institutions are contemplated or not as part of the staff (Annex 3.A1). In terms of budget, worldwide examples show that metropolitan transport institutions need significant funds. Therefore, fare box revenues need to be complemented by other sources (Annex 3.A1).
Recommendation for Lima-Callao: Secure funds for a mobility authority for Lima-Callao will require improving current practices: • Revisit the financial situation of the public transport services to be managed and regulated by the new authority. Focus on improving understanding of operating costs in the light of the higher quality and service standards set by the new authority. Analysis of the affordability of services will also be required for identifying the share of full operation and maintenance costs that could be covered by fare revenue and where subsidies would be needed. • Analyse the amount of investment for necessary expansion and service improvements. • Establishing funding requirements will also need to include an analysis of financial needs to support the new authority's staff (detailed analysis of the size and qualification of this staff will be required). Once funding needs are identified, explore national and local funds that could alternatively be allocated to the new authority.
Gain legal authority and political support
International examples: Legal authority TransLink (Vancouver) through the Greater Vancouver Transportation Authority Act in July 1988 and TfL (London) through the Greater London Authority Act in 2000 are examples of authorities that have been supported by dedicated legislation. In the case of the Syndicat des Transports Parisiens (STP) in Paris, created by decree in September 1949, jurisdiction of this authority was enlarged in 1968 to cover seven departments in the Paris region, and it was granted financial autonomy. In 2000, the Law 2000-1208 ratified the addition of the Paris region as a member of the transport authority's board, and the institution changed names to Syndicat des Transports de l'Île de France.

Table 3.1. **International experiences for achieving a successful mobility authority in Lima-Callao** *(cont.)*

Gain legal authority and political support
Political support Leadership from key political actors and/or support from other authorities, such as relevant ministries, facilitate the creation and are key to the consolidation of urban transport authorities. For instance, TransLink (Vancouver) enlarged its funding base by gaining political support from municipalities, which agreed the transfer of property tax and several transport-related levies, such as the fuel tax and parking sales tax, to the metropolitan transport authority.
Recommendation for Lima-Callao: Legal authority Work initiated by international and local organisations for the creation of the new mobility authority is already analysing the necessary reforms to the General Law for Land Transport and Traffic (Ley General de Transporte y Tránsito Terrestre). Building on this work and setting up this institution within a clear and solid legal framework will be key to its future development and effectiveness. Political support Support from the Ministry of Transport is a valuable asset. However, securing support from other ministries and political stakeholders will be important, in particular from the Ministry of Housing, Construction and Sanitation, the MEF, the municipality of Lima and the municipality of Callao.
Ensure delivery of public value
International examples: TfL's demonstrated ability to improve public transport in early years played an important role in the public acceptance of restrictions to car use implemented in later stages.
Recommendation for Lima-Callao: Recognising areas in which the new authority should focus for attaining sustainable and inclusive mobility goals in Lima-Callao will be essential for the authority to deliver public value. Key actions are advised to that end: 1) prioritise investment and road space for walking, cycling and public transport; 2) resume efforts for improving transport planning and data collection; 3) move forward with bus reform and the development of a well-integrated transport network; 4) implement transport demand management policies and effective vehicle regulation; and 5) adopt a "safe system approach" for improving road safety – that is, a holistic and pro-active approach, managed so the elements of the road transport system combine and interact to guide users to act safely.

Source: Landao, L.A., D. Hidalgo and D. Facchini et.al (2010n.d), "Curitiba, the cradle of Bus Rapid Transit", *Built Environment*, Vol. 36, No. 3, Alexandrine Press, Marcham, Oxon, available at: *http://www.sibrtonline.org/downloads/built-environment-curitiba-oct19-4db0b5ac230da.pdf*; OECD (2016), *OECD Territorial Reviews: The Metropolitan Region of Rotterdam-The Hague, Netherlands*, OECD Territorial Reviews, OECD Publishing, Paris, *http://dx.doi.org/10.1787/9789264249387-en*; Kumar, A. and O.P. Agarwal (2013), *Institutional labyrinth. Designing a way out for improving urban transport services: Lessons from current practice*, World Bank Group, Washington, DC, available at: *http://siteresources.worldbank.org/INTURBANTRANSPORT/Resources/Institutional-Labyrinth.pdf*.

Developing a strategy to realise port city benefits

The port of Callao could play an important role in fostering growth opportunities for both Lima-Callao and Peru, but efforts to harness its benefits will be essential. Ports are important economic assets as trade enablers. They can also be significant contributors to local economies since they imply large stakeholder communities and enable other economic activities. Therefore, cities located near ports can receive a range of direct and indirect economic benefits (Annex 3.A2 for more detail). However, the presence of a port also generates a number of other impacts for cities that countermand their overall benefit. Among others, one strategic issue for Lima-Callao is port-related traffic. Congestion, poor traffic management and lack of infrastructure are all responsible for competitiveness losses that affect both the port and the city. Understanding factors hindering or improving efficiency is important to maximise local economic spill-overs from the port.

Port gate solutions

A combination of port gate strategies can reduce truck wait time and congestion around the port. A truck holding area – an enclosed space for trucks to park for a limited time to wait for their pick-up time –is needed, potentially to be built on part of a 30 ha plot of government land located 2 km from the port area. It should include rest stop facilities for drivers. APMT estimates a holding area with capacity for 170 to 200 trucks would be enough to clear the gates, provide short-term parking for all drivers waiting and solve security issues.

Since bad management remains the main cause of traffic congestion in Lima-Callao, the holding area needs to be coupled with better organisation of traffic fluxes. Port gate traffic specifically can mainly be improved through the implementation of a truck appointment system, whereby drivers may book time slots for their pick-up time. Many ports have implemented this system, with varied results informative for Peru. Box 3.4 highlights the experience of US ports. For effective enforcement of such system in Peru, booking time slots for pick-up and delivery could be made mandatory. Another possibility is to set incentives for truckers to opt for this option.

Box 3.4. **Truck appointment systems at US ports**

The goal of appointment systems is to reduce road congestion at port terminals by giving preferential treatment to trucks that schedule an appointment. Appointment systems are intended to allow terminals to spread truck movements more evenly throughout the day. Terminal gate appointments are usually voluntary but have, in a few cases, been imposed by law. In 2003, California passed the California Assembly Bill (AB) 2650, requiring 13 terminals at the ports of Oakland, Los Angeles and Long Beach to create an appointment system or face a charge of USD 250 for each truck idling more than 30 minutes.

The results of terminal gate appointment systems can be positive. The Gate Entry Management system in the port of New Orleans and the WebAccess system of the Georgia Ports Authority (GPA) are considered successful. Both are web-based applications that allow dispatchers to schedule appointments and provide information for pre-clearance prior to truck arrival at the terminal. WebAccess allows customers 24-hour access to updated data on container shipments. These applications have improved traffic flow, terminal throughput and productivity for trucking companies and terminal operators. GPA has seen a 30% reduction in truck turnaround times (US Environmental Protection Agency [US EPA], 2006).

The terminal appointment system in the ports of Los Angeles and Long Beach, however, is generally considered ineffective. The majority of terminal operators did not view appointments as an effective operational strategy and did not facilitate their implementation. Only a small percentage of trucks used the appointment systems, and as the appointments were not given special priority, queues were not reduced. In addition, terminals were not able to enforce appointments, drayage operators were not willing to participate in the programme, dedicated appointment lanes were lacking and the system encountered opposition. Similar truck idling bills have been introduced in Illinois, Rhode Island, Connecticut and New Jersey. In order to realise significant time savings, a large proportion of trips would need to use appointments and priority would need to be given to trips with appointments (Giuliano and O'Brien, 2007; Giuliano et al., 2008).

Source: OECD (2014), *The Competitiveness of Global Port-Cities*, OECD Publishing, Paris, *http://dx.doi.org/10.1787/9789264205277-en.*

Looking forward, shifting traffic to rail would enable part of the cargo to bypass city congestion. Diversifying options for freight transport from the port to destination points and vice versa is in itself an effective way to prevent road congestion caused by trucks. Ports that have developed extensive rail connections to port terminals show impressive results, such as the port of Gothenburg in Sweden, which handled 48% of its container volumes by rail in 2014. The port of Callao is already connected to the national rail system, but it is not currently fit to be used for moving containers and bulk cargo from the port. Facilitating the fast upgrade of rail infrastructure would allow transport of cargo 15-17 km away from the port for pick-up by trucks. APMT is working with the Railroad Development Corporation on the development of the rail connection for that purpose. Adding rail sidings for containers will take two to three years and could be operational by 2018. The company estimates approximately 10% of containers handled annually in Callao could be moved by rail.

City-side solutions

Traffic on major road connections to the port could be smoothened through better planning and road capacity optimisation. Traffic management tools to redistribute traffic, such as lane dedication, re-routing, changing street directions or reworking the traffic light network, could be options. Spatial planning tools that incorporate land-use changes and maximise the use of road capacity could also guarantee smoother access to the port in Callao. Overall, better transportation planning and the creation of an integrated metropolitan-level transport system is necessary to ease congestion and facilitate logistics throughout the urban area, including the vital ports.

Multi-stakeholder planning

Solving port connectivity issues in Lima-Callao demands close-knit co-operation between port actors and city authorities. A port thrives only by virtue of its integration with other modes of transport. It cannot be competitive without sufficient "hinterland" or land-side support, which remains one of the criteria for port selection by shipping lines (Acciaro and McKinnon, 2013; Saeed and Aaby, 2012; Wiegmans, van der Hoest and Notteboom, 2008). Ports and cities may collaborate on a finite, short-term basis for one project (e.g. a waterfront redevelopment project) or by integrating ports in the city's long-term development (OECD, 2014). In the United States, several metropolitan planning organisations integrate ports within their metropolitan transport plans. One example is Miami Dade County's Long Range Transportation Plan (LRTP), which defines and updates priorities for Miami's transport network with a 20-year horizon every five years. The plan focuses on all transport modes, integrating the port and logistics movement with passenger transportation.

Clarifying responsibilities between local and regional authorities is necessary to facilitate decision making and project implementation aimed at reducing port-hinterland transport inefficiencies. The separation between Lima and Callao into two distinct provinces with competing assets does not facilitate co-operation. Despite its smaller size, Callao comprises the port, airport and a large naval base. Due to the way resources are assigned to local governments in Peru, this leads to resource imbalances between the two provinces. Callao receives important financial resources in the form of canon and royalties transfers (Chapter 2) from fishing activities and customs – significantly higher per capita than does Lima (OECD, 2015a).

A change in perspective concerning authorities' expectations for strategic public land concessions is required to provide opportunities for efficient and sustainable infrastructure development. The private sector's willingness to solve congestion-related issues and boost the port's efficiency can be discouraged by difficulties related to public-private partnership contracting in Peru. Often, poor or no planning decisions are taken because authorities fail to recognise links between infrastructure investments and wider socioeconomic goals. Creating a truck holding area is currently the easiest solution to the port gate bottleneck, yet government expectations are focused on maximising annual revenues from potential concessionaires, such as APMT Land Services, instead of the social and economic benefits that the project would bring. Overall, it will be important that public-private partnership contract design for this and other projects encourage the medium-and long-term social, economic and environmental benefits of infrastructure development projects.

Conclusions and policy recommendations

Several indicators of transport costs, logistics performance and transport infrastructure show Peru lagging behind OECD member countries and some benchmark countries. To address these gaps, Peru needs to shift to a multi-modal approach, improve the assessment and use of logistics, and implement other "soft" solutions to increase connectivity.

Furthermore, it is necessary to improve transport policies both nationally and in urban centres, importantly in alignment with the national development strategy. Peru should adopt a comprehensive approach to connectivity that aligns transport priorities, as well as public and private investments in the transport sector, with Peru's wider goals for economy prosperity and citizen well-being. In that context, Peru's transport strategy needs to go beyond transport infrastructure delivery.

Improvements in urban mobility will be central to enhancing living standards for a large proportion of the population and to meeting Peru's sustainability and inclusivity goals. Making them will require stronger guidance and support from the national government, which will need to develop a national policy for urban mobility. In parallel, local governments will need to improve their policies, focusing on unlocking the benefits of public transport, walking and cycling. Where urban areas have grown into metropoles, developing institutional structures for metropolitan governance will be key.

Box 3.5 summarises the main policy recommendations and requirements for each area covered in this chapter.

Box 3.5. **Main policy recommendations to improve connectivity in Peru**

1. Develop a national strategy to reduce transport costs, improve connectivity and promote multi-modality.

1.1 Design and implement a national transport plan under the auspices of the MTC and other sectors and stakeholders involved.

- Based on national objectives on environmental, social and economic aspects, present transport policies needed to achieve these targets.
- Define transport policy priorities in the transport plan and establish a budget for new public works and maintenance.
- Establish CBA, along with other assessments, to define priorities, and link with SNIP.
- Monitor the outcomes and objectives of the plan periodically.

1.2 Develop a logistics observatory to improve assessment of logistics policies needed.

- Develop data and indicators measuring components and costs of logistics at the national and sub-national level.
- Improve co-ordination between different agencies involved in logistics policies to simplify and harmonise customs procedures, and better use ICTs with the existing infrastructure.

Box 3.5. **Main policy recommendations to improve connectivity in Peru** *(cont.)*

1.3 Continue to improve the criteria determining the modality of investment (Public-Private Partnerships, public works, obras por impuestos).

- Improve the institutional framework to achieve ex ante feasibility studies and value-for-money analysis, complemented with other assessments.
- Improve the implementation of the environmental and land licensing permits; make more effective and efficiently the consultation with local communities.
- Support sub-national authorities by proving technical capacity and pursuing more accurate value-for-money analyses and assessments of public-private partnerships.

2. Develop a national urban transport policy.

2.1 Appoint the Ministry of Housing, Construction and Sanitation as lead agency, in close collaboration with the Ministry of Transport and Communications.

- Assign legal mandate for national urban transport policy.
- Strengthen technical capacity and human resources.
- Establish co-ordination mechanism with the MEF, the Ministry of Transport and Communications and the Ministry of Environment.

2.2 Focus on developing elements identified as effective policy pillars by international experience.

- Develop specific objectives, targets and guidelines for urban transport that translate the general principle of sustainable and inclusive mobility into operational goals.
- Create a national framework for the development of urban mobility master plans.
- Develop national programmes for enlarging the capacity of urban authorities to fund mobility projects.

2.3 Adjust the institutional framework to facilitate metropolitan governance of urban transport.

3. Improve policies implemented at the local level (focus: Lima Callao).

3.1 Move forward in establishing a unique mobility authority for Lima Callao, while ensuring essential conditions for its success.

- Assign it with responsibility over a range of transport policies rather than over public transport only, so it can develop integral strategies.
- Develop an institutional arrangement that guarantees co-ordination of transport, land use and housing planning and policy.
- Provide the new authority with dedicated legislation that clarifies its responsibilities, capacity and jurisdiction.
- Benefit from leadership of key political actors and foster support from other authorities:
  - The Ministry of Housing, Construction and Sanitation, given its likely role to be the lead institution for the national urban mobility policy.
  - The MEF, since new configurations for the financial framework under which the new authority will be developed will be necessary.
  - The municipalities of Lima and Callao, as the creation of the new authority will entail transferring planning and regulation competencies that are today assigned to these entities.
- Support the new authority with technical capacity, human resources and secured funding.

3.2 Once established, the mobility authority must address priority areas to deliver public value.

- Prioritise investment and road space for walking, cycling and public transport.
- Resume efforts to improve planning and data collection.
- Move forward with bus reform and development of a well-integrated transport network.

Box 3.5. **Main policy recommendations to improve connectivity in Peru** *(cont.)*

- Implement transport demand management policies and effective vehicle regulation.
- Adopt a safe-system approach for improving road safety.

3.3 Develop a strategy to realise port city benefits.

- Implement port gate solutions to reduce congestion around the port. In particular, develop a truck holding area.
- Take advantage of rail infrastructure to relieve port gate congestion by adding rail sidings to enable cargo to bypass the city by rail and be picked up away from port.
- Prioritise congestion alleviation with better traffic management tools on major road connections to the port in all urban mobility policies and strategies.
- Develop frameworks for multi-stakeholder planning and decision making, incorporating national and local public authorities, the private sector and civil society.
- Assess infrastructure development projects according to long-term social, economic and environmental objectives, rather than by short-term revenues from concessionaires only.

These recommendations for improving connectivity in Peru were also tested against the three scenarios outlined in Chapter 1. This chapter concludes with an analysis of how the scenarios might impact on incentives, create trade-offs or affect the prioritisation of policy reform in Peru in terms of connectivity.

In "Scenario 1: A new commodity super cycle", multi-modal networks would be important to advance Peru's economic and well-being objectives. However, the commodity boom could entail constraints in the implementation of such policies, as the immediate apparent policy priorities for connectivity would be to develop transport links and railway routes to deliver mining products to ports for export. In this scenario, it will be important to ensure that infrastructure that will be dedicated to the use of certain enterprises is made with their own investment, and that public funds are invested in developing a multi-modal and well-connected transport system for both freight and passengers. Depending on patterns of development, an increase of big cities or of semi-rural sub-centres, the logistics observatory will play an important role in anticipating connectivity needs.

In "Scenario 2: Increasing technology and mechanisation", logistics and connectivity would be important for Peru to position itself as a hub for technology in the region and present an opportunity to use new technologies for better planning and management (based on real-time information) for both freight and passenger transport. Developed urban mobility, green transport and multi-modality, notably at the sub-national level, would be significant attractive factors when competing for investors and firms and would foster conditions for stimulating entrepreneurship. While the scenario would entail shifting connectivity needs, the logistics observatory would play a key role in anticipating and identifying transport needs based on urban and economic planning. New developments in terms of transport-related start-ups are likely to grow in this scenario. Adequate regulation of these would need to be determined to ensure their contribution to policy objectives of improving safety, consumer welfare and sustainability in the transport sector, while addressing potential issues (e.g. labour conditions, fiscal evasion, etc.). However, even in this scenario, these services are unlikely to replace mass transit, due to both the low capacity of vehicles and the risks of social and economic exclusion of populations that could be priced out, especially in the presence of sprawl and low-density urban development and high income inequalities. This scenario presents an opportunity to invest in high-quality transport and take advantage of new technologies to improve connectivity and social and economic opportunity.

In “Scenario 3: Rising expectations of the middle class”, there is a risk that a growing middle class will lead to a further increase in cars and motorcycles and congestion. To mitigate these risks, a national transport plan with environmental, social and economic objectives will be important. The urban mobility master plans will play a key role in anticipating needs and formulating options to advance the goals of sustainable and inclusive mobility. Policies that integrate land-use and transport planning and prioritise investment and road space for walking, cycling and public transport can contribute to removing the incentives and appeal of using cars.

ANNEX 3.A1

International metropolitan transport authority frameworks, staff and budget

Institutional frameworks developed by international metropolitan transport authorities, and the staff and budget assigned to them, can inform the development of such an authority in Peru.

Overview of international metropolitan authorities

TfL – United Kingdom

TfL is a statutory body created by the GLA Act of 1999. This act gives the mayor of London a general duty to develop and apply policies to promote and encourage safe, integrated, efficient and economic transport facilities and services to, from and within London. TfL is directed by a board of 8 to 17 members appointed by the mayor of London, and decisions are made by majority vote. TfL was assigned responsibility over underground, over ground, dockland's light rail and tramway services. It is also in charge of regulating public bus, taxi and private-hire services and coach operations. In addition, it manages roads, including parking and loading regulations, and operates London's congestion charge scheme and Low Emission Zone.

The capacity for continuous investments and improvements are financially ensured by six main sources: income from fares and the congestion charge; central government funding; a proportion of London business rates; prudential borrowing; commercial development of their estate, including advertising and property rental; and development and third-party funding for specific projects.

STIF – France

France's transport authorities have been created under the 1982 law on transport planning (Loi d'orientation des transports intérieurs) with the aim of promoting urban transport alternatives to private cars. The STIF is the transport authority for the Île-de-France and it is jointly supervised by the region of Île-de-France, the departments that constitute the region and the city of Paris.

The STIF has a wide range of responsibilities in public transport planning: defining general operational and service-level targets; setting fares; and negotiating performance-based contracts with public service providers. The STIF also develops an urban mobility plan (PDU), which includes land use and transport plans that guide all subordinate levels of government. The programme of actions included in the PDU is subject to approval from regional, general and municipal councils, transport users, experts and environmental associations. Revenue from a dedicated transport tax (*versement transport*) levied on employers and based on the size of the payroll has been important in enabling the STIF to [VT]extend and maintain the public transport network and non-motorised transport facilities.

LTA – Singapore

The LTA is a statuary board under the Ministry of Transport, established in 1995 as a result of a merger of four government agencies: the Registry of Vehicles, the Road Transport Division of Public Works Department, the Land Transport Division and the Ministry of Communications and the Mass Rapid Transit Corporation. The LTA is governed by an appointed board of directors, which includes 15 representatives from business, academia, and labour and community organisations.

The LTA is responsible for planning, operating and maintaining land transport infrastructure and systems, including road safety, vehicle licensing and electronic road pricing. The LTA constantly improves and expands its current public transport network, complementing it with parking policies and electronic road pricing. The result has been in a shift from private to public transport over the last years. Investment mainly stems from government grants and operating income, such as management fees from taxes, fees and charges relating to land transport services.

URBS – Brazil

The URBS was given responsibility over all public transport modes in the metropolitan area of Curitiba in 1990. The URBS has close co-operation with IPUCC, which is the metropolitan urban development authority. Together, they ensure continuity and integrated planning of transport and land use at the metropolitan level.

URBS is responsible for planning, management, operation and control of the integrated transport network of Curitiba. Within this responsibility, it defines routes, capacity and schedules; regulates and controls the bus system; and collects fares. Bus operators are contracted to the private sector, but fare revenues are pooled and paid to providers through an integrated tariff system. In addition, URBS regulates taxis, sets parking policies and is responsible for traffic management.

Staff and budget of selected metropolitan transport authorities

Staff size

- TfL employed 3 767 staff in 2012 (total 22 452 including those working for subsidiary operating entities, such as the London Underground Limited and Victoria Station, who are also considered TfL staff members).
- TransLink (Vancouver) employed 6 800 staff in 2011 (including those in subsidiary companies).
- The STIF employed 330 staff (not including employees of operating companies, as who are not considered STIF staff members).

Budget

- In 2013, the STIF's budget was EUR 9 billion. Almost 40% came from VT, a dedicated tax levied on employers based on payroll mass, which can be collected by the STIF and other transport authorities in France. Another 40% came from fare box revenues, and 20% came from public subsidies. These subsidies are a combination of funds from the different national, regional, departmental and municipal levels of government.

- The LTA had a USD 1.05 billion budget for 2010/11. A government grant makes up almost 50% of the LTA's financing. It also receives a "management fee", which is a combination of fee revenues (e.g. vehicle registration fees, advertising fees and fines) and government funding that is subject to a periodic review of the funds needed for the LTA to carry out its core functions and responsibilities. This management fee accounts for close to 40% of the budget, while 10% is integrated by other administrative fees related to vehicle management (e.g. vehicle parking certificate fees, vocational license fees and vehicle inspection fees).
- TransLink (Vancouver) had a budget of CDN 1.46 billion in 2011. Transit fares made up 30%. In addition, B.C.'s fuel tax and property taxes contributed 20% each. Transfers from the government of Canada accounted for 13%, and parking sales tax and other small levies and taxes made up the remaining 15%. From the budget, 52% went to bus operations and 22% went to light rail (SkyTrain) operations.
- TfL's budget for 2014/15 was GBP 10.9 billion. Fares accounted for 40%, national government grants for 25%, borrowing and cash movements for 13%, and funding for the Crossrail project for 15%. Other sources contributed 7% (e.g. revenues from the congestion charge accounted for approximately 5% of the budget). During 2014/15, 60% of the total budget went to operating the transport network and 40% went to improving services (Yates, M. and Jack Thompson, 2015).[16]

ANNEX 3.A2

Economic benefits of ports to port cities

The economic impacts of ports on port cities can be categorised by degree of direct connection. Direct impacts correspond to port activities and transport services operations; indirect impacts arise from port users, as from import and export companies; induced impacts result from these activities, including creation of economic opportunities and economic multipliers. Indirect, indirect, induced and employment impacts of ports on port cities is challenging to assess and may yield large variation between ports.

Ports can generate significant value added. One meta-study of 150 port economic impact studies puts the average at USD 100/t of port throughput (Merk, forthcoming). Added value varies by cargo, cars having the highest (Table 3.A2.1).

Table 3.A2.1. **Estimated value added by cargo type (USD/t)**

Cargo Type	Average	Minimum	Maximum
Automobiles	220	116	331
Containers	90	40	149
Steel	60	23	118
Petroleum	45	11	183
Grain	20	9	37

Source: Merk, O. (forthcoming), "Meta-analysis of port impact studies", *OECD Regional Development Working Papers*, OECD Publishing, Paris.

Few studies have attempted to measure the indirect or induced economic impacts of ports, but a series of OECD case studies using uniform methodology have calculated multipliers ranging from 1.13 to 2.47 over six ports (OECD, 2015) (Table 3.A2.2). This analysis also showed that ports have a strong influence on transportation, communication, storage and energy sectors in particular.

Table 3.A2.2. **Estimated port-related multipliers in selected port cities**

Port	Leontieff multiplier
Le Havre-Rouen	2.47
Marseille	2.01
Mersin	1.79
Hamburg	1.71
Antwerp	1.18
Rotterdam	1.13

Source: Merk and Bagis (2013), Merk and Comtois (2012), Merk et al. (2011), Merk and Hesse (2012), Merk and Notteboom (2013).

The presence of a port and its added value also generate employment. Increases in traded volumes at ports are positively related to employment in port regions, with around 800 direct and indirect jobs associated to 1 million t of throughput on average (Merk, forthcoming). According to Rodrigue (2013), each direct port job is associated to three to four indirect jobs, with variations between shipping sectors. Container and breakbulk traffic, the two major activity sectors at the port of Callao, have twice the employment impacts as others.

Economic impacts vary from one region to the other as a function of local context and the type of surrounding industries utilising and supporting port traffic. However, economic benefits can be stimulated by strategies and collaboration among stakeholders to harness the added value and facilitate ports to develop to their full potential.

Notes

1. Specifically, charging users short-run marginal congestion and environmental costs.
2. In particular, Peru has a relative high share of logistics-intensive and time-sensitive exports, which account for 17% of all exports: 1.38 times higher than the OECD median (OECD, 2015a).
3. *http://lpi.worldbank.org/international* for further information.
4. *www.doingbusiness.org/data/exploretopics/trading-across-borders* for further information.
5. *http://reports.weforum.org/global-competitiveness-report-2015-2016/economies/#economy=PER.*
6. See *www.oecd.org/tad/facilitation/indicators.htm* for further information.
7. See *www.proviasnac.gob.pe/Archivos/file/Plan%20Inversiones-v7_3%20(23oct11).pdf* for further information on the Programa de Inversiones 2011-2016 Gestión Estratégica – Corredores Logísticos.
8. Based on information provided by Organismo Supervisor de la Inversión en Infraestructura de Transporte de Uso Público (OSITRAN) (2016).
9. OECD (forthcoming) for further detail on the roles and responsibilities of ministries in relation to urban policy.
10. Mass transit includes metro, light rail, tramways and BRT systems.
11. Transit-oriented development proposes building mass transit corridors that serve as the main transportation axes of cities, along with high-density, mixed land-use development along these corridors.
12. Most bus services in Peru are provided under public-private arrangements involving minimal regulation from the government. The government grants concessions to private companies, which, in turn, hire service providers. Under this scheme, government has a very limited role in route planning, management and implementation of service quality and environmental and safety regulations.
13. For instance, rather than improve the behaviour of taxi drivers, a high share of taxis avoid serving trips that go through Callao to avoid the stricter surveillance.
14. A ship's capacity is defined by the number of TEUs it can carry at once. The largest ships currently calling in Latin America have a capacity of approximately 13 000 TEUs (i.e. Maersk Edinburgh class) and are approximately 370 m long, just under 50 m wide and up to 15.5 m deep. As ship size is continuously increasing, it is likely that Latin American ports will soon have to be ready for even larger ships. Cascading effects in the shipping industry imply that introducing larger ships on the busiest route (Asia-North Europe) gradually shifts the former largest ships to other places, meaning that ships size increase and infrastructure upgrades needed to accommodate them are a concern for all ports, not only the largest in the world.
15. Port efficiency can be expressed through a number of indicators, taking into account the pace of operations at different stages of the container handling process. Shore-side operations are generally measured through ship turnaround time (the average time ships spend at the port to be unloaded and reloaded) and crane productivity (the average number of container moves per crane per hour). Land-side operations can be measured through truck turnaround time (the average time it takes trucks to operate their rotations at the port).
16. This budget do not account for Crossrail project investment.

References

Acciaro, M. and A. Mckinnon (2013), "Efficient hinterland transport infrastructure and services for large container ports", *International Transport Forum Discussion Paper*, No. 2013-19, International Transport Forum/OECD, Paris, available at *www.itf-oecd.org/efficient-hinterland-transport-infrastructure-and-services-large-container-ports.*

AFIN (2015), *Un Plan para salir de la pobreza: Plan Nacional de Infraestructura 2016-2025*, Asociación para el Fomento de la Infraestructura Nacional, Lima, available at *www.afin.org.pe/publicaciones/estudios/1079-plan-nacional-deinfraestructura-2016-2025.*

Aguilar Jaber, A. and D. Glocker (2015), "Shifting towards low carbon mobility systems", *International Transport Forum Discussion Paper*, No. 2015-17, International Transport Forum/OECD, Paris, available at *www.itf-oecd.org/shifting-towards-low-carbon-mobility-systems.*

Ardila-Gómez (2012), "Peru en el umbral de una nueva era", Volumen II, Nota 31. Transporte Urbano, World Bank, Lima office, available at: *http://documents.worldbank.org/curated/en/405581468294018630/pdf/617830v50SPANI0ptimized0es00PUBLIC0.pdf*

Barbero (2006), *Perú: La Oportunidad de un País Diferente*, World Bank, Washington, D.C., 2006, *http://siteresources.worldbank.org/PERUINSPANISHEXT/Resources/Notas_de_politica.pdf?resourceurlname=Notas_de_politica.pdf*.

Bitran, E., S. Nieto-Parra and J.S. Robledo (2013), "Opening the black box of contract renegotiations: An analysis of road concessions in Chile, Colombia and Peru", *OECD Development Centre Working Papers*, No. 317, OECD Publishing, Paris, *http://dx.doi.org/10.1787/5k46n3wwxxq3-en*.

Centro Investigacion Desarrollo Asesoria Transporte Terrestre (CIDATT) (2015), "Informalidad laboral y competitividad del transporte urbano", presentation given to the OECD delegation, Lima, December 2016.

Certu (2012), "Le Plan de déplacements urbains: pour une intégration des politiques de mobilité", *Collection Références*, No. 1, Centre d'études sur les réseaux, les transports, l'urbanisme et les constructions publiques, Lyon, *www.outil2amenagement.certu.developpement-durable.gouv.fr/IMG/pdf/PDU_cle02ad4c.pdf*.

Cervero, R. (2011), "State roles in providing affordable mass transport services for low-income residents", *International Transport Forum Discussion Paper*, No. 2015-17, International Transport Forum/OECD, Paris, available at *www.itf-oecd.org/state-roles-providing-affordable-mass-transport-services-low-income-residents*.

Citylab (2014),For Lima, There's No Simple Path to Re-Regulating Public Transportation, online article, May, 2014, available at: *www.citylab.com/cityfixer/2014/05/lima-theres-no-simple-path-re-regulating-public-transportation/8982/*.

Containerisation International (2015), Containerisation International Yearbook 2015, The National Magazine Company Ltd, London

DETR (1998), A new deal for transport: Better for everyone, *United Kingdom White Paper*, The Stationery Office, London, *www.persona.uk.com/a5dunstable/deposit-docs/DD001-DD025/DD-020.pdf*.

Dextre, J. and P. Avellaneda (2014), *Movilidad en Zonas Urbanas*, Fundación Transitemos/Fondo Editorial, Pontivicia Universidad Católica del Perú, Lima, available at *www.fondoeditorial.pucp.edu.pe/libros-impresos/109-movilidad-en-zonas-urbanas-.html#.V6yx53xTHIU*.

Elorza, J.C. (2012), "Ventanilla única de comercio exterior: Requisitos para una implementación exitosa en América Latina", *Serie Políticas Públicas y Transformación Productiva*, No. 8/2012, Corporación Andina de Fomento, Caracas, *http://publicaciones.caf.com/media/21186/caf_libro_vuce_web.pdf*.

Giuliano, G. et al. (2008), "Evaluation of the Terminal Gate Appointment System at the Los Angeles/Long Beach Ports", METRANS Project 04-06

Giuliano, G. and T. O'Brien (2007), "Reducing Port-Related Truck Emissions: The Terminal Gate Appointment System at the Ports of Los Angeles and Long Beach", Transportation Research Part D, Vol. 12, No. 7, pp. 460-473.

GIZ (2013), "Urban mobility master plans: National approaches and local practice, *Sustainable Urban Transport Technical Document*, No. 13, Deutsche Gesellschaft für Internationale Zusammenarbeit, Bonn, *www.itdp.org/wp-content/uploads/2015/06/TD13_UMP_final.pdf*.

GIZ/EMBARQ (2013), *Financing Sustainable Urban Transport – International Review of National Urban Transport Policies and Programmes*, Deutsche Gesellschaft für Internationale Zusammenarbeit/Embarq Corp., Bonn, *www.sutp.org/files/contents/documents/resources/J_Others/GIZ_SUTP_Financing-Sustainable-Urban-Transport_EN.pdf*.

Hummels, D.L., and Georg Schaur (2013), "Time as a Trade Barrier", *The American Economic Review*, Vol. 103, No. 7, pp. 2935-2959, American Economic Association, Nashville, *http://dx.doi.org/10.1257/aer.103.7.2935*.

INEI (n.d), Población estimada al 30 de junio según departamento, Instituto Nacional de Estadística e Información, webpage, Lima, available at *www.inei.gob.pe/estadisticas/indice-tematico/poblacion-y-vivienda/*

ITF (2013), *Cycling, Health and Safety*, OECD Publishing, Paris, *http://dx.doi.org/10.1787/9789282105955-en*.

IUT (India) (2014), Comprehensive Mobility Plan Toolkit, Institute of Urban Transport (India), Delhi, available at *www.iutindia.org/downloads/Documents.aspx*.

Kauppila, J. (2014), "Logistics observatories: international experiences", presentation at the Workshop on Logistics Observatory in Chile, Santiago, Chile, 2 December 2014.

Kumar, A. and O.P. Agarwal (2013), *Institutional labyrinth. Designing a way out for improving urban transport services: Lessons from current practice*, World Bank Group, Washington, DC, available at: *http://siteresources.worldbank.org/INTURBANTRANSPORT/Resources/Institutional-Labyrinth.pdf.*

Landao, L.A., D. Hidalgo and D. Facchini (2010), "Curitiba, the cradle of Bus Rapid Transit", *Built Environment*, Vol. 36, No. 3, Alexandrine Press, Marcham, Oxon, *www.sibrtonline.org/downloads/built-environment-curitiba-oct19-4db0b5ac230da.pdf*

Lima Cómo Vamos (2014), *Encuesta Lima Cómo Vamos, Quinto Informe de Percepción Sobre Calidad de Vida*, Lima Cómo Vamos, Observatorio Ciudadano, Lima, available at *www.limacomovamos.org/noticias/descarga-la-quinta-encuesta-lima-como-vamos-2014/#!prettyPhoto[inline]/0/.*

Lima Cómo Vamos (2013), *Encuesta Lima Cómo Vamos, Cuarto Informe de Percepción Sobre Calidad de Vida*, Lima Cómo Vamos, Observatorio Ciudadano, Lima, available at: *http://www.limacomovamos.org/cm/wp-content/uploads/2015/01/InformeEvaluandoLima2013.pdf*

Maersk (2014), "Latin America's new trade hub", article by John Churchill, 11th March 2015.

Merk, O. (forthcoming), "Meta-analysis of port impact studies", *OECD Regional Development Working Papers*, OECD Publishing, Paris.

Merk, O. (2014), "The Mediterranean port economy: The case of Marseille and Mersin", *International Transport Forum Discussion Paper*, No. 2014-09, International Transport Forum/OECD, Paris, available at *www.itf-oecd.org/mediterranean-port-economy-cases-marseille-and-mersin.*

Merk, O. and T. Notteboom (2013), "The Competitiveness of Global Port-Cities: the Case of Rotterdam, Amsterdam – the Netherlands", *OECD Regional Development Working Papers*, 2013/06, OECD Publishing,

Merk, O. and O. Bagis (2013), "The Competitiveness of Global Port-Cities: The Case of Mersin, Turkey", OECD Regional Development Working Papers, No. 2013/01, OECD Publishing, Paris: *http://dx.doi.org/10.1787/5k4c43014plt-en.*

Merk, O. and C. Comtois (2012), "Competitiveness of Port-Cities: The Case of Marseille-Fos, France", *OECD Regional Development Working Papers*, No. 2012/11, OECD Publishing, Paris: *http://dx.doi.org/10.1787/5k8x9b92cnnv-en.*

Merk, O. and M. Hesse (2012), "The Competitiveness of Global Port-Cities: The Case of Hamburg, Germany", *OECD Regional Development Working Papers*, No. 2012/06, OECD Publishing, Paris: *http://dx.doi.org/10.1787/5k97g3hm1gvk-en.*

Merk, O., et al. (2011), "The Competitiveness of Global Port-Cities: The Case of the Seine Axis (Le Havre, Rouen, Paris, Caen), France", *OECD Regional Development Working Papers*, No. 2011/07, OECD Publishing, Paris, available at: *http://dx.doi.org/10.1787/5kg58xppgc0n-en.*

Mesquita Moreira, M. (2013), "Too far to export: domestic transport cost and regional export disparities in Latin America and the Caribbean", Mauricio Mesquita Moreira, Juan S. Blyde, Christian Volpe, Danielken Molina (eds.), Inter-American Development Bank, Washington, D.C., available at: *https://publications.iadb.org/handle/11319/3664#sthash.bCtLCSqb.dpuf.*

Ministry of Ecology of France (2008), Circular of 9 December 2008 on the Establishment of a Quality Charter for Evaluation, available at: *http://moud.gov.in/division_work_allocation/urbantransport*

Ministry of Urban Development of India (2014), National Urban Transport Policy 2014, Government of India, Delhi, available at: *http://itdp.in/wp-content/uploads/2014/11/NUTP-2014.pdf*

Mougard, S. (2015), "STIF: The organizing authority for transport and mobility in Paris and Île-de-France", presentation at Transforming Transportation, Washington, D.C., January 2015, available at *www.slideshare.net/EMBARQNetwork/stif-the-organizing.*

MTC (2015), Parque de Motocicletas Inscritas Según Departamento, 2007-2012, Ministerio de Transporte y Comunicaciones - Oficina General de Planeamiento y Presupuesto, con datos de la Superintendencia Nacional de los Registros Públicos, Peru, 2015.

Municipalidad Metropolitana de Lima (2014), PLAN Lima y Callao 2035, Lima, Peru, available at: *www.transitemos.org/aprende-de-movilidad/plam-lima-y-callao-2035/*

MVCS (2006), *Plan Nacional de Desarrollo Urbano 2006-2015*, Ministerio de Vivienda, Construcción y Saneamiento, Lima, Peru, *www.urbanistasperu.org/inicio/normas%20legales/PLAN%20NACIONAL%20DE%20DESARROLLO%20URBANO.pdf.*

National Infrastructure Commission (2016), "The National Infrastructure Assessment, Process and Methodology, A Consultation", United Kingdom Government, London, available at: *https://www.gov.uk/government/uploads/system/uploads/attachment_data/file/525950/National_Infrastructure_Assessment_Consultation.pdf*

OECD (forthcoming), *OECD Territorial Reviews: Peru 2016*, OECD Publishing, Paris.

OECD (2016), *OECD Territorial Reviews: The Metropolitan Region of Rotterdam-The Hague, Netherlands*, OEDC Publishing, Paris, *http://dx.doi.org/10.1787/9789264249387-en.*

OECD (2015a), *Multi-dimensional Review of Peru: Volume I. Initial Assessment*, OECD Publishing, Paris, *http://dx.doi.org/10.1787/9789264243279-en.*

OECD (2015b), *OECD Territorial Reviews: Valle de México, Mexico*, OECD Publishing, Paris, *http://dx.doi.org/10.1787/9789264245174-en.*

OECD (2014), *The Competitiveness of Global Port-Cities*, OECD Publishing, Paris, *http://dx.doi.org/10.1787/9789264205277-en.*

OECD/ITF (2011), *Improving the Practice of Transport Project Appraisal*, OECD Publishing, Paris, *http://dx.doi.org/10.1787/9789282103081-en.*

OECD/CAF/ECLAC (2013), *Latin American Economic Outlook 2014: Logistics and Competitiveness for Development*, OECD Publishing, Paris, *http://dx.doi.org/10.1787/leo-2014-en.*

OECD/ECLAC (2012), *Latin American Economic Outlook 2012: Transforming the State for Development*, OECD Publishing, Paris, *http://dx.doi.org/10.1787/leo-2012-en.*

OECD/ITF (2016), "Logistics observatory for Chile: Strengthening policies for competitiveness", *Case-Specific Policy Analysis*, OECD/International Transport Forum, Paris, available at *www.itf-oecd.org/logistics-observatory-chile.*

OECD/ITF (2015a), "Logistics strategy and performance measurement: Mexico's national observatory for transport and logistics", *Case-Specific Policy Analysis*, OECD/International Transport Forum, Paris, available at *www.itf-oecd.org/logistics-strategy-and-performance-measurement-mexico%E2%80%99s-national-observatory-transport-and-logistics.*

OECD/ITF (2015b), *ITF Transport Outlook 2015*, OECD Publishing, Paris, *http://dx.doi.org/10.1787/9789282107782-en*

OECD/ITF (2015c), "The Impact of Mega-Ships", *International Transport Forum Policy Papers*, No. 10, OECD Publishing, Paris, *http://dx.doi.org/10.1787/5jlwvzcm3j9v-en.* (citation details from OECD).

Owen, B., A. Carrigan and D. Hidalgo (2012), *Evaluate, Enable Engage: Principles to Support Effective Decision Making in Mass Transit Investment Programs*, Embarq Corp., Washington, D.C., available at *www.wrirosscities.org/research/publication/evaluate-enable-engage-principles-support-effective-decision-making-mass.*

Rodrigue, J.P. (2013), *The Geography of Transport Systems*, 3rd Edition, Routledge, Abingdon-on-Thames, available at *www.routledge.com/The-Geography-of-Transport-Systems-3rd-Edition/Rodrigue-Comtois-Slack/p/book/9780415822541.*

SACTRA (1999), *Transport and the Economy*, Standing Advisory Committee on Trunk Road Assessment, The Stationary Office, London, *http://webarchive.nationalarchives.gov.uk/20050301192906/http:/dft.gov.uk/stellent/groups/dft_econappr/documents/pdf/dft_econappr_pdf_022512.pdf.*

SACTRA (1994), *Trunk Roads and the Generation of Traffic*, Standing Advisory Committee on Trunk Road Assessment, The Stationary Office, London, *http://persona.uk.com/A21Ton/Core_dox/P/P14.pdf.*

Saeed. N. and C.N. Aaby (2013), "An Analysis of factors contributing as selection criteria for users of European Container Terminals, conference paper, TRB Annual Meeting 2013, Washington, DC., January 13-17, Transportation Research Record Journal of the Transportation Research Board.

Transitemos (2015), "Autoridad Unica de Transporte y Movilidad para Lima Metropolitana y provincias conurbadas", presentation given to the OECD delegation.

U.K. Department for Transport (2009), *Guidance on Local Transport Plans 2009*, United Kingdom Government, London, available at: *http://webarchive.nationalarchives.gov.uk/20110509101621/http:/www.dft.gov.uk/adobepdf/165237/ltp-guidance.pdf*

United States Department of Commerce, Bureau of the Census (2016), *FT920 U.S. Merchandise Trade: Selected Highlights December 2015*, Bureau of the Census, Washington, D.C, available at: *https://www.census.gov/foreign-trade/Press-Release/2015pr/12/ft920/ft920.pdf.*

US EPA (2006), A Glance at Clean Freight Strategies: Terminal Appointment Systems for Drayage, SmartWay Transport Partnership, US Environmental Protection Agency, Washington DC.

Vostroknutova E. et al. (2015), *Peru Building on success: boosting productivity for faster growth*, World Bank Group, Washington, D.C., available at *http://documents.worldbank.org/curated/en/2015/10/25122535/peru-building-success-boosting-productivity-faster-growth*.

Wiegmans, B.W., van der Hoest, A. and T.E. Notteboom, T.E. (2008), "Port and terminal selection by deep-sea container operators", Maritime Policy & Management, Vol. 35, No. 6, Taylor & Francis (Routledge), UK, pp. 517-534, *http://dx.doi.org/10.1080/03088830802469329*.

World Bank (2016), "Parte 1: Resultados Agregados y Lineamientos Estratégico", *Análisis Integral de Logística en Perú Práctica: 5 Cadenas de Exportación*, Global de Transporte y Tecnologías de la Información Región de América Latina y el Caribe, World Bank, Washington, D.C., *http://ww2.mincetur.gob.pe/wp-content/uploads/documentos/comercio_exterior/facilitacion_comercio_exterior/Analisis_Integral_Logistica_Peru.pdf*.

World Bank (2014), *Connecting to Compete 2014. Trade Logistics in the Global Economy: The Logistics Performance Index and Its Indicators*, World Bank, Washington, D.C., *www.worldbank.org/content/dam/Worldbank/document/Trade/LPI2014.pdf*.

Yates, M. and Jack Thompson (2015), "Introduction to TfL Planning and Operations", presentation given to the OECD, Mexico City, 2015.

Multi-dimensional Review of Peru
Volume 2. In-depth Analysis and Recommendations

Chapter 4

Towards more formal jobs and economic activities in Peru

To promote itself to a high-income country, Peru must address the pervasive, persistent issue of informal economic activity and employment in the country. This chapter analyses informality in Peru and provides policy recommendations to mitigate the negative impacts of informality and promote more formal jobs and economic activities. Informality generally involves lower job quality and labour conditions, leaving many workers in vulnerable situations. Costs of formalisation, linked to both wages and non-wage labour costs, only partly explain informality in Peru. Low productivity levels, strongly associated with low skills levels, mean workers are not sufficiently productive to overcome the current costs of formalisation. Coupled with an economic structure concentrated in low value-added sectors, where informality is the norm, there is little opportunity or incentive for formal job creation. Peru must revise, design and implement strategic short- and longer-term policy actions to redress the underlying structural causes and consequences of informality.

Informality in Peru is high and persistent, with a pervasive impact on economic activity and on jobs. More than two-thirds of workers and almost 90% of firms are informal. Although informality has decreased, it remained high throughout the most recent period of economic expansion and progress and continues to stand among the highest in Latin America and the Caribbean. The negative impact informality has on jobs, firms and the overall economy make it one of the main barriers to inclusive development in Peru.

Informality is a complex, multi-dimensional phenomenon, both cause and consequence of the low levels of development in Peru. The broad concept refers to all economic activity that happens outside of government regulations, whether by evasion or by being beyond the scope of regulation. Weak institutional frameworks, the costs associated with formalisation, the large size of low-productivity sectors and certain cultural and socioeconomic conducts common among economic agents are some of the most relevant drivers of informality. In turn, informality has a pervasive impact on economic efficiency and productivity, tax collection, firm development and job conditions, among other consequences.

In order to promote more formal jobs and economic activity in Peru, it is crucial to better understand the complexity of this phenomenon in the country – its main causes and consequences. This chapter presents a set of strategic recommendations to increase formal jobs and economic activities while mitigating the negative impact of informality on job conditions. The first section describes informality in Peru. The second and third sections analyse its main causes. Together with an economic structure that does not generate sufficient formal job opportunities, the costs and barriers associated with formalisation, and the low levels of productivity and skills are relevant drivers of informality. The fourth section concerns the need to mitigate the impact of informality, mainly on health and pension coverage for informal workers. The chapter concludes with strategic recommendations to promote more formal job creation and economic activities and improve overall working conditions.

Informality is a long-standing, multi-faceted barrier to inclusive development in Peru

Informality is pervasive in Peru, at the centre of a cycle linking low-productivity, low-quality jobs and limited state capacity. Its causes and consequences are complex, making it particularly difficult to address with public policy. This section aims to better understand the concept, causes and consequences, and the scope of informality among both firms and workers, by disentangling this highly prevalent, multi-faceted and decades-old phenomenon that so encumbers inclusive development in Peru.

Informality is a complex phenomenon with multiple causes and consequences

In economic terms, informality refers to informal economic activity and informal employment. Informal economic activity encompasses that which happens unrecognised by the state and, therefore, does not follow the registration, recording or taxation regulations it would otherwise. Similarly, informal employment refers to that not under the protection of labour law and social security regulation. These broad descriptions encompass a range of activities and jobs, prompting much debate over the years about what constitutes informality and how to measure it. This review follows the definitions used for official statistics in Peru, which are based on those endorsed by the International Conference of Labour Statisticians (ICLS) (Box 4.1)

Box 4.1. **Defining and measuring informality in Peru**

The ICLS has adopted two definitions for measuring the importance of informality. The 15th ICLS adopted a definition of "informal sector" in 1993 using production unit characteristics. The 17th ICLS adopted a definition of "informal employment" in 2003. Together, they compose the "informal economy", as defined by the International Labour Organization (ILO) in Recommendation 204 on the Transition from the Informal to the Formal Economy (ILO, 2013).

The informal sector constitutes all unregistered and/or small-scale enterprises that produce goods or services for sale or barter and operate with the aim of providing income to their owners and employees. Small enterprises are included in this definition, as they are often exempt from employee registration and are unlikely to be taxed or subject to the enforcement of labour laws. The definition leaves significant latitude to individual countries to define the relevant criteria (size of enterprise, incorporation status, employee registration, etc.). In practice, measurement often excludes agricultural activities due to difficulties in data collection (Hussmanns, 2004), in particular ascertaining whether agricultural household produce is for the market or for consumption (subsistence agriculture is not considered part of the informal sector).

Informal employment includes all jobs which are "not subject to national labour legislation, income taxation, social protection or entitlement to certain employment benefits (advance notice of dismissal, severance pay, paid annual or sick leave, etc.)" and includes "unregistered employees who do not have explicit, written contracts or are not subject to labour legislation, workers who do not benefit from paid annual or sick leave or social security and pension schemes, most paid domestic workers employed by households and most casual, short term and seasonal workers". All employment within the informal sector is considered informal. Informal employment also includes all contributing family workers, employees in informal jobs in the formal sector, members of informal producers' co-operatives and own-account workers producing for the household. Informal employment is, therefore, composed of employment in the informal sector, informal employment within the formal sector and certain types of employment in households (informal domestic work and own-account workers producing for the household).

Methods of measuring informality vary by country. Some countries measure the informal sector by non-registered enterprises, while others use employment size. Others employ a combination of both. Measuring informal employment also varies by country, some using as the main indicator lack of social protection and others using the existence of a contract, among other means.

This chapter follows the official definitions of informal sector and informal employment set out by Peru's National Institute of Statistics (INEI). According to INEI, the informal sector refers to all unincorporated productive units not registered with the National Tax Administration (SUNAT). All unincorporated enterprises in the primary sector are considered informal. Informal employment includes all workers who present one of these conditions: 1) firm owners or self-employed workers with a unit of production that is part of the informal sector; 2) salaried workers with no social security financed by the employer (measured, in practice, by affiliation and payment of health insurance contributions); and/or 3) contributing family workers, regardless of the formal or informal nature of the productive unit that they work in (INEI, 2014a).

The impact of informality is multi-faceted and extensive, taking a toll on the economy, firms and workers alike. For the overall economy, informality results in economic inefficiencies, reduced growth and decreased productivity. Eventually, these affect government revenues through lower taxation and smaller business growth, reducing the public sector's ability to provide public services, such as education, health care, social security and infrastructure. For firms, operating in the informal sector precludes access to capital from financial institutions and credit markets, restricting growth domestically and internationally of itself and by the diversion of earned revenue towards costs associated with informality, such as penalties or bribes. Formal firms are also affected, as they face competition from informal firms with potentially lower production costs by not complying with labour, security or quality regulations. Finally, informal workers are affected directly by the poor working conditions and lack of benefits, job security and access to training associated with informal employment. In addition, informal jobs are generally low-productivity, low-wage jobs from which the transition to formal employment is difficult, in terms of proven employment history and skill levels, thereby cementing persistence in poverty and exacerbating socioeconomic inequalities, given that informal employment mostly affects disadvantaged groups and those forced to accept any available employment to meet mere subsistence-level needs.

The complexity of informality derives mainly from its multiple drivers and the fact it is both cause and consequence of many of them. That cycle represents various pitfalls for development. The variety of causes are difficult to disentangle and make its analysis, and the mitigation of its pervasive impacts, particularly difficult. Moreover, the disparity in the definition and measurement of informality in economic literature (Kanbur, 2009) makes drawing inference from international experience and research a complicated exercise. Informality is the consequence of some specific institutional factors, such as the costs of formalisation, which can probably be dealt with by adopting specific cost-reducing policies. However, it is also the consequence of broader structural issues, such as a country's low labour productivity or large agricultural sector or the predominance of micro and small firms. These correspond to a set of drivers of informality that needs to be dealt with over a long period of time and that demand policies with a broad scope of action.

Drawing up a policy agenda to address informality in Peru requires a consideration of the many different types of workers and firms that make up the informal economy and what drives each of them to operate informally. While broad policy statements can be made about informality, policy actions will need to be directed at specific groups, such as small firms, domestic workers, undeclared workers, independent workers, informal employees, informal mining operators, etc. The specific policy stance towards these different groups is also bound to vary, depending on country preferences and the consequences of their actions.

Informality is a widespread, long-standing phenomenon in Peru

Informal employment in Peru remains high and has persisted over time. It reached 72.8% of total employment in 2014 (INEI, 2015). At 68.8% when using the ILO definition applied to non-agricultural employment,[1] it is one of the highest in Latin America and the Caribbean, well above some benchmark countries (Figure 4.1, Panel A) (OECD, 2015a). Informal employment has been persistently high in Peru, even throughout the recent period of large economic expansion, when it dropped from 79.9% in 2007 to the current 72.8% (Figure 4.1, Panel B) (INEI, 2015). Most of this reduction took place in urban areas, while in rural areas, informal employment is particularly persistent. Without further action this persistence could continue, and informal employment would be placed at 50% by 2030 according to some estimations (CEPLAN, 2016).

The incidence of informal employment is unequal across socioeconomic groups. It is higher among young workers (aged 15 to 29) and older workers (ages 65+), women, those with lower levels of education and those living in rural areas (OECD, 2015a). Among the young, informality is high for all groups and particularly high for those living in poor households. For young people aged 29, approximately eight out of ten workers are informal among those living in extreme poverty households. The rates are seven out of ten among those moderately poor and five out of ten among those living in vulnerable households (Figure 4.2).

Figure 4.1. **Informal employment in Peru**

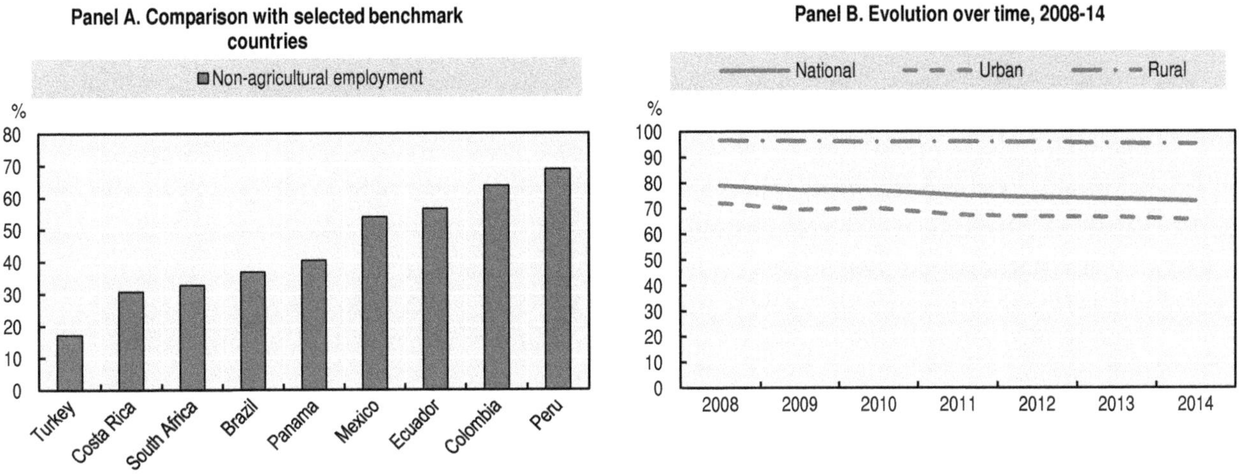

Source: OECD (2015a), *Multi-dimensional Review of Peru: Volume I. Initial Assessment*, OECD Publishing, Paris, *http://dx.doi.org/10.1787/9789264243279-en*.

StatLink http://dx.doi.org/10.1787/888933411402

Figure 4.2. **Employment status across income groups for young people aged 15 to 29 in Peru, 2014**

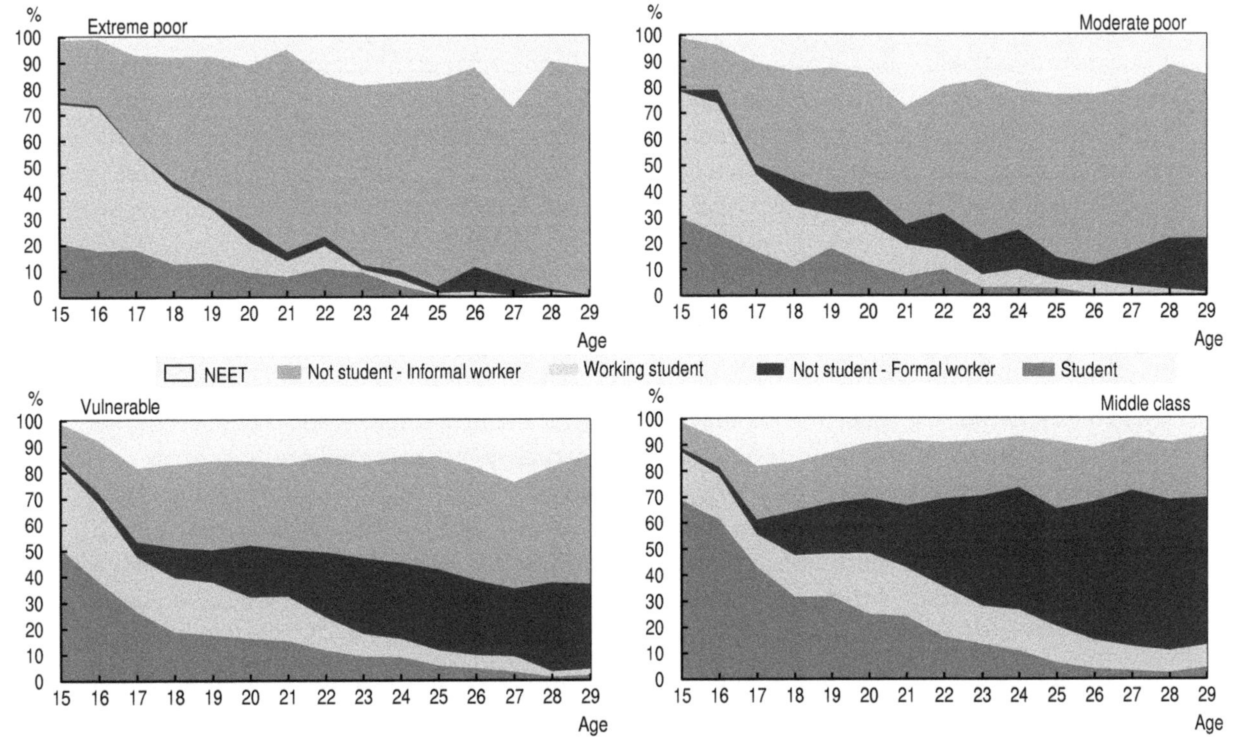

Note: NEET refer to youth Not Employed, nor in Education or Training. Socio-economic classes use the World Bank classification, and refer to youth belonging to households with a daily per capita income lower than USD 2.50 for the "extreme poor"; between USD 2.50-4.00 for the "moderate poor"; between USD 4.00-10.00 for the "vulnerable"; and higher than USD 10.00 for the "middle class". Poverty lines and incomes are expressed in 2005 USD PPP per day (PPP = purchasing power parity).

Source: OECD/CAF/[ECLAC (forthcoming 2016), *Latin American Economic Outlook 2017: Youth, Skills and Entrepreneurship for Development*, OECD Publishing, Paris.

StatLink http://dx.doi.org/10.1787/888933411411

The decline in informal employment, although limited, can be partly attributed to economic growth. Strong economic growth in Peru, particularly since 2002, led to a 44% increase in output per worker in the period 2004-12, accompanied by a modest reduction of informal employment. However, economic growth has not drastically reduced informality, likely because growth has been concentrated in sectors with high levels of productivity but little job creation. Most job creation occurred in low-productivity sectors under informal conditions (see section on productivity and economic structure). In fact, despite a net creation of formal jobs accompanied by a decreasing rate of informality in new jobs, which have been mainly formal, the trend represented a small share of total employment, and the elasticity informality-economic growth, which reflects how much impact economic growth has on the reduction of informality, has remained low in Peru (Céspedes, 2015).

Institutional changes in Peru have been another source of reduction in informal employment. These include a new obligation, as of 2007, to submit to SUNAT an electronic payroll with information on workers, pensioners or service providers, among others – information previously submitted to the Ministry of Labour. Given the greater detection capacity of the tax authority, the new obligation strongly increased the labour authority's capacity to monitor compliance with labour regulations. Other potential explanations for the reduction in informal employment are the introduction and extension of special health insurance regimes and the Law on Small and Medium-sized Enterprises (SMEs) approved in 2003 (ILO/Formalización de la Informalidad en America Latina y el Caribe [FORLAC], 2014).

Because informality in Peru is caused by diverse and sometimes structural factors, the response must be multi-dimensional. As seen, Peru has experienced only a slight reduction in informality in the economy, even over a long period of strong growth. This persistence suggests that the drivers are complex and involve both circumstantial and structural factors. Informal employment and economic activity in Peru are very heterogeneous and manifest in different ways, requiring different policy approaches, including actions to address specific barriers to formalisation in the short term, as well as longer-term strategies to create opportunities for more formal jobs and economic activities.

Informality has many faces in Peru

Informality can take place either by choice or by exclusion. Workers and firms may make a rational choice to operate informally based on a cost-benefit analysis. They may also be pushed into informality if the conditions and costs imposed by formality preclude it as an alternative, e.g. make the job unsustainable or the firm unprofitable. Three scenarios emerge based on cost-benefit rationales: 1) informality by choice, when both firms and workers perceive the costs of formality to outweigh the benefits; 2) informality for evasion, when firms remain informal, even if the benefits of formality outweigh the costs; and 3) informality by exclusion, when workers work informally, even if the benefits of formality outweigh the costs and they would be willing to assume those costs, because there are no formal jobs available (Table 4.1).

A significant share of informal employment in Peru is not voluntary. One traditional explanation in the literature is that a large share of informal employment is the result of low levels of formal job creation so that workers do not have occupational alternatives. Some part of informal employment in Peru can be deemed involuntary or the only employment alternative available; at least 11% of workers – and up to 73.8%, if a broader definition of informal is used – can be considered informal due to lack of alternatives (Tello, 2015).

Table 4.1. **Categories of informality according to different cost-benefit scenarios in Peru, 2013**

		Workers	
		Cost > Benefit	*Cost < Benefit*
Firms	*Cost > Benefit*	Choice	Exclusion
	Cost < Benefit	Evasion	Optimal formality

Source: Bosch, M., A. Melguizo and C. Pagés (2013), *Mejores Pensiones, Mejores Trabajos: Hacia la Cobertura Universal en América Latina y el Caribe* (Better Pensions, Better Jobs: Towards Universal Coverage in Latin America and the Caribbean), Inter-American Development Bank, Washington, D.C., *https://publications.iadb.org/bitstream/handle/11319/462/Mejores%20 pensiones%20mejores%20trabajos.pdf*.

Other factors may affect the cost-benefit analysis of formalisation by firms and workers, including a certain myopia in evaluating future benefits and costs, and a lack of trust in the public sector and service provision. In fact, informality also derives from the existence of weak social contracts in Latin American countries, which in turn derive from low trust by citizens in governments and in one another, low fiscal legitimacy, and weak institutional frameworks, among other factors (Saavedra and Tommasi, 2007). The variety of approaches to categorising informality has been noted, and their delineation is beyond the scope of this report. The present analysis is limited to the two main groups: informal workers and informal firms.

Informal employment can be characterised by the employment status of informal workers. Following the INEI classification adopted in this chapter, the self-employed represent the largest group of informal workers in Peru at 41% of total informal workers; 31% are informal wage workers – either *obrero* (salaried labourers) or *empleado* (salaried employees)[2] – and approximately 22% are informal family workers (Figure 4.3).

Figure 4.3. **Informal employment by group as a share of the total informal labour force in Peru, 2014**

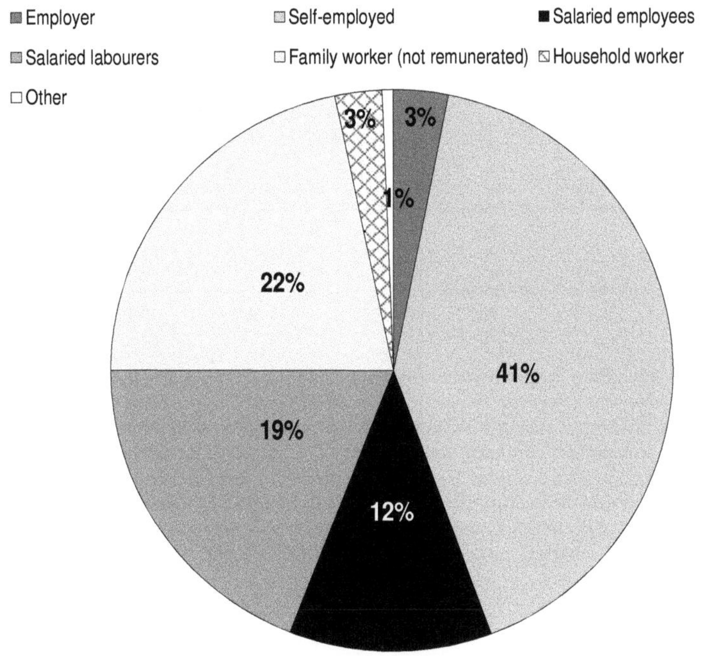

Source: OECD calculations based on INEI (2014a), *Producción y Empleo Informal en el Perú, Cuenta Satélite de la Economía Informal 2007-2012 (Production and Informal Employment in Peru, A Satellite Account of the Informal Economy 2007-2014)*, Instituto Nacional de Estadistica e Informatica, Lima, *www.inei.gob.pe/media/MenuRecursivo/publicaciones_digitales/Est/Lib1154/libro.pdf* (accessed on 29 January 2016).

StatLink http://dx.doi.org/10.1787/888933411424

Box 4.2. **An alternative approach to categorising informal workers by different socioeconomic characteristics**

Informal workers are highly heterogeneous. Recognising that not all informal workers are poor, unproductive workers without access to more productive forms of employment is important not only to describe informal employment accurately but to determine what policies will improve welfare and reduce vulnerability.

Latent class analysis is one means of profiling groups of informal workers across different dimensions, while also accounting for their specific multiple and concurrent socioeconomic and labour market barriers to formal employment. This approach follows similar work on labour market difficulties conducted, for example, by Immervoll (2013) and Fernandez et al., (2016). The analysis focuses on characteristics of different groups (or clusters) that make up the informal sector with the aim of revealing policy-relevant information about the social and economic factors facing the groups.

The informal population (as defined by the INEI, and using the National Household Survey [ENAHO] 2014) can be classified into eight clusters. Figure 4.4 shows their distribution and features.

Overall, about half of the informal workers appear to be particularly vulnerable. Individuals in this group have a higher incidence of extreme poverty and work mostly as unpaid family workers (Clusters 1 and 2: approximately 34% of informal workers), or they are older workers with a higher prevalence of disability and chronic disease and low education (Clusters 7 and 8: approximately 16% of informal workers). The other half of informal workers consists of wealthier workers overly represented in Lima (Clusters 3 to 6: approximately 51% of informal workers), some of whom are working in the formal sector as employees with a pension system (Cluster 5, for example).

Figure 4.4. **Latent class analysis of informal workers in Peru, 2014**

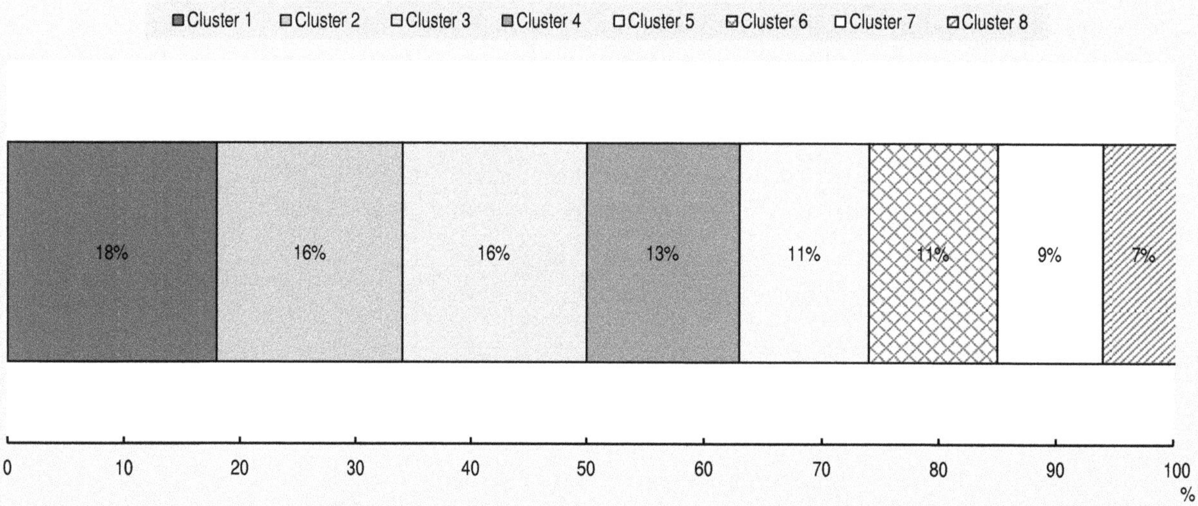

Notes: Cluster 1 = poor men, low education, large company workers. Cluster 2 = poor women, low education, family workers without pay, informal sector. Cluster 3 = wealthier, educated, independent male workers, Lima. Cluster 4 = educated workers/employees (1/3 in the formal sector), no trust, Lima. Cluster 5 = young, wealthier, educated employees with pension, large formal firms, Lima. Cluster 6 = wealthier women, low education, independent or home workers, Lima. Cluster 7 = older disabled women, low education, independent or family workers without pay, informal sector. Cluster 8 = older disabled men, low education, independent workers, informal sector.
Source: Tassot and Vazquez-Zamora (forthcoming 2017); INEI (2014a), *Producción y Empleo Informal en el Perú, Cuenta Satélite de la Economía Informal 2007-2012 (Production and Informal Employment in Peru, A Satellite Account of the Informal Economy 2007-2014)*, Instituto Nacional de Estadistica e Informatica, Lima, *www.inei.gob.pe/media/MenuRecursivo/publicaciones_digitales/Est/Lib1154/libro.pdf* (accessed on 29 January 2016).

StatLink http://dx.doi.org/10.1787/888933411432

A better understanding of the socioeconomic characteristics of these informal worker demographics can guide policy actions to better support informal workers or prevent them from being informal (Box 4.2). The incidence of informality by labour status shows that 90% of all self-employed are informal, while *obreros* and *empleados* have informality rates of 74% and 38%, respectively. Salaried house workers have an informality rate of 90%. Informality is also very high among independent workers at 90%.

The informal sector is large in Peru and remains concentrated in micro and small productive units and in the agricultural, commerce and transport sectors. In Peru, 87% of all productive units were informal in 2012. Of these informal firms, almost all have fewer than 5 workers (98.4%), suggesting a strong association between informality and firm size. Only 1.2% of firms have between 6 and 10 workers, and 0.3% of all firms have more than 11 workers (INEI, 2014b). In addition, approximately one in three informal firms (33.8%) in the agricultural and fisheries sector are informal, while in the non-agricultural sector, most informal firms belong to the commerce sector (23.9% of total informal firms) and transport (12.2%) (INEI, 2014b).

Addressing informality in Peru will require a gradual approach that recognises that some "faces" of informality are structural and likely to persist. The large share of self-employed informal workers with low earnings are a response to the tepid employment growth the country has known. Therefore, a policy agenda to address informality needs to combine 1) a short-term agenda to deal with proximate causes of informality and encourage formalisation of firms and workers, 2) a long-term agenda to address structural causes of informality and 3) an effort to address and mitigate the consequences of informality across a number of areas, especially in social protection coverage.

Informality is largely explained by weaknesses in the institutional framework

Informality is often seen as a by-product of excessive regulations and barriers to entry into the formal sector. This is the view of the legalist tradition of informality (De Soto, 1989; Djankov et al., 2002). To what extent this logic explains informality in Peru requires an analysis of the specific regulations that apply to different groups of firms and workers, the type of incentives these create, and the costs and benefits they face for formalisation.

Business registration is the first step towards formality for firms, although not necessarily the greatest obstacle in Peru. Micro and small firms in downtown Lima report a greater disadvantage of informality, yet 75% of the firms will remain informal, even when the full cost of registration is subsidised and guidance to obtaining proper registration is offered (Jaramillo, 2013). In fact, the relative ease of attaining a business licence to operate formally in Peru compared to other Latin American countries with similar levels of informality (World Bank, 2016) suggests that there must be explanations for informal activity other than entry costs. These probably relate to the prospects of the recurrent burden attached to formalisation and/or the limited growth perspectives of these firms (Vostroknutova et al., 2015). The barriers to formality that go beyond business registration have to do mainly with tax compliance, regulation compliance and some efficiency-related considerations.

Tax regimes for SMEs can be improved to provide incentives to become formal and grow

Most SMEs are informal in Peru, and they face particular barriers to becoming formal. Costs of formalisation, like those linked to taxes and the associated book-keeping and filing procedures, can be particularly hard to overcome for SMEs, given their limited size, capacity and revenues. In an effort to bridge the barriers faced by SMEs, governments have adopted special simplified tax regimes with narrower tax bases tailored, in theory, to encourage formalisation through cost reduction and ease of compliance. Tax compliance costs average PEN 915.80 (Peruvian soles) for a business to adhere to special taxation regimes, which is a significant reduction relative to PEN 7 489.00 for firms to adhere to the general tax regime (SUNAT, 2015). These measures address the cost of tax compliance and, to some extent, special regimes have lowered efficiency hurdles for firms, but they generally do not enhance labour inspection capacities or address other regulatory hurdles.

Peru has several tax regimes targeted at a similar base, which are often redundant and bias occupational categories (Table 4.2). There is a general regime and two simplified special tax regimes for SMEs. The single simplified regime (RUS) has been in force since 2004. RUS is a presumptive tax regime open to individuals and single-owner firms aimed at encouraging small producers and retailers to become formal through the payment of a small monthly fee contingent on the level of annual sales being less than PEN 360 000 and assets being less than PEN 70 000. As a benefit, these SMEs are entitled to enrolment in and use of the Comprehensive Health Insurance (Seguro Integral de Salud [SIS]) in exchange for a single, flat tax that ranges from PEN 20 to PEN 600 per month. The second special regime for SMEs is an income tax regime (RER). It applies to small producers whose sales are less than PEN 525 000 with assets less than PEN 126 000 and fewer than 10 employees. Under this regime, firms are liable for 1.5% of net profits, compared to 28% in the general regime for corporate taxation.

Table 4.2. **Tax regimes for individuals or firms with businesses in Peru, 2016**

	RUS	RER	General Regime
Scheme description	A tax regime created for small retailers and producers, which replaces payment of various takes, allowing them to pay a fixed monthly fee based on their purchases and/or income. This scheme is aimed at individuals who make sales of goods or services to final consumers. Individual limited liability companies can also benefit from the RUS.	A tax regime aimed at individuals and firms with some sector restrictions.	Applies to income attained from business activities, either by a formally established firm or an individual. In general, this income is the combination of labour income and labour.
Allowances to the tax base	None	Cost of inputs to produce or maintain the source of income	Cost of inputs to produce or maintain the source of income Depreciation of equipment Research and innovation investments
Tax rates or tax liability	Tax liability varies according to the level of income: up to an income of PEN 60 000, tax liability is PEN 240; up to PEN 96 000, tax liability is PEN 600; up to PEN 156 000, tax liability is PEN 2 400; up to PEN 240 000, tax liability is PEN 4 800; up to PEN 360 000, tax liability is PEN 7 200 Includes access to the Entrepreneur SIS (healthcare system)	1.5% of net income	28% of net income
Annual thresholds	PEN 360 000 per year	PEN 525 000 per year	
Other implied costs	Does not allow for tax credits due to value-added tax (VAT) and does not require bookkeeping		Requires bookkeeping consistent with international financial reporting standards

Source: OECD based on SUNAT (2016), *Estadísticas y Estudios (Statistics and Studies)* (database), La Superintendencia Nacional de Aduanas y de Administración Tributaria, Lima, *www.sunat.gob.pe/estadisticasestudios/index.html* (accessed on June 2016).

The overlap among regimes can generate perverse incentives. RER users can use invoices to deduct intermediate inputs and to recover VAT, while RUS users cannot. This turns the VAT into a *de facto* cost, hurting efficiency for firms under this scheme. Moreover, given the duplication and the tax benefits of these schemes, firms (single proprietor or larger) might opt for horizontal disaggregation (i.e. some firms split into two or more parts when they reach the maximum size to continue in the most advantageous tax regime), creating tax dwarfism (Inter-American Development Bank [IDB], 2013). There is plenty of anecdotal evidence supporting this claim; however, finding the supportive evidence is more elusive, given the high rate at which SMEs appear and disappear and the volatility of their incomes.

Reduction of formalisation costs to SMEs might have encouraged an increase in registered taxpayers, but the special regimes have not raised significant tax revenues. The number of registered taxpayers increased significantly during the last decade, especially users of the RUS and the RER. This was particularly the case for RER after the fiscal reform of 2007 (Decree No. 968), which raised the threshold for access and removed barriers to register in the regime. However, tax revenue collection as a percentage of GDP from these programmes remained modest, despite the increase in taxpayer numbers.

Informality remains stubbornly high for SMEs, despite these special tax regimes. A reason why SME legislation (mainly the Law on SMEs approved in 2007) has not been more effective in reducing informality among SMEs and promoting compliance is that some of its elements have not been implemented, such as the social protection regime for workers of SMEs. In addition, some of the advantages (such as the general health insurance provided through the SIS) were already accessible without having to bear the costs of formalisation.

Labour costs of formalisation represent a barrier to formality for low-income groups in Peru

In Peru, the cost of pension and healthcare programmes represent 17.5% of total labour costs for salaried workers, 10.1% of which is paid by the employee, and 7.4% by the employer. "*Taxing wages in Latin America and the Caribbean*" (LAC) allows a comparison of taxes paid on wages in twenty economies in Latin America and the Caribbean (Box 4.3). Relative to other countries in the region, in Peru the share of the social security burden to both employee and employer is low. Collusion between the employer and employee might arise to lessen the tax burden on both (i.e. they both agree not to contribute to pension and healthcare such that the employer reduces the total labour cost, while the employee increases the net payment in the short-run), thereby encouraging informality.

Box 4.3. **Taxing wages: Estimating labour costs and tax burdens in Latin America and the Caribbean**

Taxing Wages in Latin American and the Caribbean is a new high-profile report detailing taxes paid on wages in 20 LAC economies:

- Personal income taxes and social security contributions paid by employees
- Social security contributions and payroll taxes paid by employers
- Cash benefits received by in-work families

The purpose is to illustrate how these taxes and benefits are calculated in each country and examine how they affect household incomes. The results also enable quantitative comparisons of labour costs and the overall tax and benefit position of single persons and families at different income levels.

Box 4.3. **Taxing wages: Estimating labour costs and tax burdens in Latin America and the Caribbean** *(cont.)*

The publication shows the amount of taxes and social security contributions levied and cash benefits received for different family types, which vary by a combination of household composition and household type. It also presents the resulting average and marginal tax rates (i.e. the tax burden).

Average tax rates show the part of gross wage earnings or total labour costs that is taken in tax and social security contributions (both before and after cash benefits). Marginal tax rates show the part of a small increase of gross earnings or total labour costs that is paid in these levies.

Informal workers earn 68% less than formal workers in Peru, thus raising the implied relative costs of formalisation for the former group. In Peru, the interaction of minimum contributions to social security programmes and the minimum wage lead to large costs of formality for informal workers at the lower end of the income distribution. The difference highlights the exclusion caused by floors mandated by regulatory schemes. This is not exclusive to Peru; it is prevalent throughout Latin American economies, with the exception of Argentina (Table 4.3).

Table 4.3. **Implied formalisation costs to formal and informal salaried workers in selected countries, 2013 (employee plus employer contributions to old-age and health insurance programmes as % of wage earnings)**

Country	Average cost for a formal worker (%)	Formalisation costs for an informal worker (%)				
		Q1	Q2	Q3	Q4	Q5
Argentina	39.2	39.8	37.0	39.2	39.2	39.2
Bolivia	21.5	47.7	25.8	25.7	25.7	25.7
Brazil	28.0	100.7	44.7	28.6	28.0	29.5
Chile	18.5	53.7	22.4	18.5	18.5	18.5
Colombia	27.5	148.3	53.3	32.8	27.9	27.5
Costa Rica	25.3	283.7	97.6	53.6	35.1	25.7
Dominican Republic	20.1	62.9	34.5	25.9	20.5	20.1
Ecuador	15.5	51.1	24.5	18.7	15.5	15.5
El Salvador	22.5	55.8	33.0	25.0	23.5	23.5
Guatemala	9.6	46.3	29.2	20.9	14.3	11.5
Honduras	9.2	98.9	39.3	25.2	16.1	8.7
LATAM	**21.2**	102.7	41.9	29.0	23.6	22.5
Mexico	16.2	163.2	35.7	23.7	19.3	15.2
Nicaragua	17.7	127.1	47.2	31.9	22.3	19.3
Panama	27.7	210.5	82.7	52.0	34.7	30.0
Paraguay	22.0	80.7	38.7	26.8	22.1	22.0
Peru	**20.2**	118.5	36.9	23.6	20.2	20.2
Uruguay	29.4	129.8	56.8	38.0	29.9	29.4
Venezuela	11.9	29.9	14.5	12.4	11.9	11.9

Sources: OECD calculations based on IDB (2015a), *Base de datos Sociómetro-BID: Sistema de Indicadores Sociales de América Latina y el Caribe*, IDB, Washington, DC., available at *www.iadb.org/en/research-and-data//sociometro-bid,6981.html* (accessed on 7 July 2016); OECD/IDB/CIAT (2016), *Taxing Wages in Latin America and the Caribbean*, OECD Publishing, Paris, *http://dx.doi.org/10.1787/9789264262607-en*.

In some cases, contributions to social security programmes are too costly relative to income, effectively thwarting any possibility of adhering to social security programmes by those workers. For informal salaried workers who earn an average labour income of the first decile (the lowest in the income distribution), the cost of contributing to social security programmes would be 124% of his/her labour income, rendering it unaffordable (Figure 4.5,

Panel A). The cost of becoming formal diminishes as incomes rise, evidencing the positive association between higher social security contributions as a share of income and higher levels of informality within the Peruvian economy. The price of social security contributions stabilises at the level of the minimum wage (sixth decile); however, overall levels of informality remain high even after costs for social security schemes become constant. Despite lower costs, informality persists in 14% of the population, even among those in the highest income decile, again suggesting the existence of other explanatory factors for informality.

Figure 4.5. **Informality and formalisation costs in Peru, 2014-16**

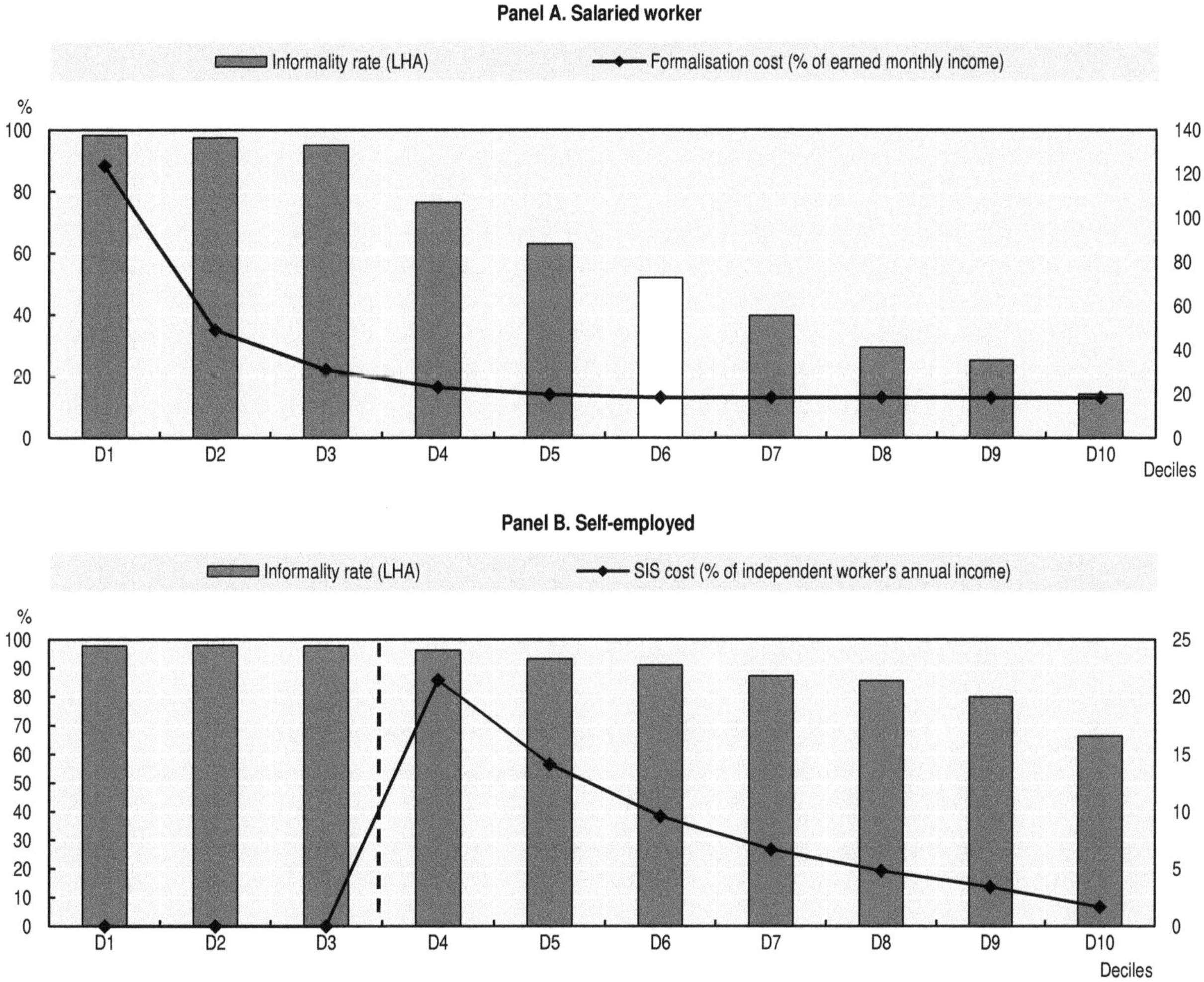

Notes: The white bar in Panel A represents workers earning minimum wage (PEN 750, although it rose to PEN 850 in May 2016). In Panel B, the poverty threshold to be eligible for the free SIS for 2014 – illustrated by the vertical dotted line – was established at 161 soles per month for every member of a household.

Source: OECD calculations based on IDB (2015a), *Base de datos Sociómetro-BID: Sistema de Indicadores Sociales de América Latina y el Caribe* and OECD/IDB/CIAT (2016), *Taxing Wages in Latin America and the Caribbean* for Panel A; OECD based on ENAHO (INEI, 2014b), *Encuesta Nacional de Hogares (ENAHO) (National Household Survey)* (database) for Panel B.

StatLink http://dx.doi.org/10.1787/888933411442

Self-employed workers with lower incomes have zero cost for formalisation, but the cost is still large for self-employed in the mid-range of the income distribution. Most informal workers are not subject to the general regime, given that a large share of them are self-employed. Independent workers in the first three deciles qualify to access the free SIS. After the fourth decile, workers have to contribute almost 90% of their income to social security programmes. This percentage declines for workers with higher income, but is still relatively high and represents a particularly large barrier to participation in social security for those in the third, fourth and fifth decile (Figure 4.5, Panel B). This creates a large gap and may create incentives to remain self-employed and not declare a share of income in order to remain with free access to SIS, which diminishes the benefit of being formal. In addition, when comparing costs of formalisation for salaried vs. independent workers (Panels A and B, respectively), the high costs of formalisation for salaried workers in low-income groups not only limits their access to social security but may also create incentives away from salaried work and towards self-employment for that group, given the free access to social security that can be enjoyed under the latter status.

There is a bias against income derived from formal employment that may encourage informality among salaried workers. This can be seen through a simulation of tax and social contributions for a taxpayer who earns PEN 60 000 annually, by tax regime (Figure 4.6). For the purposes of simplicity, let us assume that an individual abiding by formality can choose between providing a service as an independent worker or as an employee, and also that this individual can opt to provide this service as a small firm, rather than an independent individual, and so can adhere to the RUS or RER. The decision the individual faces will be influenced largely by the costs the different available tax regimes entail, namely: the fourth and fifth categories for the labour regime, and the RUS and RER for firms. The results show that the fifth category (dependent salaried workers) incurs a slightly higher cost (PEN 1 597) than the independent regime, even though they entail performing the same activity compliant with social security contributions.[3] The cost difference increases to approximately PEN 10 000 relative to the RUS and RER schemes. Although the higher price of formality entitles the worker to a different set of benefits, it raises the question of how agents value these benefits. Nevertheless, under the definition of tax compliance (income tax and social security programmes), the individual is formal at very different costs, illustrating how tax schemes, in the short run, may play a role in the kind of occupational category the worker may select.

Figure 4.6. **Tax liability by tax regime in Peru, 2016**

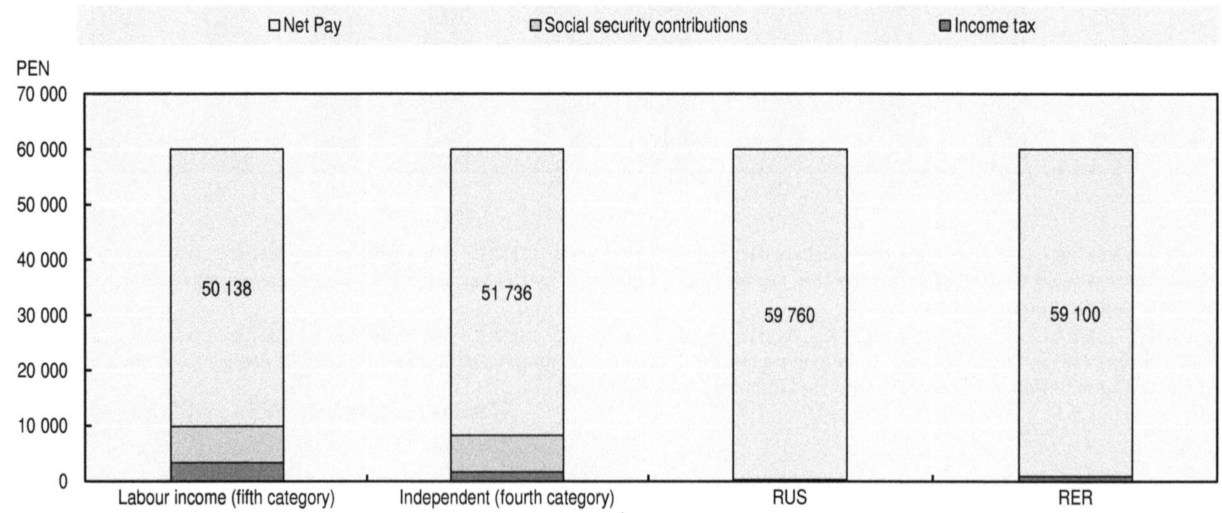

Source: OECD calculations based on OECD/IDB/CIAT (2016), *Taxing Wages in Latin America and the Caribbean* and SUNAT (2016), *Compendio de tasas impositivas*.

StatLink http://dx.doi.org/10.1787/888933411451

There are other regulatory costs or barriers to formalisation – such as the minimum wage or dismissal costs – that also play a role in the decision to formalise. A labour standard aimed at protecting the lowest-paid workers, it can be a cause of unemployment or informality. If set too high with respect to average wages, a great majority of the population can be excluded via the cost of social security programmes and thereby labelled informal. However, it is more relevant to analyse the impact of the minimum wage on informality by linking it to labour productivity levels (next section). Employment protection legislation (EPL) rigidity is also positively correlated with informality in Latin America and is mentioned frequently as a barrier to formal employment creation. The labour rigidities associated with regulations and non-wage costs can increase informality, especially for low-skilled workers (IDB, 2015b). EPL restrictiveness for individual dismissals is relatively low in Latin American countries and OECD economies but perceived as constraining by employers, given the lack of clarity in labour legislation regarding economic causes of fair dismissal for individual workers. However, the severance an employer is required to pay in Peru is high, compared to other Latin American countries, potentially preventing employers from entering into formal employment arrangements. In the case of dismissal, severance as a percentage of wages depends on years of employment. These range from 37.5% to 125% in the case of Peru. The corresponding range for LAC countries is 9.4% to 74.5%.

In sum, the regulatory framework creates incentives for firms to remain small and workers to be self-employed, with negative consequences to formality. In fact, the special tax regimes created to increase formality may, in some instances, have a perverse effect. Firms have incentives to remain small, given the advantages they enjoy and the significant burdens they face by growing and bearing the costs of formality. This can provide favourable conditions for small firms, that do not have the capacity to grow and create formal jobs, to remain small and continue operating informally. Conversely, firms with the potential and ambition to grow, which could be the drivers of formal job creation, may also face a disincentive to expand, given the significant extra costs they will have to bear and the unfair competition they will have to face from firms operating in the informal sector.

Informality as a result and hurdle in a low-productivity, primary-based economy

Informality is strongly linked to the structure of the economy and to low levels of productivity. Among the many drivers of informality, certain structural factors are key to explaining its prevalence and persistence. Low levels of overall productivity driven by low skills, the dynamics of job creation and atrophy, and the structure of the economy are among the critical factors. This approach to informality is concerned with supply-side and demand-side considerations. From a labour supply-side perspective, low labour productivity leads to a large share of jobs being cost-effective only in the context of informality. From a demand-side perspective, most jobs will be created in low-productivity sectors and through self-employment, mostly in subsistence and informal jobs, ultimately with little formal job creation. In this context, the large share of informality will not decrease unless productivity rises and diversification and structural change take place.

Low labour productivity is a strong barrier to formal employment

Informality is largely related to the low levels of productivity of the labour force in Peru. Although it has been growing since 2002, labour productivity in Peru has remained low in the last decades and its gap with the United States remains large; labour productivity in Peru represents 24% of the labour productivity in the United States (Chapter 2). The most direct connection between low productivity and informality is that low-productive workers do not produce enough value-added to cover the costs of being hired formally. Their production remains profitable only under informal working conditions. Evidence confirms this strong correlation between low productivity and high informality, with higher levels of informality concentrated in developing countries (La Porta and Shleifer, 2014).

Productivity levels of a large share of informal workers lead to an output per worker that does not cover minimum regulatory costs of formal hiring (i.e. the minimum wage). If labour income is used as a proxy for labour productivity, then the productivity of a significant share of workers in Peru is below the minimum wage they would need to be paid if they were hired formally. Low productivity, then, is a functional barrier to formality for this share of workers, as employers will not readily bear the costs of the formalisation of workers who do not produce enough to cover them. In fact, labour income of more than half – around 52% – of informal wage earners (dependent workers) remains below the minimum wage of PEN 750.[4] The productivity of formal dependent workers appears sufficient to bear these costs. Only 7% of formal wage workers earn monthly salaries close to or below the minimum wage (Figure 4.7). Although it appears that the minimum wage is too low to be binding for most formal sector jobs, it may affect the formalisation decision of a significant share of workers. The minimum wage plays a benchmark role, which can be seen by the density of informal workers earning close to the minimum wage.

Figure 4.7. **Labour income of formal and informal workers and its distribution relative to the minimum wage in Peru (in PEN), 2014**

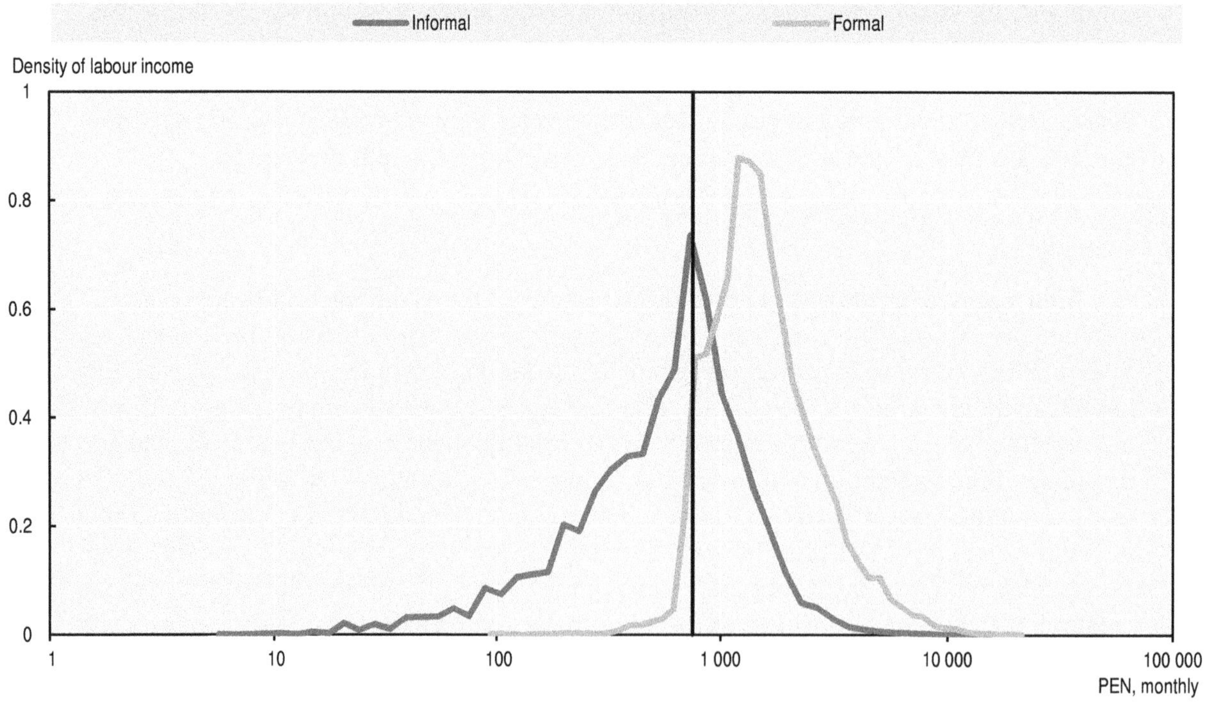

Notes: Kernel estimates of monthly-equivalent labour market incomes for dependent workers depending on their classification as formal or informal on the basis of the INEI methodology. The black bar represents the minimum wage (PEN 750, although it was set at PEN 850 in May 2016).

Source: OECD calculations based on ENAHO (INEI, 2014b), *Encuesta Nacional de Hogares (ENAHO) (National Household Survey)* (database).

StatLink http://dx.doi.org/10.1787/888933411469

Differences in informality rates across regions are closely linked to differences in productivity levels as well as to the proportion of social security over total labour costs. There are significant differences in total labour costs and the wedges on workers' wages (implied formalisation costs – that is, the portion of the total labour costs that goes towards paying taxes and social security contributions) between departments, urban and rural settings, and geographic areas (Figure 4.8). In general, urban settings have higher labour costs. Formalisation costs are proportional among all departments, although there is greater variance with respect to total labour costs. Informality tends to be lower in geographic locations where the total labour cost is further away from the minimum labour cost. In this regard, the presence of large, competitive, productive industries and the rich commodity resources within a department is a better indicator of higher levels of income and, thus, of higher labour costs and lower levels of informality. In these regions, social security costs represent a smaller fraction of total labour costs (Céspedes, Lovado and Ramirez, 2016; OECD, 2015a).

Figure 4.8. **Total labour costs by geographic location in Peru, 2014**

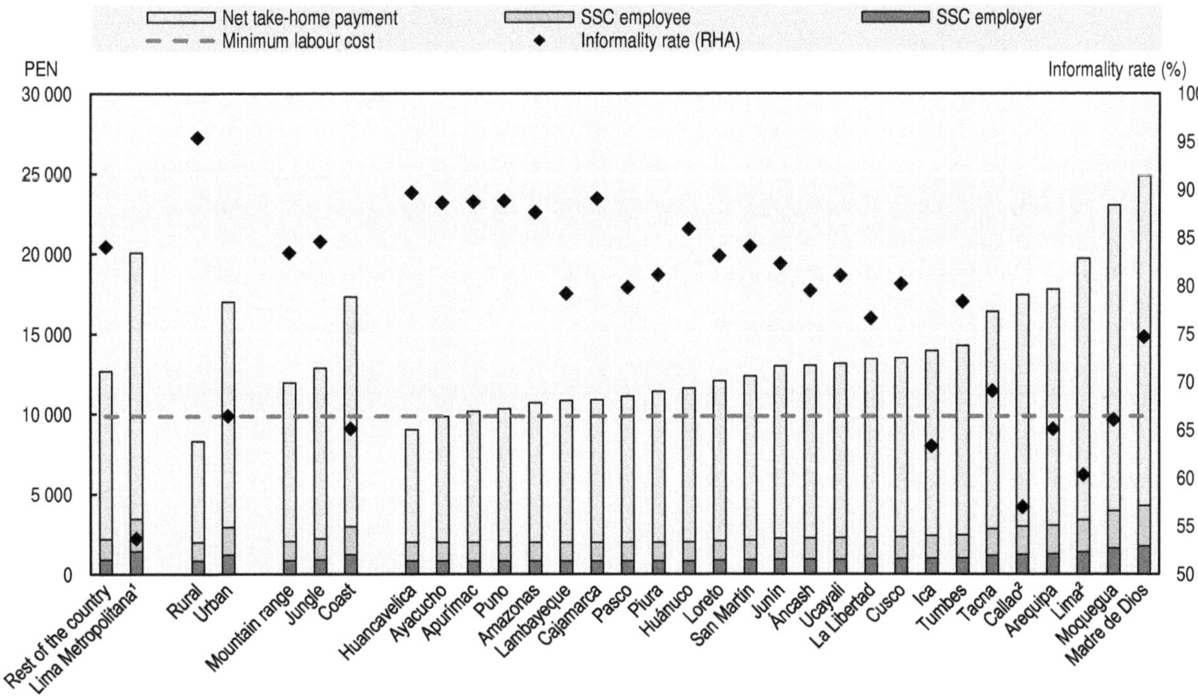

Notes: [1]Encompasses the province of Lima and the constitutional province of Callao. [2]Up to the year 2006. The results of the ENAHO were presented for the department of Lima, which included the constitutional province of Callao. Independent measures for Lima and the Callao were collected after 2007.

Source: OECD calculations based on OECD/IDB/CIAT (2016), *Taxing Wages in Latin America and the Caribbean* and INEI (2014b) *Encuesta Nacional de Hogares (ENAHO) (National Household Survey)* (database).

StatLink http://dx.doi.org/10.1787/888933411473

Upgrading skills levels is vital to break the cycle of low productivity and informality

High informality and low skills reinforce each other in Peru. Low skills levels are both cause and consequence of informality (Figure 4.9). Higher skills levels lead to higher productivity levels, which lead to better access to formal jobs and even to their creation. The correlation between the use of skills at the workplace and productivity is very significant (OECD, 2016a). By the same token, informality limits the expansion of the pool of skills as, in a context of informality, certain skills tend to deteriorate or remain limited to a low value-added range, and access to training and intermediation services in the informal sector is scarce.

Figure 4.9. **The circular relationship between skills, productivity and informality**

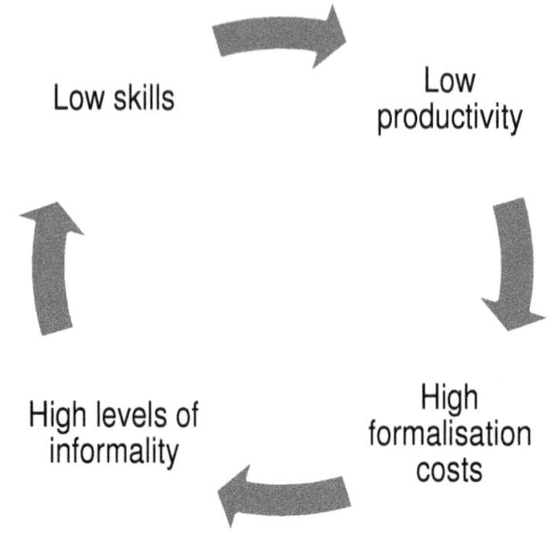

Source: Authors' elaboration.

StatLink http://dx.doi.org/10.1787/888933411480

In Peru, low skills and informality are strongly connected, decreasing as workers attain higher levels of education (Figure 4.10). Most workers with less than primary education are informal, and approximately 23% of workers with secondary education have a formal job. Conversely, formality is almost 70% among workers who completed higher education.

Figure 4.10. **Informal and formal employment by level of education in Peru, 2014**

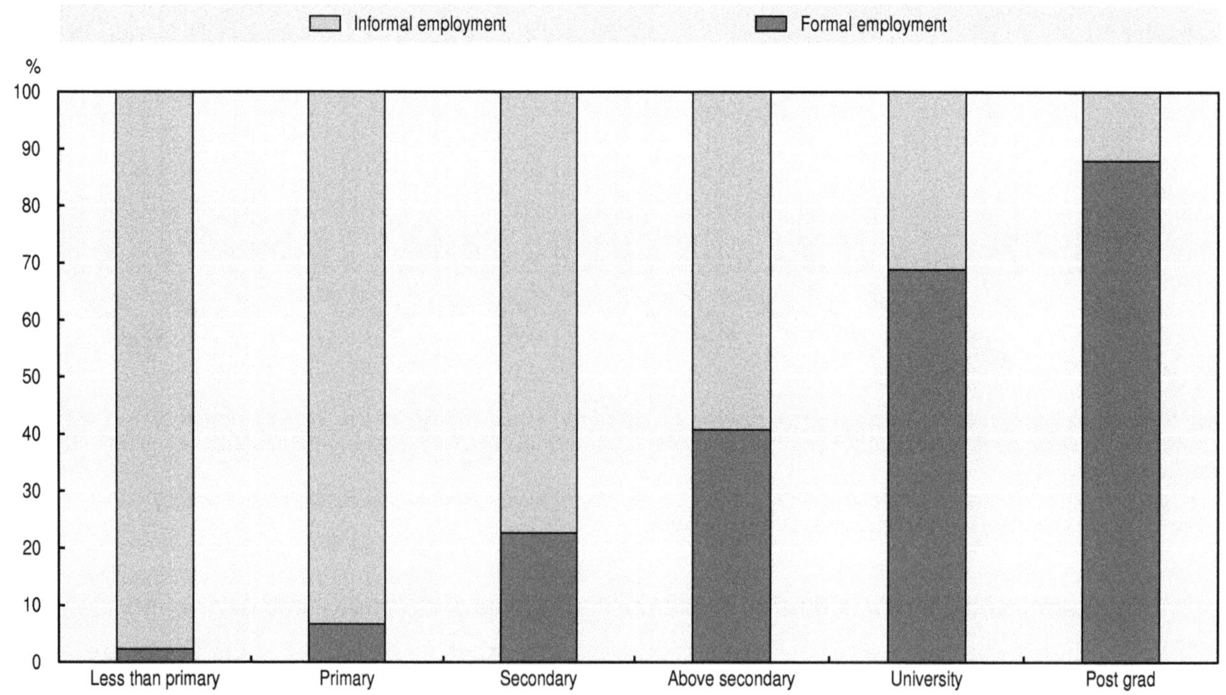

Source: OECD calculations based on INEI (2014a), *Producción y Empleo Informal en el Perú, Cuenta Satélite de la Economía Informal 2007-2012 (Production and Informal Employment in Peru, A Satellite Account of the Informal Economy 2007-2014.*

StatLink http://dx.doi.org/10.1787/888933411496

The available pool of skills in Peru is poor and disconnected from the demands of the productive sector. Results from the Programme for International Student Assessment (PISA) indicate the poor quality of education in Peru, which represents a good proxy for skills levels. An average 15-year-old student in Peru is behind the average Latin American student by the equivalent of eight months of secondary schooling and is approximately three years behind the average OECD member country student (OECD/CAF/ECLAC, 2014).

Vocational education and training (VET) is also poor in Peru; 70% of students who finish secondary education and continue with higher education choose to enter university rather than the VET system (OECD, 2015a). The disconnection between the demand and supply of skills is also large, leading to poor labour market outcomes. From the demand side, between 28% (World Bank, 2010) and 68% (ManpowerGroup, 2015) of firms face difficulties in finding a workforce with requisite skills. Despite a demand for science, technology, engineering and mathematics (STEM) skills, together with more experience and soft skills, students in tertiary education display a bias towards law, administration and business instead (OECD, 2015a). The disconnect is clear: of the nearly 2 million Peruvians with technician-level degrees, only 15% work as technicians, while only half of all technicians have completed formal training (OECD, 2016a).

Informality also limits the development of skills. First, labour market segmentation in Peru is high, and the transition from informal to formal jobs is rare. In fact, over 2007-2012 less than 4% of workers made the shift to formal employment (Vostroknutova et al., 2015). This can be harmful for skills development, as persistence at unskilled labour or low value-added tasks in the informal sector may lead to a deterioration or stultification in skills not called upon. Second, workers in the informal sector are more difficult to identify and reach with training and active labour market policies, while training at informal workplaces is almost non-existent (OECD, 2016b forthcoming).

Upgrading skills and improving their link with the productive system can raise labour productivity levels and, together with recognition of skills acquired in informal employment, favour access to formal jobs. Improving overall skills levels is critical. A curricula generally more focused on developing STEM, technical and soft skills, and a stronger connection between the education system and skills demands in the economy, are critical to raising skills levels and productivity in Peru (OECD, 2016a). Recognition and certification of skills acquired in the informal sector can be another critical area for policy action, while moving towards a national qualifications framework could be a relevant policy goal in the medium term.

The primary structure of Peru's economy is not conducive to formal job creation

Informality is also directly linked to Peru's economic structure, which relates to the country's low productivity levels. An economic structure concentrated in primary and/or low-productivity sectors that employ large shares of the population in low-quality informal jobs impedes the expansion of formal employment (La Porta and Shleifer, 2014). This is the economic structure seen in Peru, coinciding with a dualist view of informality, which suggests the informal and formal sectors are largely separated, with a large informal sector consisting of many uneducated entrepreneurs running small, unproductive firms that add little value to productivity and a smaller formal sector of educated entrepreneurs who run bigger, more productive firms.

In Peru, employment is concentrated in low-productivity, informal sectors, while more productive and formalised sectors create little employment. Labour productivity varies widely across the economic sectors. Mining, finance, energy and water, and telecommunications have high labour productivity, while productivity in retail and restaurants and agriculture is particularly low. In particular, in 2013, mining was the most productive sector, with labour productivity more than 10 times the average for Peru and more than 40 times the level for agriculture. However, the few economic sectors with high labour productivity, like mining, employ a small fraction of the labour force. In contrast, retail and restaurants and agriculture employ most workers in the country and remain the lowest productivity sectors in Peru (Figure 4.11). This demonstrates both the inverse relationship between productivity and informality in Peru, and that Peru's economy is not currently conducive to increased formal job creation.

Figure 4.11. **Labour productivity in Peru's economic sectors, 2013**

Relative value-added as a percentage of workers and employment by economic sector (y axis: 100 = total labour productivity; x axis: % of employment)

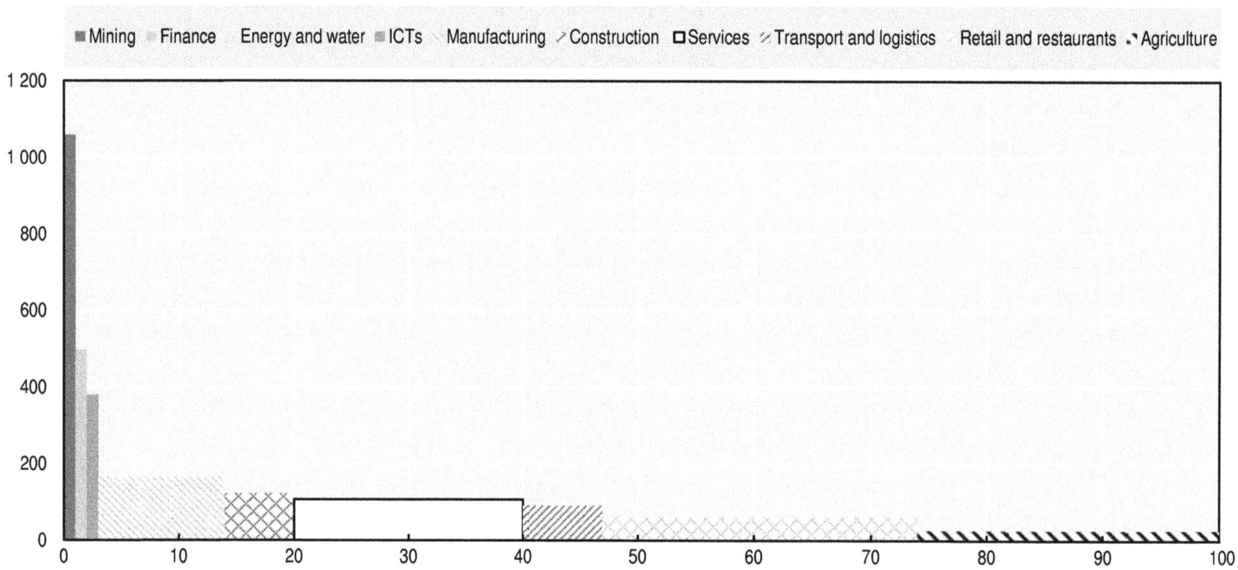

Note: Number of workers based on INEI's ENAHO. "Energy and water" is the item with the lowest employment contribution, representing less than 0.5% of total employment.

Source: OECD calculations based on INEI (2014b) *Encuesta Nacional de Hogares (ENAHO) (National Household Survey)* (database).

StatLink *http://dx.doi.org/10.1787/888933411505*

Job creation in the recent period of economic expansion had a limited impact on formality. Between 2003 and 2013, the main structural change in employment was a movement away from the agricultural sector towards services. Most formal job creation in this period took place in the government services sector, followed by the wholesale and retail sectors, all of them sectors with productivity levels below the country average. The main source of loss of informal jobs was the agricultural sector. Overall, informal jobs accounted for approximately 60% of total job creation in the period 2002-13, with an increase in the share of formal jobs in the total economy. However, most informal job creation occurred between 2002 and 2006. After 2006, formal job creation outpaced informal job creation (Bulmer et al., 2015).

Informality also varies across sectors and geographical location, exhibiting a high correlation with agricultural activities. Departments where agricultural sectors employ the vast majority of workers exhibit higher levels of average informality and lower levels of productivity and wage earnings, reinforcing the idea that the economic structure and productivity levels are key determinants of informality rates (Figure 4.12).

Figure 4.12. **Employment composition by sector and geographical location in Peru, 2014**

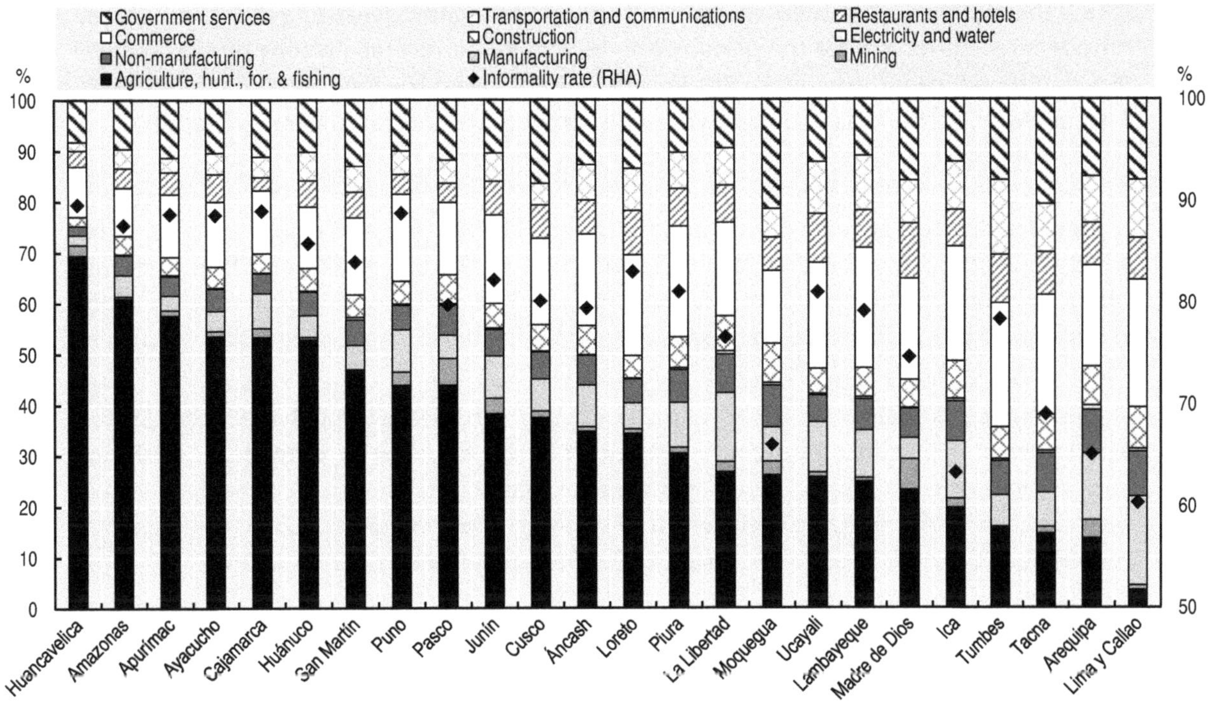

Source: OECD calculations based on INEI (2014b) *Encuesta Nacional de Hogares (ENAHO) (National Household Survey)* (database).

StatLink http://dx.doi.org/10.1787/888933411519

A more diversified economy can support formal job creation

The noted link between informality and productivity levels, along with Peru's economic structure, indicate productive diversification as a key policy area to promote more formal jobs in the medium to long term. Efforts to favour more formal job creation should be integrated into longer term planning, with a strong link to the broader national development strategy. Creating formal jobs requires the promotion of an economy which, from the supply side, has workers with higher levels of productivity and skills and, from the demand side, can create good-quality formal jobs to absorb those workers. This will have to be linked with the development strategy and the productive diversification strategy in a broader sense (Chapter 2).

Promoting formal job creation, boosting productivity and providing equal opportunities for all Peruvians necessitates expanded economic diversification. Several measures aimed at bolstering economic diversification should also positively affect the labour market. For instance, market regulations designed to promote entrepreneurship may result in further formal jobs and consolidate new firms and activities in Peru. In addition, improvements in the allocation of commodity-based transfers according to the level of development of Peruvian departments and investment in broad based policies to increase competitiveness should support formal jobs. In this direction, a large number of national strategic plans have been developed, some referencing the necessity to reduce informality and create formal jobs. These include the Plan Estratégico de Desarrollo Nacional Actualizado: Perú hacia el 2021; the National Plan for Productive Diversification; the National Strategy on Development and Social Inclusion: "Incluir para Crecer"; and the Agenda de Competitividad 2014-2018. In particular, a key objective of the Plan Estratégico is to increase economic diversification, boost qualified workers and lower informality. The main objective of the Agenda de Competitividad 2014-2018 is to boost competitiveness to increase formal jobs and the well-being of the population. Among its main targets for the period 2014-18, two are to increase labour productivity by 15% and to reduce informality by 5%. Recently, the Consejo Nacional de Competitividad y Formalización (CNCF) has included within its competencies a plan for formalisation.

Informality leads to lower-quality jobs and limits the reach of social protection

Informality has adverse consequences to social protection and labour conditions for informal workers and the population. As informal workers are excluded from national labour laws and social security regulations, they are less likely to have access to pensions and health insurance systems. They also face more difficult working conditions, in particular lower wages and greater difficulty in finding sufficient work.

Recent reforms have resulted in an increase in health coverage through the multiplication of avenues and subsidised programmes. The poor are targeted by programmes offering health coverage free of charge. Better-off households have greater chances of being in formal work and, therefore, enjoying social security coverage. However, a significant proportion of Peruvians in the middle of the income distribution are left outside the system.

Informality is linked to poor working conditions and underemployment

Informal jobs are generally of poorer quality than formal jobs. Not only is this the case for average earnings (see e.g. Jütting and de Laiglesia, 2009), but it is found to be the case across a range of labour quality indicators in the OECD job quality framework. This framework measures job quality in three building blocks: earnings quality, which includes the level and distribution of earnings; labour market security, which considers the likelihood of income loss; and the quality of the working environment, which, for emerging economies, is implemented on the basis of working time data (OECD, 2015b).

Informal workers earn less than formal workers

Informal workers earn significantly less than formal workers, in terms of wages, job stability and contracts. Among employed persons with a contract working more than 30 hours per week, formal workers earn hourly wages 24.3% higher than informal workers and monthly wages 22.3% higher (Jaramillo, 2013). This disparity is amplified by the fact that, of the workers considered, formal workers work fewer hours – about one day less per month (Jaramillo, 2013).

Not only are earnings lower for informal workers, they are more unequally distributed. The OECD framework's measure of earnings quality penalises inequality, giving a much lower quality of earnings assessment for informal workers in Peru (Figure 4.13).

Informal workers face higher risks in the labour market

Unemployment risks are low in Peru but are higher for informal workers. The unemployment rate is low at 3.7% in 2014, relative to comparable countries. Moreover, duration of unemployment is also low (less than one month on average). As a result, the risk of income loss through loss of employment is very low in Peru, compared to other emerging economies, despite the lack of an unemployment insurance scheme. Despite the generally low level of labour market risk (understood as the risk of income loss due to loss of employment), informal workers are almost twice as likely as formal workers to transition to unemployment and three times as likely to abandon the labour force (OECD, 2015a).

Figure 4.13. **Earning equality by formality in Peru**

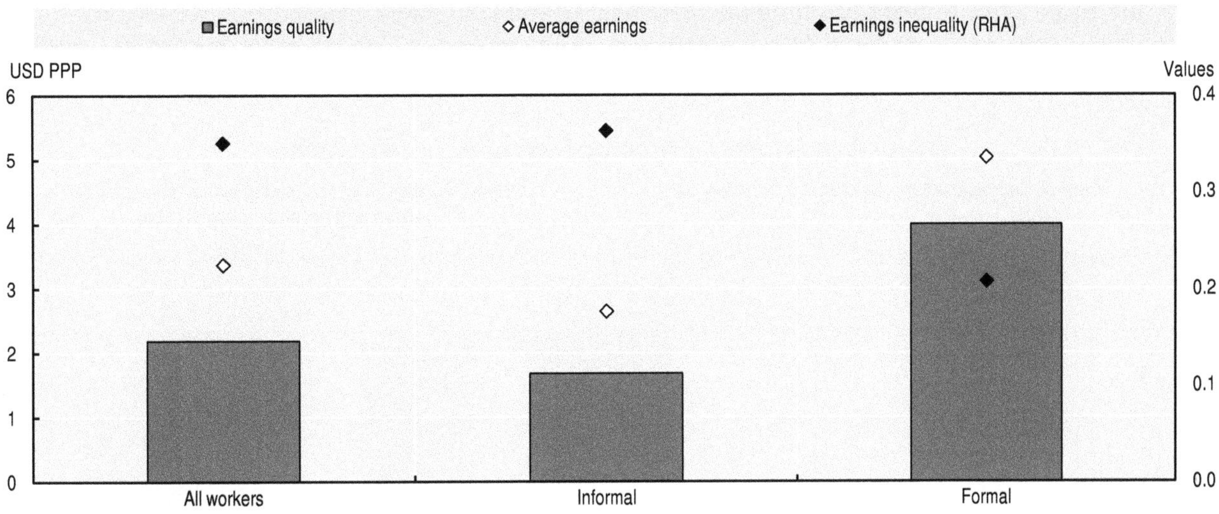

Note: Earnings inequality is measured by the Atkinson index of hourly net labour earnings, with a parameter alpha = 0, which corresponds to the relative difference between the arithmetic and harmonic mean. Earnings quality is the general Atkinson mean of the same parameter. The methods follow those implemented in OECD (2015b).

Source: OECD calculations based on INEI (2014b), *Encuesta Nacional de Hogares (ENAHO) (National Household Survey)* (database).

StatLink http://dx.doi.org/10.1787/888933411528

On the other hand, informal workers are at severe risk of receiving extreme low pay. As many as 17% of informal workers earn an hourly net income below the USD 1 purchasing power parity (PPP) threshold used by the OECD (2015b) to determine extreme low pay. The corresponding figure for formal workers is much lower at 2.5%. Moreover, income support measures for able-bodied working-age people in Peru are widely insufficient to cover the risk of income loss through low earnings.

Working time patterns are also challenging for informal workers

Full-time work at a primary occupation is less likely for informal workers. While almost 40% of formal workers work between 30 and 48 hours per week at their primary occupation, only 26% of informal workers do (Figure 4.14, Panel A). Over 40% of informal workers work part-time – or between 0 and 30 hours per week – at their principal occupation, compared to just 10% of formal workers. Informal workers are also more restricted in terms of work hours. Almost 50% of informal workers work fewer than 30 hours per week at their principal occupation, compared to just over 20% for formal workers. Formal workers are also more likely to work overtime at their principal occupation; 50% of formal workers work over 48 hours per week, while only 32% of informal workers work long hours at their primary occupation. Approximately 16% of informal workers state wanting to work more hours than their usual weekly load, compared to 14% of formal workers (INEI, 2014b).

As such, informal workers are much more heavily affected by a need to work two jobs to earn sufficient income; 17% of informal workers have a secondary occupation, compared to 14% of formal workers (INEI, 2014b). To compound matters, the majority of secondary occupations are informal (93%). Even for workers whose primary occupation is formal, 81% of secondary occupations are informal (INEI, 2014a)

The pattern of working hours differs across the income distribution and between formal and informal workers. Informal workers are more likely to work short hours (Figure 4.15), but among those at higher income levels, fewer work short hours and more work long hours (over 48 hours per week). By comparison, formal workers in higher income quintiles are more likely to work full time (30 to 48 hours), and a significant proportion works over 48 hours in a normal week. These patterns suggest that the earning potential of informal workers heavily influences the quality of their jobs.

Figure 4.14. **Working time by formality in Peru, 2014**

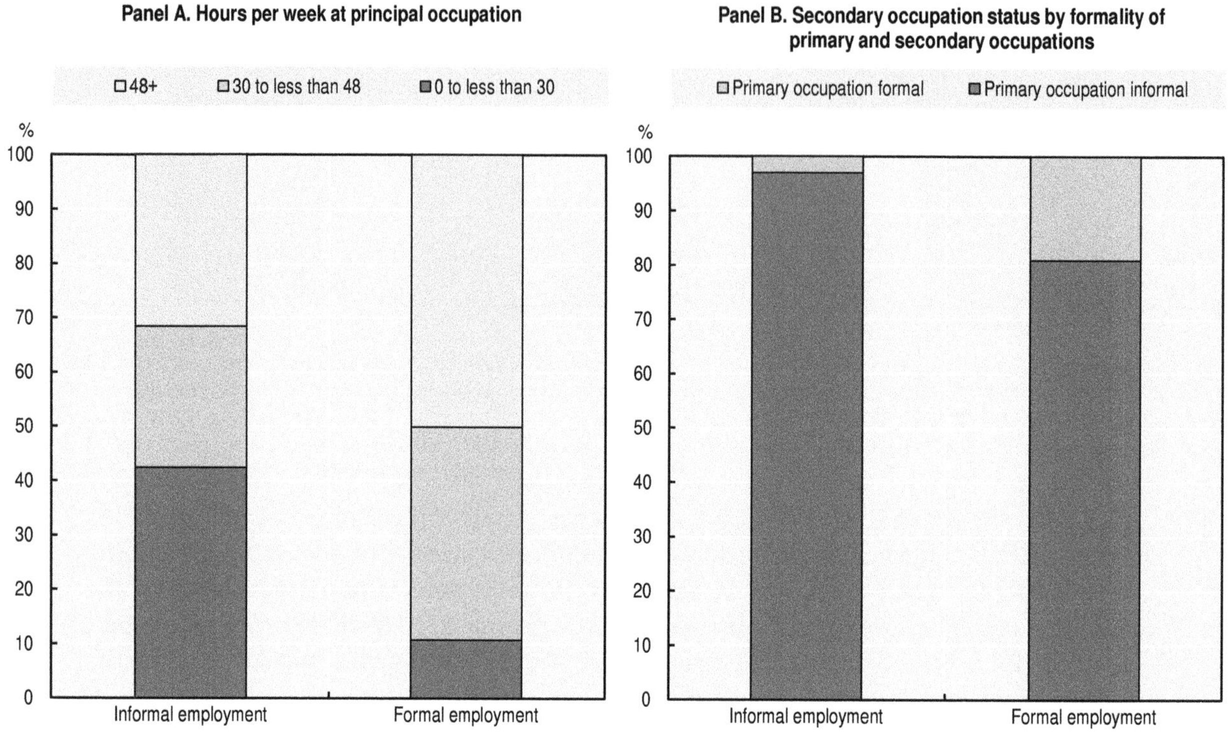

Source: INEI (2014b), *Encuesta Nacional de Horages (ENAHO) (National Household Survey)* (database), Instituto Nacional de Estadística e Informática, Lima, *http://webinei.inei.gob.pe/anda_inei/index.php/catalog/247* (accessed on 9 March 2016).

StatLink http://dx.doi.org/10.1787/888933411530

Figure 4.15. **Hours worked at primary occupation by formality and income quintile Peru, 2014**

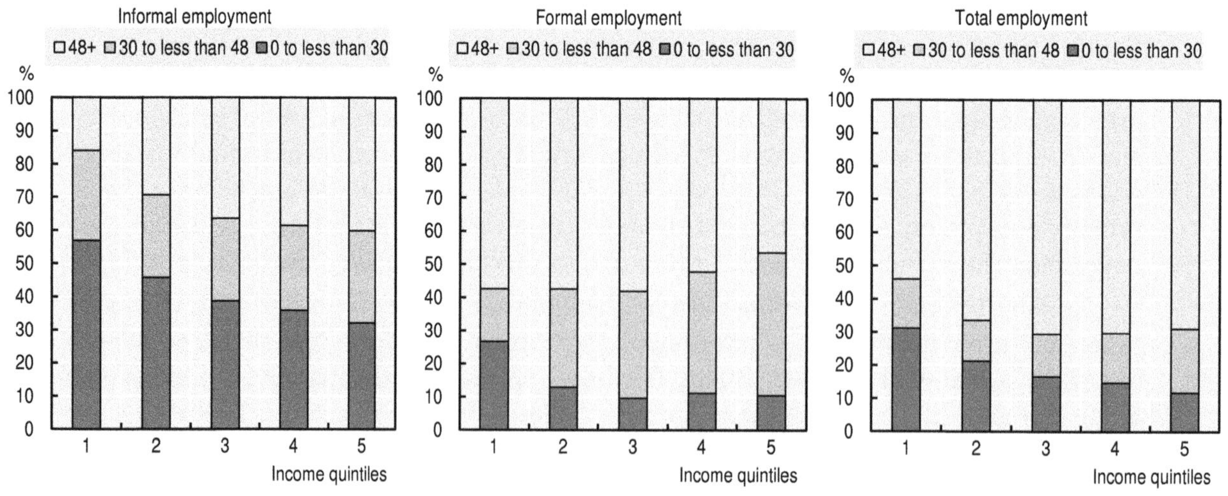

Note: Income quintiles are defined over household per capita income for all individuals.

Source: INEI (2014a), *Encuesta Nacional de Horages (ENAHO) (National Household Survey)* (database), Instituto Nacional de Estadística e Informática, Lima, *http://webinei.inei.gob.pe/anda_inei/index.php/catalog/247* (accessed on 9 March 2016).

StatLink http://dx.doi.org/10.1787/888933411544

At the other end of the spectrum, a relatively large number of workers in Peru work very long hours (Figure 4.16, Panel A). About 15% of workers worked over 60 hours over the reference week.[5] Long working hours are used as a proxy for poor working conditions. Domestic workers are one of the groups that systematically work long hours. The overwhelming majority of domestic workers are women (96%) and most are informal (90%). In this case, long working hours clearly signal poor working conditions. The number of hours worked by independent workers is not systematically higher than for employees in Peru, in contrast to comparable countries. In fact, formal self-employed workers are much more likely to work very long hours (36%) (Figure 4.16, Panel B). For this group, the use of long working hours as a proxy for poor job quality is questionable, as they potentially have greater agency in determining their working conditions.

Figure 4.16. **Incidence of very long working hours in Peru, 2014**

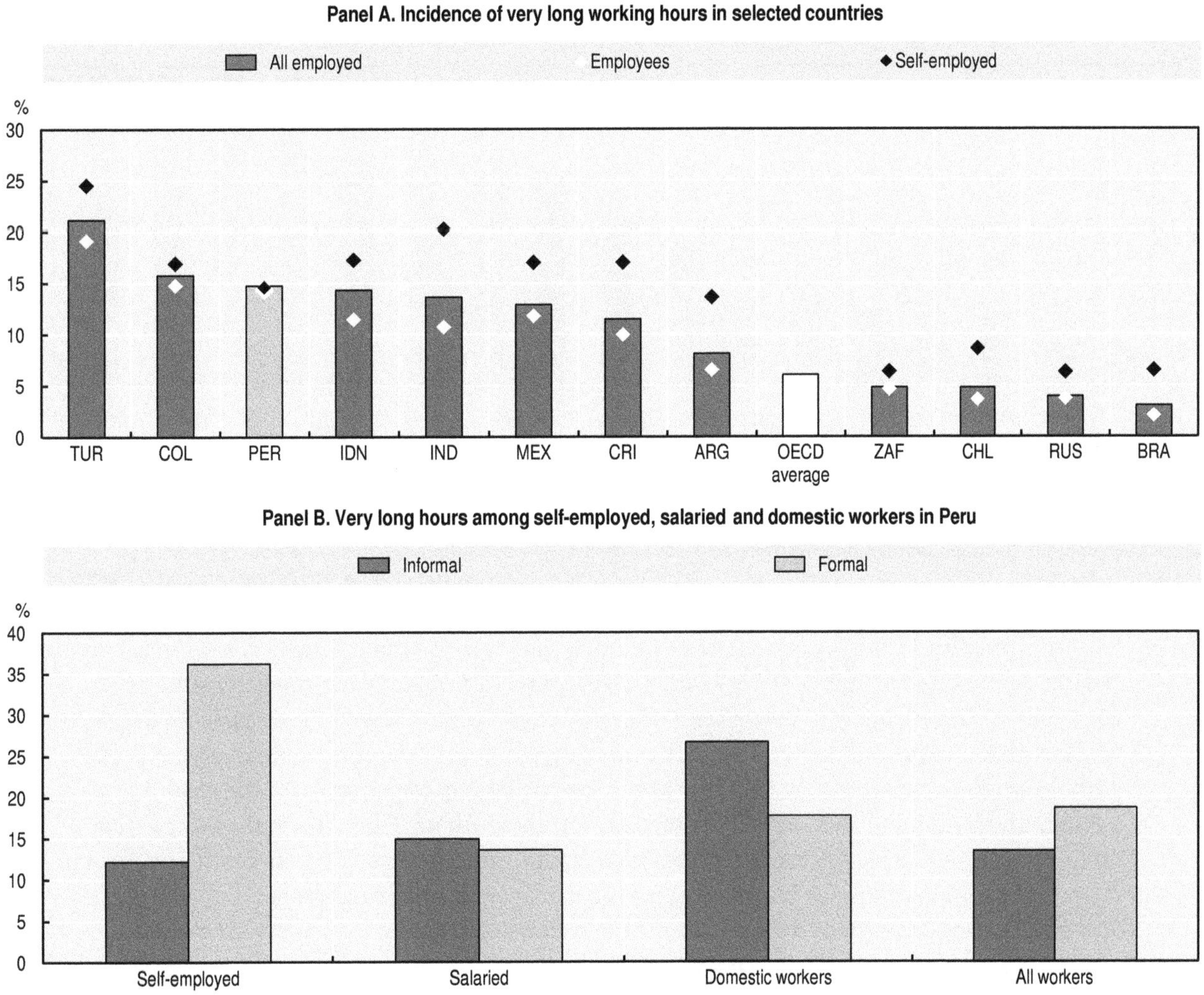

Note: A worker is considered to work very long hours if they work over 60 hours per week.

Source: OECD calculations based on INEI (2014b), *Encuesta Nacional de Horages (ENAHO) (National Household Survey)* (database) for Peru and OECD (2015b), *OECD Employment Outlook 2015*, for other countries.

StatLink http://dx.doi.org/10.1787/888933411550

Informality limits the reach of social protection

Health coverage has progressed, but coverage of informal workers remains a challenge

Health coverage remains low across Peru. As many as 31% of Peruvians do not have health insurance coverage (Figure 4.17). Health insurance in Peru is provided through contributory social security (*Seguro Social de Salud* [EsSalud]) as well as the subsidised *Seguro Integral de Salud* (SIS). Almost 40% of the population is covered by SIS, while 25% is covered by EsSalud. Other schemes insure 5% of the population. By age group, young adults have the lowest coverage, with 46% of those aged 18 to 25 having no coverage at all. The various health insurance systems that automatically cover dependents do not cover the beneficiary's children if they are over 18, unless they are disabled or otherwise unable to work.

Figure 4.17. **Health insurance coverage in selected countries**

2014 or latest available

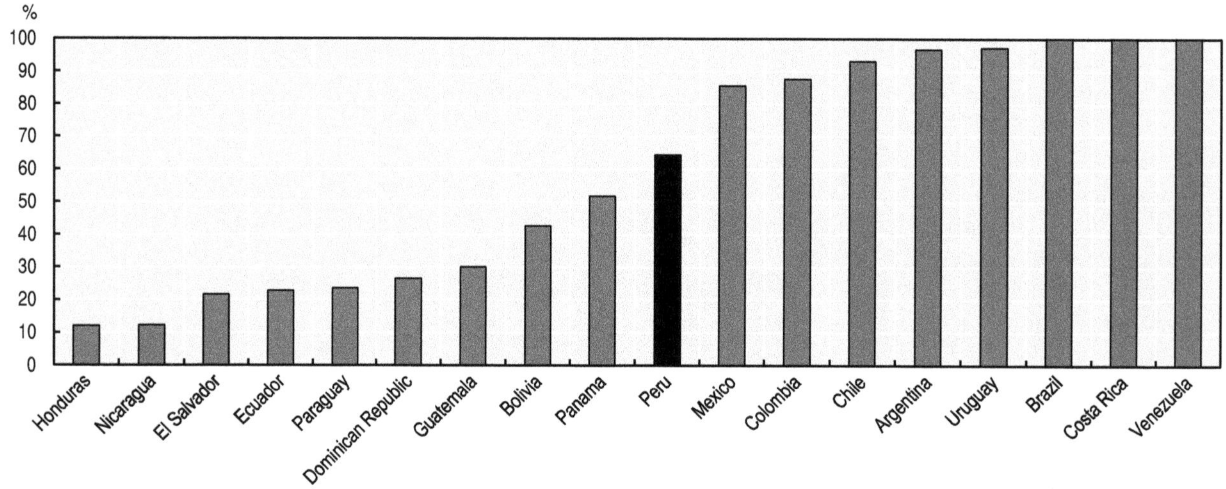

Source: ILO (2014a), *World Social Protection Report: Building Economic Recovery, Inclusive Development and Social Justice, 2014/15*, International Labour Organization, Geneva, *www.ilo.org/wcmsp5/groups/public/---dgreports/---dcomm/documents/publication/wcms_245201.pdf.*

StatLink http://dx.doi.org/10.1787/888933411569

Informality and the prevalence of self-employment are the main causes of relatively low health insurance coverage. Of the 9.7 million Peruvians estimated to lack health insurance in 2014, only 2.6% were living in households with no active workers. Even among the poor (e.g. in the first income quintile), only 9% of citizens without health insurance are in households with no workers, a percentage that is lower the higher the income level. On the other hand, 6.3 million were living in households with no formal workers. Figure 4.18 shows coverage rates and Figure 4.19 shows the contribution of formal and informal workers to the coverage rates. The gap in coverage for formal workers is exclusively made up of independent workers;[6] 50% of formal independent workers do not contribute to any social security scheme.

Health protection coverage displays a U-shaped pattern, with both the poor and the better-off enjoying better coverage than the middle quintiles. This pattern is largely driven by informal workers. While 22% of workers in the first quintile are informal workers without coverage, 38% of workers in the third quintile are informal workers without coverage. At higher income levels, there are fewer informal workers. Moreover, approximately 10% of workers in the upper two quintiles are indirect EsSalud beneficiaries and work informally. Both of these conditions reinforce the U-shaped coverage pattern.

Figure 4.18. **Health insurance coverage rates by income per capita quintiles in Peru, 2014**

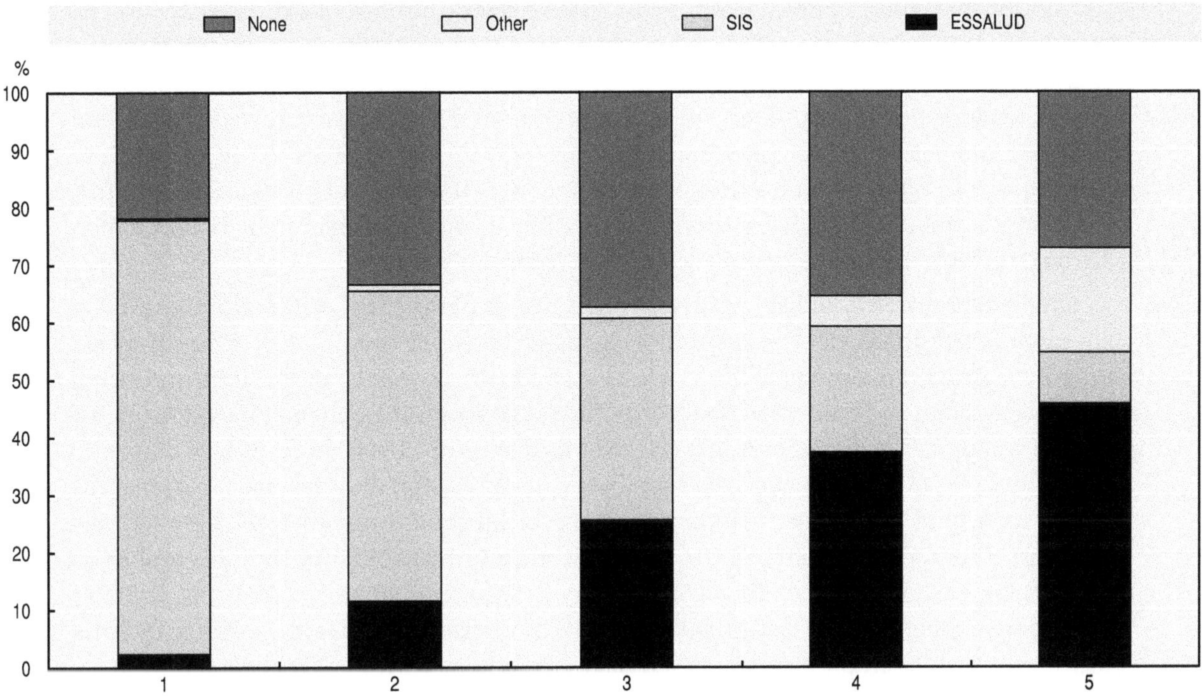

Note: The "other" category includes: private insurance, private healthcare provider, armed forces and police, university insurance, and private school insurance.

Source: INEI (2014b), *Encuesta Nacional de Horages (ENAHO) (National Household Survey)* (database), Instituto Nacional de Estadística e Informática, Lima, *http://webinei.inei.gob.pe/anda_inei/index.php/catalog/247* (accessed on 9 March 2016).

StatLink http://dx.doi.org/10.1787/888933411576

Figure 4.19. **Health insurance coverage rates by formality and income per capita quintiles in Peru, 2014**

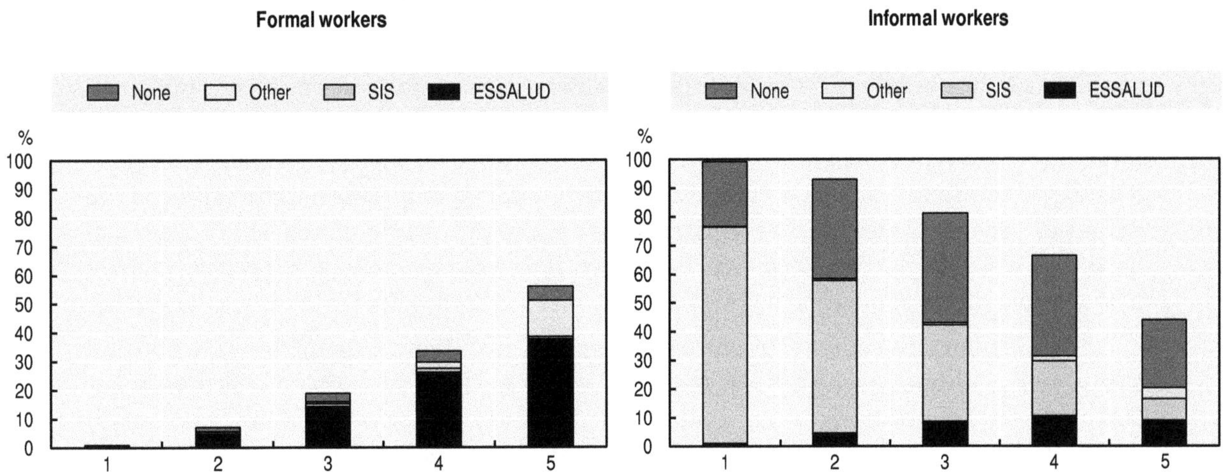

Note: The "other" category includes private insurance, entidad prestadora, armed forces and police, university insurance, private school insurance.

Source: INEI (2014b), *Encuesta Nacional de Horages (ENAHO) (National Household Survey)* (database), Instituto Nacional de Estadística e Informática, Lima, *http://webinei.inei.gob.pe/anda_inei/index.php/catalog/247* (accessed on 9 March 2016).

StatLink http://dx.doi.org/10.1787/888933411581

The type of health coverage differs greatly by income quintile and between income quintiles for formal and informal workers. EsSalud covers almost 70% of formal workers. The subsidised SIS, created in 2002 to cover children and older citizens without coverage and then extended to the poor and extreme poor, covers 70% of workers in the first income quintile. Other types of insurance, including private and university insurance, are more prevalent among those with higher incomes, especially formal workers, covering less than 1% of those in the first income quintile but up to 15% of those in the fifth income quintile. Over 20% of formal workers have another form of insurance, approximately half of which is through private insurance, compared to 7% of informal workers.

Smaller enterprises, which hire a larger percentage of informal workers, are less likely than larger enterprises to offer insurance. Smaller firms are more likely to be informal, as the benefits to remaining small – such as avoiding discovery by authorities and being forced to pay fines and compensation – oftentimes outweigh the benefits of expansion. Of informal workers, 92% work in firms with fewer than 20 employees, whereas 54% of formal workers work in firms with over 100 employees (INEI, 2014b). As informal firms are less likely to offer health coverage, informal workers in informal firms are less likely to have coverage; 91% of those without health coverage work in firms with fewer than 20 employees (INEI, 2014b). Additionally, health providers vary between small and large firms. EsSalud covers more workers as firm size grows, from 13% of workers with health coverage in firms with fewer than 20 employees to almost 50% of workers with health coverage in firms with 21 to 50 employees, and over 70% of workers with health coverage in firms with over 500 employees (INEI, 2014b). SIS, however, covers 45% of workers with health coverage in firms with fewer than 20 employees (INEI, 2014b).

Health coverage has progressed significantly due to universal insurance reforms undertaken in the past 15 years. Coverage progressed from 37% in 2004 to 65% in 2013 (Casalí, Cetrángolo and Goldschmit, 2015). The progressive implementation of the SIS, first aimed exclusively at poor citizens and gradually extended to other categories, played an important role in increasing coverage. More Peruvians are insured through SIS than through contributive social security since 2007. Since 2011, SIS is also accessible to a number of other categories of vulnerable workers for a small fee, subject to a means test. There are subsidised health insurance schemes for independent workers, microenterprises and entrepreneurs. The cost for independent workers is PEN 15 per month plus PEN 14 per month for every immediate family member who is covered. The cost to cover microenterprise workers is PEN 30 per month for each employee, the cost being split equally between the state and the employer. Each employee must be registered by the employer, and children and spouses can benefit as well. The success of SIS has been such that coverage rates in rural areas (where a large share of the population belongs to the target group) are higher than in urban areas.

The creation of a scheme for entrepreneurs has given new impetus to SIS. Uptake of subsidised contributive schemes has remained very low. Of all those covered by SIS – about 50% of the total population of Peru – only 2% fall under the partially-subsidised or voluntary group. Of those covered by SIS, 72% are from the original target group of poor and extreme poor, while the remainder of those covered by SIS were able to enter the programme as non-poor or through other channels. However, since 2013, operators of unincorporated enterprises who are registered tax payers in RUS are automatically granted coverage under SIS. This led to a jump in affiliation to semi-contributive regimes in 2013, from 25 000 to 224 000. However, these numbers remain small relative to the significant coverage gap.

The fragmentation of the health sector in Peru challenges coverage

The health insurance system in Peru is highly fragmented, which potentially limits its reach to certain categories of informal workers. Table 4.4 presents the main components of the health insurance system. The contributive system is the social security regime. Private providers can be contracted (at the establishment level) to provide basic care, which is financed by a partial transfer of contributions. The system also includes special regimes for agricultural workers and a voluntary regime for independents. This scheme, created under the framework of the Universal Coverage Law, was under revision at the time of writing. SIS includes as its main component a free, means-tested regime, which has been complemented by a number of specific regimes targeted at own-account workers and their families: (SIS Emprendedor), independents (SIS Independiente) and operators and workers in microenterprises (SIS Microempresas).

Table 4.4. **Fragmentation in the health insurance system in Peru as of December, 2015**

Regime	Beneficiaries	Contribution (monthly)	Coverage (thousands)
Contributive regime (EsSalud)			**10 755**
Regular regime	Formal dependent workers, pensioners, civil servants	9% of income (minimum of 9% of minimum wage	10 143
Agricultural regime	Agricultural workers:		579, of which
	Dependent	4% of income	535
	Independent	4% of minimum wage (PEN 34)	29
Voluntary regime	Independent workers, other voluntary (students, etc.)	PEN 64 (individual) and up to PEN 228 (3 or more dependents)	32
Subsidised regime (SIS)			**16 773**
Free regime	Poor and extreme poor	Free	16 534
SIS Emprendedor	Entrepreneur with no dependent workers enrolled in the simplified tax regime (RUS)	Free (if the entrepreneur has paid tax dues)	219
SIS Independiente	Means tested, citizens with no other insurance	PEN 39 (individual) and up to PEN 115 (3 or more dependents)	16
SIS Microempresas	Enterprises registered in the microenterprise registry: entrepreneurs and their workers	PEN 15 for workers and their family (paid by the employer)	4

Note: Coverage as of December, 2015.

Sources: EsSalud (2016), *http://www.essalud.gob.pe/* Seguro Social de Salud del Perú (Peru's Social Health Insurance), Lima, *www.essalud.gob.pe/*; Seguro Integral de Salud (2016).

The complex array of special regimes has failed to increase coverage significantly for microenterprises and their workers, while the free, means-tested regime has led to large increases in coverage. The uptake in independent schemes has been low, both in SIS and the social security regime. These two have significant overlap, all the more considering that the means test is not predictable for many workers as the methodology, while transparent, is complex and not easily visible to the public. Moreover, the voluntary social security regime suspended new affiliations in October 2015 (resolution 30-GCSPE-EsSalud-2015) to examine its viability, as it was being, *de facto*, subsidised by contributions to the regular regime. For agricultural workers, the subsidised regime is accompanied by stringent eligibility criteria (e.g. the need to present property deeds), which may go some way to explain its low uptake rate.

The articulation of the various regimes should be re-examined in light of universal coverage objectives. For example, the current system for microenterprise workers has so far not had much success in extending coverage. Although this is partly due to its late implementation, consideration should be given to whether the payment and registration requirement are consistent with the drive to extend coverage. This is particularly true considering the worker cannot directly access this system but has to be enrolled by the employer or seek coverage under the alternative system for independents, thereby fulfilling the employer's obligation.

The progressive implementation of compulsory universal insurance needs to be accompanied by a well-articulated set of schemes that offers greater clarity on subsidy levels. The multiplicity of regimes also manifests itself in the span of coverage and even in the access to different providers. EsSalud and the SIS have different networks for health service provision. A network of service provision agreements is closing the gaps in actual service, but its effective implementation should be monitored. Current regimes offer different levels of subsidised access to health insurance, but as the example of the "regimes for independents" shows, these are not necessarily consistent.

The creation of a social regime for entrepreneurs in effect creates a single contribution for that category. Experiences in Brazil and Argentina have been positive in terms of the increased affiliation – and, to a lesser degree, contributions – attained through the *SIMPLES* and *monotributo* regimes. But in Peru this regime has appeared as if by accident through the provision of SIS, rather than by design, as a means to consolidate the fulfilment of social security and fiscal obligations. It has also not received the same degree of publicity.

The multiplicity of regimes could generate disincentives to firm growth and does create a complex overlap of eligibility conditions. Coverage for partially subsidised regimes is contingent on sales (for the microenterprise regime for new firms), number of employees (for microenterprises established before 2013) or turnover and asset value (for the entrepreneur regime), while eligibility for the subsidised independent regime depends on a relatively complex means test operated by the targeting authority, Sistema de Focalización de Hogares (SISFOH). For a microenterprise employing eight workers, going over the threshold that grants eligibility (just under PEN 50 000 in monthly sales) would imply a jump in monthly labour costs of PEN 520 in social security contributions alone.

Informality challenges pension provision and finance

Peru has one of the lowest rates of affiliation to the pension systems in Latin America. Only 40.5% of employed urban workers was affiliated to a pension system in 2013 (ILO, 2014b). While this is an improvement over the very low coverage rates of a decade ago (26.7% in 2005), the improvement has been much slower than for health coverage and has slowed down since 2010 (Casalí, Cetrángolo and Goldschmit, 2015). The low coverage of the pension system is largely driven by informality. Formal workers are much more likely to have access to pensions than informal workers. While only 16% of informal workers are affiliated to a pension system, 83% of formal workers are affiliated. Contributions are, in fact, compulsory for dependent formal workers. Since younger workers are more likely to be informal, coverage is lower for those aged 15 to 29, with 81% not covered. Coverage improves for those 30 and over, although 64% lack affiliation.

Low levels of affiliation and contribution lead to low coverage of contributory pensions. Only 34% of Peruvians aged 65 and above receive a contributory pension (AAFP, 2015). The contributory pension system in Peru is composed of two parallel systems: the defined-benefit public system (Sistema Nacional de Pensiones [SNP]) and the privately-managed defined contribution system (Sistema Privado de Pensiones [SPP]). The majority of affiliated workers are in the SPP, which was created in 1993. As a result, most pensioners who receive a contributory pension receive it from the SNP. Even for those affiliated to the pension system, contribution densities are low, with 49% of affiliated workers contributing less than half of the time spent working (Bosch, Melguizo and Pagés, 2013).

Minimum pensions exist in both systems but require long validation periods. A retiring worker has to have contributed for 20 years to receive a pension at retirement age. Given the low levels of formality and low contribution densities, this penalises workers who transit between formal and informal employment and is likely to lead to significant numbers of older people without pension benefits.

Several reforms aimed to increase coverage have not been implemented

Social pensions contribute to extending coverage. Pension 65 is a means-tested social pension for Peruvians over 65 identified as being in extreme poverty. Created in 2011, the programme covers 23% of the over-65s, making an important contribution to old-age income security. The transfer is relatively modest at PEN 125 per month, but it represents 53% of per capita rural household expenditures nevertheless (Casalí, Cetrángolo and Goldschmit, 2015).

Given the high share of self-employment in Peru, extending pension coverage to independent workers is a major challenge. The 2012 reform of the pension system (Law 29903) made pension affiliation and contributions compulsory for a subset of independent workers (in particular professional service providers). However, the policy was reversed only months after its implementation began (in September 2014). In 2014, only 14% of self-employed workers were affiliated to a pension system.

A matching contribution system is planned for Peru. The legislation to favour microenterprises established a subsidised pension regime (Sistema de Pensiones Sociales [SPS]) for microenterprise workers and operators. The SPS would receive contributions of up to 4% of the minimum wage, which the state would match with equal contributions into personal accounts. To date, this system has not been implemented. If it were to give entitlements to the same pensions as the general regime, this would imply a significant subsidy (contributions to private or public pensions regimes are 13% of wages) without a means test, as eligibility is based on not having previous affiliations to the pension system and the characteristics of the enterprise.

Avenues for extending pension coverage and preserving incentives

Incentivising pension savings while preserving incentives for formality should be a concern of pension reform and, more broadly, social protection reform that seeks to increase coverage. To this end, it is important that programmes are not systematically designed as residual – that is, requiring lack of coverage or lack of previous coverage for eligibility. It is also important to examine the effective marginal reduction in benefits from increases in income and from formalisation. Step increases in contributions can provide incentives against formalisation, in particular when there is high mobility between formal and informal work.

The coverage of non-contributory pensions could be extended. The Pension 65 social pension aims to cover the extreme poor over 65. Since the end of 2015, Pension 65 reached 500 000 beneficiaries, which is the limit set by the credits allocated. Given the coverage gap among older adults, the progressive universalisation of the social pension should be considered – that is, extending the programme to all adults above retirement age, beginning with those subsisting under the poverty line. Realising this in a financially sustainable manner would require taxing pension income and possibly progressively reducing the amount of the social pension for those receiving contributory pensions.

Avenues to incorporate independent workers into the pension system should be provided. Given the policy reversal on obligatory contributions, any policy mandating affiliation or contributions from independent workers should be matched with a greater communication effort and a design that allows for greater flexibility in payments and payment schedules so as to provide a suitable vehicle for retirement savings for independent workers. Ultimately, independent workers should be included in the system and their contributions made compulsory at a level that ensures the financial sustainability of the pension system.

The matching contribution system should be significantly revised prior to implementation. As described in law, the system would create a parallel system with significant subsidies. This alone is likely to generate adverse incentives by limiting worker mobility out of the large and largely unproductive microenterprise sector. More worryingly, the condition of no previous affiliation implies that, in order to benefit from the system, the worker would have to have been informal continuously prior to affiliation, thereby reinforcing incentives to be informal, especially for younger workers. Experience with matching contributions systems is mixed and suggests that the creation of parallel systems is generally not advisable (Bosch, Melguizo and Pagés, 2013).

Incentives for retirement savings can also be given via direct subsidies to contributions. Akin to matching contributions, subsidies to contributions can help incentivise participation in the pension system and help to decrease the cost of formality for low-earning workers. Providing public financing this way rather than by, *ex-post*, financing funding gaps in the pension system, contributes to providing incentives for individual workers. Subsidies could be tapered as a function of contributions or could be a fixed amount for all contributors, so that the relative weight of the subsidy is large for those with low earnings and lower (in relative terms) for higher income earners.

Conclusions and policy recommendations

Informality is a widespread and persistent issue in Peru. At 72.8%, informal employment is one of the main barriers to inclusive development in the country. Informality undermines social protection, labour conditions and the creation of better job opportunities. It affects the economy, firms and workers by reducing productivity, efficiency and competition. It also undercuts government revenues and, therefore, the quality of public services.

To promote more formal jobs and mitigate the negative effects of informality, public policy should recognise the aspects of informality that can be addressed in the short term and those more structural aspects that will require longer-term targets and plans. Four main policy areas for action are recommended to promote formal, better quality jobs and formal economic activities in Peru (Box 4.4).

These recommendations were informed by the three future-state scenarios outlined in Chapter 1. This chapter concludes with an assessment of their implications to incentives, trade-offs and prioritisation of policy reforms towards increased formalisation in the case of each global trend.

Box 4.4. Main policy recommendations to promote formal economic activities and employment and mitigate the impacts of informality in Peru

1. Mitigate the pervasive impact of informality on jobs and labour conditions.

1.1 Move towards universal basic health coverage.

- Implement a universal basic health package provided for free or for a fee based on existing means tests and complemented by contributory cover.
- Alternatively, move towards a unique health regime, gradually unifying SIS and EsSalud coverage plans, fee structures and service provision, progressively expanding its coverage to all citizens.
- Rationalise the collection of existing coverage plans and their eligibility conditions to ensure a complete set of articulated plans is available to formal workers. In particular, ensure that adequate coverage plans exist for self-employed workers.

1.2 Extend pension coverage.

- Consider extending the coverage of non-contributory pensions (Pension 65); move towards universal coverage by first expanding Pension 65's beneficiary set.

1.3 Improve working conditions.

- Increase the capacity of the labour inspectorate to address issues of safety at work for informal workers and firms through provision of information; accompany their formalisation.
- Provide for financial education and foster the creation of savings and insurance instruments for vulnerable groups (e.g. insurance against occupational hazards, crop insurance, etc.).

2. Promote the formalisation of jobs.

2.1 Strengthen systems of inspection and supervision.

- Increase efforts to supervise informal workers in the formal sector as potential 'low-hanging fruit' to increase levels of formality, especially given the implementation of new tools (planilla electronica) and programmes (Programa RETO). Ensure appropriate protocols exist to exploit the various enforcement tools managed by SUNAT, the labour inspectorate (SUNAFIL) and the Ministry of Production (in particular, the REMYPE - Registro Nacional de la Micro y Pequeña Empresa).

2.2 Increase the incentives of being formal by reducing the costs of formal hiring, increasing the benefits of being formal (monetary and/or services) and making it easier (more flexible), particularly for groups where these are clearly binding.

- Establish a clearly defined mechanism to determine minimum wages in order to reduce current discretion, linking its future evolution to productivity and price levels.
- Explore the possibility that this mechanism incorporates the option of having a different evolution of minimum wages across regions.
- Subsidise social contributions of low- and low-middle income workers.
- Match contributions, combined with immediate benefits (e.g. insurance).
- Provide alternatives to incorporate independent workers in the pension system, which should be compulsory again but accompanied by 1) more information and possibilities for gradual incorporation to the system and 2) allowances for specific contribution patterns (e.g. less regular contributions).

2.3 Improve communication and financial knowledge, highlighting the benefits associated to formal employment.

- Associate inspection and supervision with an information campaign and counselling, along the lines of efforts for Ferias de la formalidad and Bus de la Formalidad.
- Communicate the benefits of formality and the risks of informality.

Box 4.4. **Main policy recommendations to promote formal economic activities and employment and mitigate the impacts of informality in Peru** *(cont.)*

3. Promote the formalisation of firms by providing incentives for and reducing the costs of formalisation.

3.1 Reduce incentives not to formalise (and to remain small, which encourages firm informality).

- Simplify and reduce SME regimes; reduce current multiplicity and pervasive incentives to remain in the RUS. Align eligibility criteria for special tax, labour and social protection regimes. Reevaluate sector exclusions from special tax regimes.
- Reduce the gaps in employment protection across sectors and firm sizes.
- Extend the use of invoicing, including in special regimes and hitherto excluded sectors (e.g. agricultural sector); consider imposing a requirement to issue invoices.

3.2 Reduce the costs and increase the incentives of formalisation.

- Reduce red tape and administrative/recurrent costs associated with formal status.
- Facilitate transition to formality by a reduction (or full discount) of costs associated with the recognition of past benefits of workers that are formalised, which could be fully or partially subsidised.

4. Create the conditions for formal job creation and formal job opportunities.

4.1 Improve labour productivity through upgraded and more pertinent skills levels.

- Finalise the application to the Ley de Institutos de Educación Superior to improve the quality of the technical path and its reputation.
- Establish a mechanism for recognition of skills acquired in the informal sector and advance towards a National qualifications framework, following recommendations in the OECD Skills Strategy for Peru (OECD, 2016b).

4.2 Improve labour market institutions to improve matching in labour markets and increase the dynamism of the Peruvian labour market.

- Reinforce the link between active labour market policies and formal jobs, mainly by strengthening programmes, such as Jóvenes Productivos, to prevent the mass entry by young people into informality, which has lasting impact on working lives.
- Favour information mechanisms regarding returns to different studies; continue the expansion of Ponte en Carrera.

4.3 Link efforts to create formal jobs with broader productivity diversification strategies and skills strategies.

- Co-ordinate institutional efforts to promote better-quality formal jobs with the recommendations in Chapter 2 on productive diversification and the Skills Strategy for Peru (OECD, 2016b forthcoming).
- Set efforts for formalisation as a key item within the broader national development strategy to coordinate action across line ministries and agencies. Following the inclusion of a plan for formalisation within the competencies of the Consejo Nacional de Competitividad y Formalización (CNCF), the CNCF is well placed to play this coordinating role.

In "Scenario 1: A new commodity super cycle", there is a risk job creation linked to the commodity boom would occur in the informal sector, creating conditions that make addressing the structural causes of informality more challenging. On one hand, revenue generated from mining exports could fund policies aimed at formalisation, such as, for example, subsidising social contributions of low- and low-middle income workers or matching workers' contributions combined with immediate benefits. However, diminished incentives for formal job creation would need to be alleviated, and policy would need to focus on the creation of formal jobs. In terms of making the most of new Chinese markets,

Peru could take certain steps to ensure that jobs that are created are formal, and encourage formalisation by extending the coverage of the Law on SMEs to some sectors currently not covered, such as agriculture, and which could have a great potential for expansion and integration into global value chains.

"Scenario 2: Increasing technology and mechanisation" would entail the decline of mid-skilled jobs and the increasing division of the labour force into high-skilled and low-skilled workers. This shift, however, would also present opportunities for formal job and formal firm creation around these new technologies. In view of the dramatic impact of technology on labour, it would be important for Peru to pursue active labour market policies and skills and training, and to ensure these are specifically linked to technical education. Technology innovation centres could play a role in carrying out these functions. In this environment, policies that foster a positive environment for start-ups could lead to formal job creation.

In "Scenario 3: Rising expectations of the middle class", improvement in public services and increased social spending puts pressure on labour costs, services and the pension system. Policy incentives to extend non-contributive social protection and pensions would be significantly diminished, while the consequences of limiting redistribution would be increased costs in the long term.

Notes

1. Informal employment in non-agricultural activities is used in this case for the sake of comparability, given the international availability of this indicator.
2. According to the INEI, "empleado" describes a worker who usually performs non-manual work for a public or private employer for a monthly salary; "obrero" describes a worker who usually performs manual work for a public or private employer for a weekly wage.
3. Total labour costs are also higher for employees, since employers have to contribute to social security programmes.
4. Formal and informal workers' earnings in 2014 when minimum wage was PEN 750.
5. The figure is not altered substantially if "normal" hours are taken instead. The former is preferred because it refers to a specific job, while normal hours for Peru are only available together for all occupations.
6. The definition of formal work used by INEI and this review identifies informality for dependent workers on the basis of their employers' contribution to social security.

References

AAFP (2015), *Solo la Mitad de los Adultos Mayores del País Cuenta con una Pensión (Only Half of the Elderly in the Country Have a Pension)*, Asociación de Administradoras de Fondos de Pensiones, Lima, *www.asociacionafp.com.pe/wp-content/uploads/140910-AAFP-SDR-4-Cobertura-en-el-SPP-FINAL.pdf*.

Bosch, M., A. Melguizo and C. Pagés (2013), *Mejores Pensiones, Mejores Trabajos: Hacia la Cobertura Universal en América Latina y el Caribe (Better Pensions, Better Jobs: Towards Universal Coverage in Latin America and the Caribbean)*, Inter-American Development Bank, Washington, D.C., *https://publications.iadb.org/bitstream/handle/11319/462/Mejores%20pensiones%20mejores%20trabajos.pdf*.

Bulmer, E.R. et al. (2015), *Jobs in Peru: Dynamics, Constraints and Policy Implications*, World Bank, Washington, DC.

Casalí, P., O. Cetrángolo and A. Goldschmit (2015), *Análisis Integral de la Protección Social en el Perú (Comprehensive Analysis of Social Protection in Peru)*, Office for the Andean Countries, International Labour Organization, Lima, *www.ilo.org/wcmsp5/groups/public/---americas/---ro-lima/---sro-lima/documents/publication/wcms_392037.pdf*.

CEPLAN (2016), "Economía Informal en Perú: Situación y Perspectivas" ("Informal economy in Peru: situation and perspectives"), Serie Avance de Investigacion N. 8, CEPLAN.

Céspedes, N. (2015), "Crecer no es Suficiente para Reducir la Informalidad" ("Growth Is Not Enough to Reduce Informality"), *Working Paper*, No. 2015-005, Banco Central de Reserva del Perú, *www.bcrp.gob.pe/docs/Publicaciones/Documentos-de-Trabajo/2015/documento-de-trabajo-05-2015.pdf*.

Céspedes, N., P. Lavado and N. Ramírez Rondán (eds.) (2016), *Productividad en el Perú: Medición, Determinantes e Implicancias (Productivity in Peru: Measurement, Determinants and Implications)*, Universidad del Pacífico, Lima, available at *http://repositorio.up.edu.pe/handle/11354/1083*.

Cruz-Saco, M. A., J. Mendoza and B. Seminario (2014), "El Sistema Provisional del Perú: Diagnóstico 1996-2013, Proyecciones 2014-2050 y Reforma" ("Peru's Pension System: Diagnostic 1996-2013, Projections 2014-2050 and Reform"), *Documento de discusión*, DD/14/11, Universidad del Pacífico, Lima, *http://srvnetappseg.up.edu.pe/siswebciup/Files/El%20sistema%20Previsional%20del%20Per%C3%BA_%20Diagn%C3%B3stico,%20Proyecciones%20y%20Reforma%20(1).pdf*.

De Soto, H. (1989), *The Other Path: The Invisible Revolution in the Third World*, HarperCollins, New York.

Djankov, S. et al. (2002), "The Regulation of Entry", *Quarterly Journal of Economics*, Vol. 117, No. 1, Oxford University Press, Oxford, pp. 1-37, *http://dx.doi.org/10.1162/003355302753399436*.

EsSalud (2016), website, Seguro Social de Salud del Perú (Peru's Social Health Insurance), Lima, *www.essalud.gob.pe/*.

Hussmanns, R. (2004), *Defining and Measuring Informal Employment*, Bureau of Statistics, International Labour Office, Geneva, *www.ilo.org/public/english/bureau/stat/download/papers/meas.pdf*.

IDB (2016), *Numbers for Development* (database), Inter-American Development Bank, Washington, D.C., available at *https://data.iadb.org/* (accessed on 13 July 2016).

IDB (2015a), *Base de datos Sociómetro-BID: Sistema de Indicadores Sociales de América Latina y el Caribe*, Inter-American Development Bank, Washington, D.C. Available at *www.iadb.org/en/research-and-data//sociometro-bid,6981.html*. (accessed on 7 July 2016).

IDB (2015b), "Empleos para Crecer" ("Jobs for Growth"), webpage, Inter-American Development Bank, Washington, D.C., *www.iadb.org/en/topics/labor-and-pensions/jobs-for-growth/jobs-for-growth-how-to-promote-social-development-through-labor-policies-in-latin-america-and-the-caribbean,18751.html* (accessed May 2016).

IDB (2013), *More Than Revenue: Taxation as a Development Tool*, Inter-American Development Bank, Washington, D.C., available at *www.iadb.org/en/research-and-data/dia-development-in-the-americas-idb-flagship-publication,3185.html?id=2013*.

ILO (2014a), *World Social Protection Report: Building Economic Recovery, Inclusive Development and Social Justice*, 2014/15, International Labour Organization, Geneva, *www.ilo.org/wcmsp5/groups/public/---dgreports/---dcomm/documents/publication/wcms_245201.pdf*.

ILO (2014b), *Panorama Laboral 2014: América Latina y el Caribe (Labour Overview 2014: Latin America and the Caribbean)*, Regional Office for Latin America and the Caribbean, International Labour Organization, Lima, *www.ilo.org/wcmsp5/groups/public/---americas/---ro-lima/documents/publication/wcms_334089.pdf*.

ILO (2013), *Measuring Informality: A Statistical Manual on the Informal Sector and Informal Employment*, International Labour Organization, Geneva, *www.ilo.org/wcmsp5/groups/public/---dgreports/---dcomm/---publ/documents/publication/wcms_222979.pdf*.

ILO/FORLAC (2014), "Evolución del empleo informal en Perú 2004-2012", International Labour Organization/Formalización de la Informalidad en America Latina y el Caribe.

INEI (2015), "Evolución de los Indicadores de Empleo e Ingreso por Departamentos, 2004-2014", Instituto Nacional de Estadística e Informática, Lima, *https://www.inei.gob.pe/media/MenuRecursivo/publicaciones_digitales/Est/Lib1294/index.html* (accessed in May 2016)

INEI (2014a), *Producción y Empleo Informal en el Perú, Cuenta Satélite de la Economía Informal 2007-2012 (Production and Informal Employment in Peru, A Satellite Account of the Informal Economy 2007-2014)*, Instituto Nacional de Estadistica e Informatica, Lima, *www.inei.gob.pe/media/MenuRecursivo/publicaciones_digitales/Est/Lib1154/libro.pdf* (accessed on 29 January 2016).

INEI (2014b), *Encuesta Nacional de Hogares (ENAHO) (National Household Survey)* (database), Instituto Nacional de Estadística e Informática, Lima, *http://webinei.inei.gob.pe/anda_inei/index.php/catalog/247* (accessed on 9 March 2016).

Jaramillo, M. (2013), "Is There Demand for Formality Among Firms? Evidence from Microfirms in Downtown Lima", *Avances de Investigación* (Research Progress Paper), Grupo de Análisis para el Desarrollo, Lima, *http://repositorio.grade.org.pe/bitstream/GRADE/42/1/AI13.pdf*.

Jütting, J. and J. de Laiglesia (2009), *Is Informal Normal? Towards More and Better Jobs in Developing Countries*, OECD Publishing, Paris, *http://dx.doi.org/10.1787/9789264059245-en*.

Kanbur, R. (2009), "Conceptualising Informality: Regulation and Enforcement", *Indian Journal of Labour Economics*, Vol. 52, No. 1, Springer (India), New Delhi, *www.arts.cornell.edu/poverty/kanbur/Conceptualizinginformality.pdf*.

La Porta, R. and A. Shleifer (2014), "Informality and Development", *Journal of Economic Perspectives*, Vol. 28, No. 3, American Economic Association, Nashville, pp. 109-126, *http://dx.doi.org/10.1257/jep.28.3.109*.

Loayza, N., A.M. Oviedo and L. Serven (2005), "The Impact of Regulation on Growth and Informality – Cross-Country Evidence", *World Bank Policy Research Working Paper*, No. 3263, Washington, D.C., *http://dx.doi.org/10.1596/1813-9450-3623*.

ManpowerGroup (2015), *2015 Talent Shortage Survey*, ManpowerGroup, Milwaukee, *www.manpowergroup.com/wps/wcm/connect/db23c560-08b6-485f-9bf6-f5f38a43c76a/2015_Talent_Shortage_Survey_US-lo_res.pdf?MOD=AJPERES*.

OECD (2016a), *Avanzando Hacia Una Mejor Educación en Perú (Moving Towards a Better Education in Peru)*, Making Development Happen, No. 3, OECD Publishing, Paris, *www.oecd.org/dev/Avanzando-hacia-una-mejor-educacion-en-Peru.pdf*.

OECD (2016b forthcoming), *Skills Strategy for Peru*, Diagnostic Report, OECD Publishing, Paris.

OECD (2015a), *Multi-dimensional Review of Peru: Volume I. Initial Assessment*, OECD Publishing, Paris, *http://dx.doi.org/10.1787/9789264243279-en*.

OECD (2015b), *OECD Employment Outlook 2015*, OECD Publishing, Paris, *http://dx.doi.org/10.1787/empl_outlook-2015-en*.

OECD/CAF/ECLAC (forthcoming 2016), *Latin American Economic Outlook 2017: Youth, Skills and Entrepreneurship for Development*, OECD Publishing, Paris.

OECD/CAF/ECLAC (2014), *Latin American Economic Outlook 2015: Education, Skills and Innovation for Development*, OECD Publishing, Paris, *http://dx.doi.org/10.1787/leo-2015-en*.

OECD/IDB (2013), *Employment Protection Database* (database), 2013 update, OECD/Inter-American Development Bank, Washington, D.C., available at *www.oecd.org/els/emp/oecdindicatorsofemploymentprotection.htm* (accessed on June 2016).

OECD/IDB/CIAT (2016), *Taxing Wages in Latin America and the Caribbean*, OECD Publishing, Paris, *http://dx.doi.org/10.1787/9789264262607-en*.

Saavedra, J. and M. Tommasi (2007), "Estado y Contrato Social en América Latina", *Revista Internacional del Trabajo*, Vol. 16, No. 3-4, OIT, Blackwell publishing Ltd, pages 315-329, *http://dx.doi.org/10.1111/j.1564-9148.2007.00016.x*

SUNAT (2016), *Estadísticas y Estudios (Statistics and Studies)* (database), La Superintendencia Nacional de Aduanas y de Administración Tributaria, Lima, *www.sunat.gob.pe/estadisticasestudios/index.html* (accessed on June 2016).

SUNAT (2015), *Memoria Anual 2015*, La Superintendencia Nacional de Aduanas y de Administración Tributaria, Lima, Lima *http://www.sunat.gob.pe/institucional/publicaciones/memoria2015.pdf* (accesed on June 2016)

Tassot, C. and J. Vazquez-Zamora (forthcoming 2017), "The faces of informality in Peru. Describing informal groups by using Latent Class Analysis", OECD Development Centre Working Papers, OECD Publishing, Paris.

Tello, Mario D. (2015), "¿Es la Informalidad una opción voluntaria o la última alternativa de empleo en el Perú?" ("Is informality a voluntary option or the last alternative to employment in Peru?"), Departamento de Economía de la Pontificia Universidad Católica del Perú), Lima, pp. 19-25, *www.cies.org.pe/sites/default/files/files/articulos/economiaysociedad/03-tello_ok.pdf*.

Vostroknutova, E., A. Rodriguez, P. Saavedra and J. Panzer (2015), *Peru - Building on success: boosting productivity for faster growth*, World Bank, Washington, DC, *http://documents.worldbank.org/curated/en/600921467995400041/Peru-Building-on-success-boosting-productivity-for-faster-growth*

World Bank (2016), *Doing Business 2016: Measuring Regulatory Quality and Efficiency*, World Bank, Washington, DC, *http://dx.doi.org/10.1596/978-1-4648-0667-4*.

World Bank (2010), *World Bank Enterprise Surveys* (database), World Bank, Washington, D.C., available at *www.enterprisesurveys.org/*

ORGANISATION FOR ECONOMIC CO-OPERATION AND DEVELOPMENT

The OECD is a unique forum where governments work together to address the economic, social and environmental challenges of globalisation. The OECD is also at the forefront of efforts to understand and to help governments respond to new developments and concerns, such as corporate governance, the information economy and the challenges of an ageing population. The Organisation provides a setting where governments can compare policy experiences, seek answers to common problems, identify good practice and work to co-ordinate domestic and international policies.

The OECD member countries are: Australia, Austria, Belgium, Canada, Chile, the Czech Republic, Denmark, Estonia, Finland, France, Germany, Greece, Hungary, Iceland, Ireland, Israel, Italy, Japan, Korea, Latvia, Luxembourg, Mexico, the Netherlands, New Zealand, Norway, Poland, Portugal, the Slovak Republic, Slovenia, Spain, Sweden, Switzerland, Turkey, the United Kingdom and the United States. The European Union takes part in the work of the OECD.

OECD Publishing disseminates widely the results of the Organisation's statistics gathering and research on economic, social and environmental issues, as well as the conventions, guidelines and standards agreed by its members.

OECD DEVELOPMENT CENTRE

The OECD Development Centre was established in 1962 as an independent platform for knowledge sharing and policy dialogue between OECD member countries and developing economies, allowing these countries to interact on an equal footing. Today, 27 OECD countries and 24 non-OECD countries are members of the Centre. The Centre draws attention to emerging systemic issues likely to have an impact on global development and more specific development challenges faced by today's developing and emerging economies. It uses evidence-based analysis and strategic partnerships to help countries formulate innovative policy solutions to the global challenges of development.

For more information on the Centre and its members, please see *www.oecd.org/dev*.

OECD PUBLISHING, 2, rue André-Pascal, 75775 PARIS CEDEX 16
(41 2016 16 1P1) ISBN 978-92-64-26466-3 – 2016

www.ingramcontent.com/pod-product-compliance
Ingram Content Group UK Ltd.
Pitfield, Milton Keynes, MK11 3LW, UK
UKHW051503290926
15471UKWH00008B/1393

9 789264 264663